Consumer Protection
A Classical Case Study

Consumer Protection

A Classical Case Study

H. R. Bangia

Hony. Secretary,
Indian Institute of Public Administration,
Haryana Regional Branch
Gurgaon

ADHYAYAN

ADHYAYAN PUBLISHERS & DISTRIBUTORS
New Delhi-110002

Published by
ADHYAYAN PUBLISHERS & DISTRIBUTORS
4378/4B, 105, J.M.D. House, Murari Lal Street
Ansari Road Darya Ganj, New Delhi - 110002
Ph.: 011-23263018, 011-23277156, Fax: 23280028
Email: adhyayanpublishers@yahoo.com

Consumer Protection: A Classical Case Study

Edition 2011
ISBN 978-81-8435-263-4

Printed in India

Published by Harish Chandra Yadav for Adhyayan Publishers & Distributors, Delhi. Laser Typesetting at Jain Computers and Printed at Tarun Offset Printers. Delhi

भारतीय लोक प्रशासन संस्थान
इन्द्रप्रस्थ एस्टेट, रिंग रोड, नई दिल्ली-110 002 स दूरभाष : 23702400 (15 लाइन)
INDIAN INSTITUTE OF PUBLIC ADMINISTRATION
INDRAPRASTHA ESTATE, RING ROAD, NEW DELHI-110002 (INDIA)

T.N. Chaturvedi
Chairman, IIPA
Former Governor of Karnataka
Former Member of Parliament (R.S.)
Former Comptroller & Auditor General of India

Tel : 011-23705927 (O)
011-23702400
95120-4214025 (R)

Foreword

Here is a book of an unconventional and unusual type. It is not a dissertation or exposition of first principles of administration or good governance. There is no attempt at discussion of the theory of case study. It goes to the heart of the problem of good governance - the need for understanding of their rights and duties by citizens. Again the other aspect is the easy comprehension of the ways and means through which the citizen can assert his rights and get his due. Another point that emerges is the need for citizen's inflexible determination to pursue the stipulated course to obtain justice. This is what makes this book by H.R. Bangia of general significance.

The raw material of the case study embodied in the book comes from his personal experience. He has meticulously maintained the record of the case and it is this that leads to his ultimate success against heavy odds. In India the approach to redressal of grievances is possible for the citizen as a consumer in a speedy and less expensive manner. This has been made possible through the Consumer Protection Act, 1986. But it needs awareness and vigilance on the part of citizen along with patience and perseverance. The encounter of Bangia has been not with a trader or businessman either big or small, but with the authority of the State represented through its missions at various levels and of different disciplines and background. He brings out the obduracy of the bureaucracy of Haryana Urban Development Authority (HUDA) which is required to help citizens meet their genuine for housing. All this has been brought out vividly by H.R. Bangia in the presentation of his case study. In a way the treatment received from authorities by Bangia is not an isolated one, or rare and exceptional. Unfortunately that is the day-to-day experience in general of citizens as most of public authorities afflicted with this evil trait in general. Hence Bangia's book has wider implications and importance. He projects the common bureaucratic malady adversely affecting citizens through the case study rooted in his personal experience, agony but with triumph after prolonged struggle.

The Consumer Protection Act, 1986 with three subsequent amendments has come to the help of citizens in the redressal of a large numbers of their grievances. Through his case study Bangia brings out succinctly the rationale of the consumers protection legislation, the mechanism and its procedures, the care and caution that a citizen with grievance has to observe. The book is educative in its impact. The case study by Shri H.R. Bangia is a useful tool for teaching and training in government - public relations. The ugly interface with cussed governmental authorities can be changed through citizen's own continuing awareness and logical and intense personal effort while trying to obtain one's due entitlement. Such a book should initiate a process of self-introspection in all public authorities and also help to promote enlightened and active citizenship. It can serve as an instrument for positive change and help the faceless bureaucracy to improve its image.

Shri H.R. Bangia had been for long associated with activities of the IIPA, Delhi and now he actively participates in the activities of its Regional branch at Gurgaon. Shri H.R. Bangia has done commendable public serve by writing a book based on his own experience. It is a simple and realistic study avoiding legal jargon and has an inspirational value for others. I congratulate him for setting such an example for others and showing the way aggrieved citizens can follow to get justice from unresponsive and unheeding authorities. Shri Bangia's book is a contribution to good governance. It can also be effectively used to spread consumers' awareness in society that is so sorely required today.

February 10, 2010

T.N. Chaturvedi

(T.N. CHATURVEDI)

Introduction

Why is it a classical case study after all? It is because it is a case where there was a public auction and the plot was allotted to the highest bidder, under such circumstances, the grievances of the bidders cannot be considered to be a consumer dispute.

A case in point is that the State Consumer Disputes Redressal Commission has no jurisdiction to entertain complaints regarding the transactions of shops/kiosks having been purchased in auction from the Delhi Development Authority; ***Kashyap Constructions (Pvt.) Ltd. Vs Delhi Development Authority, 2001 (1) CPR.128.***

In another case the State Consumer Disputes Redressal Commissions have no jurisdiction in matters involving outright sale of immoveable property at an auction; ***Allied (Garments) Exports Industries Pvt. Ltd. Vs Delhi Development Authority, II (1992) CPJ 505 (NC).***

But the author himself had gone through the case at all stages and had valid reasons that he got relief from the National Consumer Disputes Redressal Commission as well after the case was decided in his favour by the District Consumer Disputes Redressal Forum and the Haryana State Consumer Disputes Redressal Commission.

Remember it is not you alone who was cheated, it happens with every one whosoever is the consumer. Cheating the consumers is not of recent origin but is a very old profession of businessmen who are not honest in their dealings with public and whose conscience does not prick them in their heart by doing so. Their motive is to make money by hooks or crooks. Making or minting money likewise has innumerable tricks and methods. Piracy is also one of the methods of making money which is very simple and easy way to get duplicate copies of CDs. People are happy to get pirated CDs at a very cheap rate than the original CDs. Here there is the role of the administration to book the defaulters businessmen but not those who purchase such items.

Abraham Lincoln, Former U.S. President said "Discourage litigation. Persuade your neighbours to compromise whenever you can".

John F. Kennedy, also the former President of United States of America made a historic declaration at the U.S. Congress in 1982 as follow:

> "Consumers, by definition, include us all. They are the largest economic group in the economy, affecting and affected by almost every public and private economic division......But, they are the only important group.....whose views are often not heard."

He spelt out four basic consumer rights:

- Right to safety
- Right to information
- Right to choice
- Right to representation

From the time immemorial the consumers were targeted by the traders big or small to make money and the consumers found no way out but to accept it as their fate or destiny.

Supreme Court in India in 1976 observed that the protection of the consumers is the need of the society. It stated: "We hope the vigilant Legislature will activise itself on behalf of the little man and the law and make quick moving, easily accessible and free-of-cost consumer protection measures".

After a long cherished independence the state of affairs of consumers in India was not different but it began to develop a consumer movement after two decades.

The consumer movement as a movement came to light when an Asian Seminar on 'Consumer Protection' was organized some time in 1982. Indira Gandhi, the then Prime Minister of India realized the need of it and as such included it on the national agenda for protecting the interests of the consumers. By the time many NGOs and activists voiced the need of protecting the interests of the consumers. It was for the first time that the Central Government, during the tenure of Rajiv Gandhi as the Prime Minister that the Consumer Protection Bill having been passed by both the Houses of Parliament received the assent of the President on 24th December, 1986. It thus came on the Statute Book as THE CONSUMER PROTECTION ACT, 1986 (68 OF 1986).

The following is the list of amending acts:

1. The Consumer Protection (Amendment) Act, 1991 (34 of 1991)
2. The Consumer Protection(Amendment) Act, 1993 (50 of 1993)
3. The Consumer Protection (Amendment) Act, 2002 (62 of 2002)

The Complainant had purchased a plot of land in auction as he was the highest bidder from HUDA, Gurgaon and paid the amount of earnest money. On inspection of the site it was discovered that the plot was not **"Prime"** located as advertised in Times of India It did not qualify for auction as per HUDA rules and regulations. All his efforts to recover the amount through administrative action failed that he had to evoke the relevant provisions of the Consumer Protection Act, 1986 from District Forum to National Commission for about five years that he could get relief. The account of these exercises is contained in this Case Study for the readers to know as to how difficult it is to entangle with Haryana Urban Development Authority.

It is not only difficult to deal with such housing boards in India but it happens with other service providers like Railways, Electricity, Water, Municpal bodies, Postal Services, Telephones, Transportation, Airlines, Banking. etc.

The very purpose to render simple, speedy and inexpensive justice, for which these fora have been set up is defeated where avoidable delay hampers justice to the aggrieved in a reasonable time.

Though writing a case study is not an interesting one, but this case study has been attempted to give the readers the details as to how to contest the case independently. It also gives an account as to how the respondents - HUDA manipulated the matter at every stage which is supposed to ensure speedy and economic development of urban areas in the State of Haryana.

Consumer Protection Act, 1986 may be gone through for comprehensive study. However, for ready reference the addresses of State Consumer Disputes Redressal Commissions and District Consumer Disputes Redressal Forum are given in the Appendix alongwith suggested reading material.

I am indebted to all concerned authors/organisations/individuals whose materials are also being purposely included in public interest for the benefit of the readers.

For detail clarifications, readers may contact: Department of Consumer Affairs, Ministry of Consumer Affairs, Fwd and Public Distribution at http://fcamin.nic.in

January 14, 2010 **H.R. BANGIA**

Preface

Case studies depict administrative reality and thus provide reflection on administration. They are, thus, the best tools of in-service administrative training. The case study has been captioned "**Consumer Protection - A Classical Case Study**" because it is a case where there was a public auction and the plot was allotted to the highest bidder, under such circumstances, the grievances of the bidders cannot be considered to be a consumer dispute. But the author himself had gone through the case at all stages and had solid reasons to get the relief from all the Fora. As such case studies are not only motivational but also pathfinder which the readers and researchers can make it significant for contributions to introduce positive and qualitative changes in administrative procedures and practices.

The case study contained in this volume is about the protection of the rights of the consumers under the Consumer Protection Act, 1986 and has a focus exclusively on the functioning of the District, State and National Consumer Disputes Redressal Fora. It is a complex and an interesting study because the stand taken by the District Consumer Disputes Redressal Forum was also agreed to by the State Commission but the respondent choose to take up the matter with the National Commission when the respondent did not get relief from the State Commission against the order passed in First Appeal by the State Consumer Disputes Redressal Commission, Haryana, Chandigarh. The respondent went back and forth to gain time and did not comply with the orders of any of the Fora that the appellant had to evoke contempt of courts thrice that the respondent had to comply with the orders of the National Consumer Disputes Redressal Commission, New Delhi after a lapse of four years of the order passed by the District Forum. Whereas this legislation is also called **'People's Act'** and is expected to give cheap and quick relief to the consumers.

The study reveals that the Haryana Urban Development Authority spared no stone unturned to not comply with the orders of Fora. It was only due to the concerted efforts of the Consumer that he contested the case thirty nine times at all the Fora. The study gives the practical ground realities which the consumers have to face against the prevailing situations created by the big business community and as such it is high time to know the intricacies involved in dealing with the traders. Apart from spreading slogan *Jago Grahak Jago* together with educating the consumers to defend their cases themselves without involving the pleaders, even if the amount involved is insignificant, is the need of the hour to fight against rampant corruption and misleading offers of the business community.

Every care has been taken to avoid any mistake in the script because the same was typed and edited even up to final stage by me. I shall, however, appreciate the suggestions of the readers to improve it in the next edition.

I am grateful to Shri T.N. Chaturvedi for writing Foreword of this case study.

All in all, it is such a study which would be found useful by a common man, administrators, researchers, trainers, and students alike, especially with reference to administration of public sector undertakings and autonomous institutions and their dealing with consumers at large.

I am to indebted to Adhyayan Publishers and Distributors to bring it out which will go a long way in spreading consumer consciousness in the society.

H.R. Bangia

Gurgaon : 14th January , 2010

Contents

1

About HARYANA URBAN DEVELOPMENT AUTHORITY (HUDA)

Haryana Urban Development Authority was set up under Act.No. 13 of 1977. An Act to provide for the establishment of an Urban Development Authority for undertaking urban development in the State of Haryana and or matters ancillary thereto

STATEMENT OF OBJECT AND REASONS

It has been felt necessary to constitute a statutory authority in place of department of Urban Estate for ensuring speedy and economic development of urban areas in the State of Haryana. At present, the work of land acquisition and development of urban areas of various places throughout Haryana is being done by the Urban Estates Department. While the planning of the urban areas is done by the Town and Country Planning Department, the land is acquired by the urban estate department and the development of the land so acquired is carried out by the various departments and bodies like the Public Health Department, B & R Department, Electricity Board, etc.

It has been observed that the involvement of several agencies in the development of urban estates at various places gives rise to problems of co-ordination, with the result that the growth of most of the urban estates becomes slow and causes unnecessary dissatisfaction among the plot holders, in particular, and the public in general. Further, as the department has to follow the financial rules and regulations of the Government, the arrangement of finances and sanctions of estimates take a long time and the development works have not kept pace with the required physical development of the estates.

Being a Government department, the Urban Estates Department is unable to raise resources from various lending institutions although, there are various financial institutions in the country willing to finance urban land development programmes which can be made self-financing.

In order to overcome all these difficulties and to achieve expeditious development of the estate, it has been felt necessary that an Urban Development Authority should be set up.

This Bill seeks to achieve the aforesaid objects. Published in Haryana Govt. Gazette dated 23.3.1977

Be it enacted by the Legislature of the State of Haryana in the Twenty-eighth year of the Republic of India......

Thereafter Haryana Urban Development (Disposal of Land and Buildings) Regulation, 1978 was instituted.

2

Purpose of the Case Study

1. To empower, education and enlighten the citizens for redressal of their grievances under the Consumer Protection Act, 1986
2. To equip with the latest rules and regulations of CP Act and to make them aware of various provisions available to them. That is why it is called 'THE PEOPLE'S ACT'.
3. To make aware the citizens of India under the Right to Information Act, 2005 to know about the workings of three organs of the redressal machinery which are functioning at District, State and National levels.
4. To contest the case themselves without involving advocates in the District Consumer Disputes Redressal Forum, State Consumer Disputes and Redressal Commission and the National Consumer Disputes and Redressal Commission.
5. To disseminate the information to their friends, neighbors and the aggrieved who happen to be in search of quick, cheap and easy solutions of their grievances and above all.
6. to avoid the redressal of their grievances through the regular courts of law and to explicit transparency and accountability of institutions dealing with consumers.

3

Methodology

1. The names of the persons, places, buildings etc. involved have also been depicted under the RTI Act, 2005 and to avoid confusion to understand the case in its proper prospective. For example, if the Complainant takes up the case to the District Forum and the other party i.e. the Defendant takes up the matter to State Commission or further to the National Commission for getting relief then the original Complainant becomes the Respondent in that case and the original Defendant becomes the Complainant i.e. .Appellant
2. Further care has been taken to describe the case in the manner in which it proceeded. Invariably the Respondents also plead the cases at State Commission and at National Commission when the cases are not decided in their favour at the District Fora. In this case also the defendant could not get the relief from State or National Commission even then the case was lingered on for almost five years, on one pretext or the other through the courtesy of the Counsel of the defendants, by giving false affidavit and by making frivolous excuses. Whereas the provisions of the Act are very simple and the

procedure is not cumbersome. Even then the Respondent was neither fined with cost nor punished under Section 27 of the CP Act, 1986.

3. The Study of the Case would be of great help to the readers to understand the intricacies involved in this classical case of **H.R. Bangia Vs HUDA** and Vice Versa.

4

Objectives

1. Consumers must know this social legislation and understand the provisions of the CP Act, 1986, which are very simple and easy to understand and follow.
2. In order to bring transparency and accountability of business community it is must for consumers to spare their time from their busy schedule to defend their cases themselves even if the amount involved is insignificant; failing which the business community would continue to take advantage of their ignorance.
3. It is utmost necessary to make use of it as the consumers have to deal with global business community as well
4. *Jago Grahak Jago* cannot become successful slogan unless all consumers become aware of their rights to exert their pressure to get for what they pay to any trader, how big or small the transaction may be.
5. To make others aware of it because some one has also made you aware in one way or the other.
6. Yo become the ideal citizens under Article 51A of the Constitution to discharge such functions as are enumerated under Fundamental Duties of the citizens.

5

Participation in Auction of a Plot of HUDA, Gurgaon

An advertisement in the Times of India on 23rd November 1997 **(Annexure XXIX)** for auction of **Prime** located commercial and residential Plots in various sectors in Gurgaon tempted H.R. Bangia that is the author to go to Gurgaon from New Delhi. The auction was held in the lawn of Administrator HUDA in Sector 14 Gurgaon on 27.11.97. Colourful pamphlets giving the details of the plots were also displayed at the counter. He was the highest bidder for Plot No.1578 in Sector II at Rs.7300/-p.mtr for *6 marla* and paid an amount of Rs. 1 lac as Earnest Money on 27.11.97 **(Annexure I).**

Immediately thereafter on inspection of the site, it was discovered that no house could be constructed on that plot due to various deficiencies. It was not even fit for auction, as per HUDA's rules and regulations. The Estate Officer, HUDA, Gurgaon was contacted for refund of the earnest money of Rs. 1 lac. It was informed that the auction was just over and that the case will be put up to the Chief Administrator, HUDA based in Chandigarh and thereafter the amount will be refunded. Accordingly, an application dated 27.11.1997 **(Annexure II)** giving all details was submitted to the Estate Officer for refund of the earnest money of Rs. 1 lac. As no action was taken the following procedure had to be adopted for recovery of the amount.

6

Administrative Action Initiated for Refund of Earnest Money

Not satisfied with the reply of Estate Officer, Gurgaon the complainant approached Shri R.S. Verma, I.A.S., the then Chief Secretary, Haryana with the request to help him for getting refund vide letter dt. 30.11.97. **(Annexure III)**.

At the instance of Chief Secretary, Haryana, the Chief Administrator instructed the Estate Officer vide his letter dt. 19.12.97 (in Hindi) to look into the matter, as per rules and dispose of the case under intimation to him and to the party. Copy of it was forwarded to H.R. Bangia to contact the Estate Officer, HUDA, Gurgaon. **(Annexure IV).**

The applicant approached the Estate Officer (EO) and handed over letter dt. 22.12.97 **(Annexure V)** along with the letter of Chief Administrator, Haryana dt. 19.12.97 for consideration.

In the meantime he received Allotment letter vide Memo No. 294 dated 18.12.1997 **(Annexure VI)** for remittance of Rs. 1,49,112.50 in order to make 25% price of the said plot /building within 30 days from the date of allotment letter. The payment was to be made by a bank draft payable to the Estate Officer, Gurgaon and drawn on any scheduled Bank at Gurgaon. It was also mentioned that in case of failure to deposit the said amount within the above specified period, the allotment shall be cancelled and the deposit of 10% bid money deposited at the time of bid shall stand forfeited to the Authority and against which there shall be no claim for damages. In addition to other conditions it was lastly mentioned that on payment of 25% he may obtain possession on any working Wednesday.

Thereafter it was also mentioned that any other condition not incorporated above but announced at the time of auction to be indicated. Interest @ 18% would be charged for the delay period of installments.

The allotment letter was in FORM 'CC' underneath was mentioned (See Regulation 6(2). No details of what is Regulation 6(2) were mentioned at the time of auction or in the letter of Allotment.

When the plot was not developed and high tension wire was passing through the plot besides other deficiencies, it was not understood as to how it could be allotted if 25% amount is paid, when such plots do not qualify for auction, as per their rules on this behalf.

In view of the above, the matter became serious and he sent a Telegram to the Estate Officer on 31.12.1997 (Regd. No.8469), as per the details:

ESTATE OFFICER
HUDA GURGAON

REF LETS NOV 27, 30 AND DEC 22 FOR REFUND OF AMOUNT PAID FOR PLOT 1578 SECTOR 15 PART II (.) KINDLY CONVEY ORDERS FOR REFUND AND SEND COPY OF REPLY IF ANY SENT TO CHIEF ADMINISTRATOR

HR BANGIA

NOT TO BE TELEGRAPHED:
COPY BY POST IN CONFIRMATION TO: Estate Officer, HUDA, Gurgaon.

Reference is also invited to letter No. A-5-97/41350-51 dated Dec 19, 1997 from the Office of the Chief Administrator, Sector 6, Panchkula. It is requested to kindly refund the amount at your earliest. Also kindly send a copy of report if any sent to C.A. for not refunding.

Sd/-
H.R. Bangia
D-3, NIPCCD Campus,
Opp. Police Station,
Hauz Khas,
New Delhi-110016

Dec. 31. 1997

He also sent Speed Post letter (SPP 3664) dated 21st January 1998 **(Annexure VII)** to the Administrator, HUDA, Gurgaon bringing out all the facts of the matter.

7

District Consumer Disputes Redressal Forum Gurgaon

Application on 3.3.1998 before District Consumer Disputes Redressal Forum, Gurgaon

Since the applicant was not having any plot or house either in Delhi or in Gurgaon or any where in India and was due to retire in June 1998, he was in dire need of shelter on urgent basis. Moreover no reply from any quarter was received that he had no option but to file an Application with a nominal Fee to the District Consumer Disputes Redressal Forum, Gurgaon on 3.3.1998. The details are given in **(Annexure VIII).**

However the salient features are as under:

1. That there was encroachment over this plot by the houses of an already existing unauthorized colony.
2. that a high tension live wire was passing by the side of the plot.
3. that the said plot was not qualifying for adjective **"Prime"** as advertised in Times of India dated 23rd Nov. 1997 (Annexure XXIX).
4. that the length of the plot was also not 18.2 metrs as specified in the auction.
5. that it was not two side open as was declared at the

time of auction and above all it was not worth the cost and place to raise construction over the said plot.

The first hearing was fixed on 15th April 1998. No one from the opposite party attended the case nor was any reply furnished by them to the District Court.

The next date of hearing was fixed on 15.6.1998.

8

Decision of District Consumer Disputes Redressal Forum

The complainants' application was given case **No. CPA387/ 3.3.98** by the District Consumer Disputes Redressal Forum. No any reply of E.O. or their Counsel was received by the Forum and the case was decided on 15.6.1998, as per the following order:

1. The complainant filed this complaint under consumer jurisdiction for directing the respondent to refund him the amount of Rs. 1,00,000/- deposited by him with the respondent on 27.11.97
2. Briefly stated the facts of the case are that the complainant bid the auction of a plot in Sector 15-II and he turned out to be the highest bidder for plot bearing No.1578 so he deposited Rs.1,00,000/- as earnest money. But soon thereafter he visited the plot and found that there was a live high tension electricity wire passing over the plot and the plot was full of dirty water. He at once changed the idea of purchasing the plot and applied for the refund. But the respondent has not taken any action as yet. Hence he filed this complaint.
3. The respondent contested the complaint on the

grounds that the complainant himself offered the bid for the highest amount and deposited Rs.1 lac as 10% of the tentative price. Thus he filed an application for the refund of this money. As the money was not refundable, he was issued the allotment letter.

4. We have heard the parties and have gone through the documentary evidence on the file. Even in the case of draw of lot a period of one month is given to the applicant whether he accepts the plot or not. So in the case of open auction that option should be available as the plots are not shown before the auction. When the complainant saw the plot it was found not worth the auction. No house could be built at that plot. So he immediately applied for the refund of his earnest money. Thus it is ordered that the amount of Rs. 1,00,000/- be refunded to the complainant with interest at the rate of 15% per annum from the date of deposit till the date of repayment.

(The text of the orders dated 15.6.1998 are given at Annexure IX)

9

Follow up of the Case

Letter dated 20th July, 1998 **(Annexure X)** along with the orders of the District Forum dated 15.6.1998 addressed to the Estate Officer, HUDA Gurgaon were handed over to his office duly acknowledged by his office, for compliance of orders of the District Forum, Gurgaon dated 15.6.1998.

Since no reply was received from the Estate Officer, a Registered letter No.L/SP/MPC04/5021574 dated 09.09.1998 **(Annexure XI)** along with the copy of the letter dated 20 July, 1998 and the copy of District Court Order No.CPA No.287/3.3.98 were sent again to him for compliance and repayment of the amount.

In the absence of any action by the Estate Officer, Gurgaon, the applicant approached the media and sent his grievances to the Press in the column "Letters to the Editor" to **Hindustan Times** which appeared on **November 2, 1998** under the heading **"Encroached HUDA plot"** The contents of the same are reproduced below:

> *"Having failed to get a peace of land from DDA as applied for on 26.3.1981 Application No.116368), Priority No. 8193, I participated in HUDA's auction of residential plots held in Gurgaon on 27.11.1997 as I was unsuccessful in all its public draws.*
>
> Being the highest bidder I was allotted plot no.1578

in Sector 15 Part II, Gurgaon which was advertised as one of the prime residential plots. But it was discovered the same day to be encroached and not fit for use. My request for refund of earnest money so fraudulently fetched by HUDA was not considered.

Will the authorities help me get back my hard-earned money? I am at present residing in a Government accommodation which is due to be vacated by theend of this month."

H.R. BANGIA
D-3 NIPCCD Campus,
Opp. Police Station,
Hauz Khas,
New Delhi-110016

10

First Contempt of Court Case

Application filed on 9.11.98 under Section 25 & 27 of the Consumer Protection Act, 1986

As no any report of HUDA to the Hindustan Times under the column 'HT Action Line' appeared to defend the allegations made by the complainants, as is normally the case that the opposite parties clarify the allegations and as no action to refund the amount was taken by the Estate Officer, HUDA, Gurgaon, the Complainant had no option but to take up the matter **for contempt of courts under Section 25 & 27 of CPAct, 1986 vide his Petition dated 9.11.1998 (Annexure XII)**

It was also mentioned in the petition that the non-payment caused a great mental agony and tension to the complainants and **he suffered a heart attack** on 4.3.1998. District Forum Registered this Petition as CPA No.1899/9.11.98 and issued the orders on 12.10.1999 as contained in Annexure XIII.

11

Orders of District Consumer Disputes Redressal Forum Dated 12-10-1999

Concluding remarks of orders are reproduced below.

> "On notice the ADA of HUDA put in appearance on 23.12.98 but till this day no reply has been filed. Rightly so because they have no excuse to make. Hence they did not file any reply. In this view of the matter the respondent & HUDA is afforded another opportunity to refund the amount of Rs. One Lac with interest @ 15% p.a. from the date of deposit till payment within 25 days of the order of this case; failing which the HUDA and its concerned functionaries will be proceeded against as per provisions of Sections 25/27 CP Act."

12

Article on "HUDA and the Role of M.R.T.P.C." – A Document is at Annexure XXXI

Keeping in view the fact that HUDA's Rules & Regulations had lot of discrepancies, the author in the meantime, conducted a mini case study of their rules and regulations which is given in the Annexure XXXI.

13

Reported the Matter to M.R.T.P.C. and Media about Non-Compliance of Orders by HUDA

Copy of Article on "**HUDA and the Role of MRTPC** was also sent for information and necessary action to Chairman, M.R.T.P.C., Kota Annexe, Shahjahan Road, New Delhi-110011 under Regd. Post No. A-1356 dated 20.11.98. **(Annexure XIV).** Shri I.S. Sain, Deputy Director, MRTPC rang him up on 6.4.1999 and accordingly the following documents were sent to the Director, (Research) MRTPC, New Delhi for going through the complaint pending at HUDA for disposal:

1. Form 'CC' i.e. Allotment letter dated 18.12.97 containing the terms and conditions of allotment.
2. Order of District Consumer Disputes Redressal Forum, Gurgaon dt. 15.6.98 directing HUDA, Gurgaon to refund the amount of Rs. 1 lakh with 15% interest from the date of payment till the date of repayment.
3. Photocopy of Times of India Advertisement dated 23.11.97.
4. Photocopy of the letter dated 27.11.97 addressed to

Estate Officer, HUDA, Gurgaon for refund of the earnest money of Rs. 1 lac.

5. Photocopy of 'letter to Editor Hindustan Times' dated 2.11.1998 which stated that Plot No. 1578 Sector 15 II was encroached.

14

Follow Up of Cases

The Complainant appeared before District Forum on 26.11.99 for follow up.

Since nothing was heard from the office of the MRTPC, reminder was sent on December 18, 1999 and February 11, 2000.

The purpose of it was to try and to get relief from all quarters for which such Authorities and Commissions are set up by the Government for giving relief to the people. It was later discovered that MRTPC did not reply because it was being replaced by **Trade Related Competition Commission of India (TRCC).**

The complainant sent a write-up in Times of India about the functioning of Consumer Courts in the column of "letters to the Editor" **Times of India** which appeared on 22nd December 1999 under the heading **"Consumer Protection"**. The contents of the same are reproduced as in to next page in box:

CONSUMER PROTECTION

It is very satisfying to know that the Employees' Provident Fund Scheme has now come under the purview of the Consumer Protection Act through a landmark Supreme Court judgment on December 17. Even in the CP Act there are innumerable hurdles in giving relief to the aggrieved. It is a people's Act. Those who wish to and who can, should be allowed to defend their cases in person themselves rather than hiring lawyers to ensure quick disposal of cases.

So far no one has been executed for contempt of court in the district forums. Lax administration and a thriving nexus among lawyers and the judges of the district forums have seriously hampered dispensation of justice. Decisions are not honoured and no one is pulled up for contempt of court. The very purpose for which the Consumer Protection Act was formulated and enacted is defeated as the decisions of the District Forums are not taken seriously. Under the circumstances, it **is no use trying to extend the scope of the Act unless care is taken to provide quick relief while dealing with grievances.**

H.R. Bangia

22.12.1999
New Delhi.

15

Second Contempt of Courts Application dated 12.11.1999 Filed

Having failed to get relief, second contempt of courts application dated 12.11.1999 was filed before the District Consumer Disputes Redressal Forum, Gurgon under Section 25 & 27 of C.P.Act, 1986. The case was registered as **Execution Appl.No.207/12.11.99. The details are given in Annexure (XV).**

16

Orders dated 7.3.2000 of District Consumer Disputes Redressal Forum, Gurgaon

Orders of District Consumer Disputes Redressal Forum, Gurgaon dated 7.3.2000 are given at Annexure XVI.

However, concluding orders are reproduced below :

"But when the compliance was not made, the applicant filed this 2nd execution application."

Notice of the application was given to the respondent and the respondent appeared through their ADA and filed reply taking the plea that that the complainant gave highest bid for plot No. 1578/15 II, Gurgaon and also deposited Rs.1 lac being 10% of the total cost at the time of auction. The complainant had given bid in open auction so he is not a consumer as per settled law. The orders passed by Hon'ble DCF, Gurgaon have been **challenged in the Hon'ble National Commission, New Delhi** through Sh.Ravindra Bana, Advocate. It is submitted that the orders of the DCF Gurgaon shall be complied with the prior approval of the competent authority.

We have heard the complainant in person and the counsel for the respondent and have gone through the evidence and record on the file.

The complainant had purchased plot Number 1578 Sector 15-II in a public auction held on 27.11.97. He had deposited Rs. One lac but the said plot was not fit for construction. So the complainant approached the respondent for the refund of Rs. One lac but the respondent failed to do so so far. So the complainant filed C.P.A. No.287/3.3.98decided on 15.6.98 but all in vain. The complainant again filed execution application under Section 25 & 27 C.P .Act in which it was ordered that the respondent shall refund the amount of Rs. One lac with interest @15% from date of deposit till the date ofpayment within 25 days of the order dated 12.10.99. HUDA again failed to comply with the order passed by this Forum. So the applicant again filed an execution application against the order dated 12.10.99.

> **Several show cause notices were given to the respondent for comply with he order but the respondent stated that the order passed by this Forum ave been challenged in the Hon'ble National Commission but no copy of stay order has been placed on the file. No** copy of complaint has been placed n the file. No any proceedings of Hon'ble National Commission in respect of the complaint had been filed by the respondent-HUDA. No affidavit in this regard has been filed by the HUDA.

So in these circumstances, the respondent is directed to refund the amount of Rs. One lac to the complainant with interest @ 15% per annum from the date of deposit till the date ofpayment within 25 days from today; **failing which HUDA shall pay Rs. 100/- per day to the complainant and strict action will be taken."**

No order as to costs

(The above orders were recorded at District Forum: 1181 dt. 22.3.2000).

17

Follow Up of the Second Contempt of Court Case

As a follow up, the Complainant appeared before District Forum on 26.11.99, 28.12.99, 18.1.2000, 14.2.2000 and 15.2.2000 to know about the progress in the case.

Copies of the orders dated 7.3.2000 were sent by Registered Post No. RL C8191 dt.7.4.2000 from Kalkaji PO, New Delhi on 7.4.2000 and Faxed at Phone 916-323211 to Shri Anurag Aggarwal, the then Administrator, HUDA also to inform him that the complainant had not received the refund of Rs. One lakh with interest @ 15% p.a. It was also informed to note the change in address.

18

National Consumer Disputes Redressal Commission, New Delhi

HUDA CHALLENGED THE ORDERS DATED 15.6.1998 OF THE DISTRICT CONSUMER DISPUTESD REDRESSAL FORUM, GURGAON BEFORE THE NATIONAL CONSUMER DISPUTES REDRESSAL COMMISSION, NEW DELHI. through Revision Petition No. 491 of 1999.

HUDA challenged the orders dated 15.6.98 of the District Consumer Disputes Redressal Forum, Gurgaon in the National Consumer Disputes Redressal Commission, New Delhi.

No information as to how HUDA went to National Consumer Disputes Redressal Commission, New Delhi without the knowledge of the complainants and the District Forum before taking up the matter before Haryana State Consumer Disputes Redressal Commission, Chandigarh

Notice for Revision Petition No. 491 of 1999 (Against the Order dated 24.7.1998) in Appeal No. 837/98 of the Haryana State Consumer Disputes Redressal Commission, Chandigarh dated 12th July, 2000 was received by H.R. Bangia, the Complainant in District Consumer Disputes Redressal Forum, Gurgaon. He became the Respondent in this case as the opposite party went for Revision Petition against order dated 24.7.1998 in above said appeal of the State Consumer Disputes Redressal Commission, Chandigarh. The detailed contents of the Notice are given in Annexure XVII.

19

Appeal Against Revision Petition Before National Consumer Disputes Redressal Commission, New Delhi

Appeal dated 22.8.2000 against Revision Petition No.491 of 1999 filed by H.R. Bangia against Opposite Party Before National Consumer Dispute Redressal Commission, New Delhi is given at **ANNEXURE XVIII.**

Reply/version of respondents was sent vide Speed Post Receipt Regn. No. EE00021887 dated 22.8.2000 and also got delivered personally on 22.8.2000. Recorded Receipt No.9080 dt. 22.8.2000 duly stamped.

20

HUDA Challenged the Orders of District Consumer Disputes Redressal Forum, Gurgaon dated 7.3.2000 before the Haryana State Consumer Disputes Redress Commission, Haryana

HUDA challenged the orders dated 7.3.2000 of District Consumer Disputes Redressal Forum, Gurgaon before Haryana State Consumer Disputes Redressal Commission. in Revision Petition No. 36 of 2000. The details are given in **Annexure XIX.**

The Estate Officer, HUDA, Gurgaon sent by hand Summon/Notice to the respondents i.e. H.R. Bangia and Smt. Subhash Bangia separately vide his Memo No.13267 **dated 6.9.2000** on **11.9.2000 at 7.00** p.m. stating to kindly find enclosed herewith the *Dasti* Summon/Notice passed by the Hon'ble State Commission, Haryana Chandigarh for appearing on **13.9.2000 at 11.00 a.m**. before Hon'ble State Commission Haryana, Chandigarh. The receipt of it was also acknowledged as desired by Estate Officer, HUDA Gurgaon.

The Respondent accordingly attended and contested the case on 13.9.2000 at Haryana State Consumer Disputes Redressal Commission, Chandigarh.

The case was fixed for hearing on 4.12.2000 but was adjourned to 21.12.2000'

It was thus contested on 21.12.2000.

21

Orders dated 15.2.2001 of Haryana State Consumer Disputes Redressal Commission, Chandigarh

The orders of the Haryana State Consumer Disputes Redressal Commission, Chandigarh were given on 15.2.2001 and are at Annexure XX.

However the concluding orders of the Haryana State Consumer Disputes Redressal Commission, Chandigarh dated 15.2.2001 are reproduced below:

> "We have heard the counsel for the petitioner as well as respondent in person and have also perused the impugned order. After taking into consideration their respective submissions, we are convinced that there was no justification for imposing penalty of Rs. 100/- per day upon the petitioner - HUDA and the same is waived off. The rest of the order is maintained. The impugned order is modified in the manner indicated above and the revision petition stands disposed of accordingly. However, it is made clear that order of the District Forum is to be implemented within one month from the receipt of the copy of the order; failing which penal action will be initiated under Section 27 of the Consumer Protection Act against the petitioner - HUDA."

22

Follow up for Recovery

Chief Administrator HUDA, Panchkula vide Regd. Letter No. RL F-3438 dated 27.3.2001 **(Annexure XXI)** and Estate Officer, Haryana Urban Development Authority, Sector 14, HUDA OFFICE COMPLEX, Gurgaon (Haryana) vide his Regd. Letter Nos. RL F-7439 dated 27th March 2001 **(Annexure XXII)** were sent copies of above orders of State Consumer Disputes Redressal Commission, Haryana, Chandigarh in respect of the Revision Petition No. 36 of 2000 **(decided on 15.2.2001)** in respect of **HUDA Vs. H.R. Bangia** & Subhash Bangia both residents of E-99 (Top Floor), Lajpat Nagar II, Central Market, New Delhi-110 024 for favour of their kind perusal with the request to kindly comply with the orders accordingly.

Reminded vide Regd. Letter No. RL 1113 dated 10 April 2001 (Annexure **XXIII)** to Estate Officer for compliance and also invited his attention to refer to earlier registered letter dated March 27,2001 (see Annexure XXII) on the same subject.

23

Third Contempt of Court Application Dated 20.6.2001 Under Section 25 and 27 filed at District Consumer Disputes Redressal Forum, Gurgaon

Contempt of Courts Application dt. 20.6.2001 was filed before the District Consumer Disputes Redressal Forum, Gurgaon again bringing out the facts that the defendant had not complied with the orders of various Fora as per details: (Full Text given at **Annexure XXIV**)

(i) Order dated 15.6.98 of Gurgaon Distt. Forum
(ii) Order dated 24.7.1998 of Haryana State Commission
(iii) Order dated 12.10.1999 of Gurgaon Distt. Forum
(iv) Order 7.3.2000 of District Forum, and
(v) Finally order dated 15.2.2001 of Haryana State Commission.

When the above case came up for hearing on 23.10.2001 the HUDA Counsel instead of complying with the orders, submitted application dated 23.8.2001 objecting to replacing page No. 7 of the Contempt application dt. 20.6.2001 about which the complainant had made a request with his application dated 23.8.2001.

The District Forum vide their order dated 6.9.2001 **(Annexure XXV)** allowed the complainant to replace the page as the Defendant had not complied with the latest order about which the mention was to be made in the application dt. 20.6.2001. The case was adjourned to 8.10.2001.with the instructions that EO HUDA may appear in person on 8.10.2001.

Estate Officer did not appear in person on 8.10.2001 as such Dasti dt. 23.10.2001 **(Annexure XXVI)** was issued by the President of the District Forum to the Estate Officer to appear in person before the Forum on 8.11.2001 with the relevant records of the case for compliance. A copy of the *Dasti* was also obtained by the Complainant on 24.10.2001 for records and reference.

Estate Officer appeared in person on 9.11.2001 instead of on 8.11.2001.

District Forum issued orders on 14.12.2001 **(Annexure XXVII).**

Details of the orders are also reproduced hereunder:

> HR Bangia Vs HUDA Present: Complainant in person
> Shri Satbir Singh Tanwar, Counsel for the complainant

Vide Order dated 23.10.2001 the Estate Officer, HUDA Gurgaon was directed to appear in person before this Forum for compliance of the order passed by this Forum on dated 15.6.1998 by which the respondent-HUDA was directed to refund the amount of Rs. 1,00,000/- to the complainant with interest at the rate of 15% per annum from the date of deposit till the date of payment and failing which strict action will be taken. Thereafter, the opposite -party-HUDA went in appeal against that order and the following order was passed by the Hon'ble State Commission on dated 15.2.2001

> "We are convinced that there was no justification for imposing penalty of Rs.100/- per day upon the

petitioner-HUDA and the same is waived off. The rest of the order is maintained."

In compliance to the order of this Forum, Sh. Pardeep Kumar, Estate Officer, HUDA has appeared before this Forum on dated 9.11.2001 and made a statement that he will comply with the order of the Forum after receiving the approval of Chief Administrator, HUDA, Chandigarh within a month. But no action has been taken by the opposite party till date. So notice be issued to the Chief Administrator, HUDA, Chandigarh with the direction to approve the case and approval of the same be sent before this Forum on or before 15.1.2002 so that compliance of the order is made accordingly.

In connection with the compliance of above order the Estate Officer, HUDA, Gurgaon furnished the following letter which he addressed to The Chief Administrator, HUDA, Legal Cell, Panchkula on 30.1.2002.

From

The Estate Officer,
HUDA, Gurgaon.

To

The Chief Administrator,
HUDA, Legal Cell, Panchkula.

Memo No. 1807

Dated: 30.1.2002

Sub: Execution Case - H.R. Bangia V/S HUDA (Plot No. 1578/15-II, Gurgaon.

Ref: This Office memo No. 11213 dated 5.11.01

It is submitted that plot No. 1578/15-II, Gurgaon was allotted in open auction in the name of Sh. H.R. Bangia. The allottee deposited 10% amount. The allottee moved an application for refund of earnest money which was deposited by him. The allotment letter issued on 18.12.97. The allottee filed a consumer complaint before DCF, Gurgaon. The DCF(G) ordered that the earnest money be refunded. The entire matter was referred to the H.Q. vide memo No. 11331 dated 2.7.98. Complainant filed an execution application for executing the court orders. The DCF heard the matter at length and ordered that refund of Rs. 1.00 lac may be made to the complainant with interest @ 15%p.a. from the date of deposit till the date of payment. The allottee earlier also filed an execution petition and the entire matter was referred to the H.Q. from time to time. Now the case is pending in National Commission New Delhi and Sh. Ravinder Rana Advocate has been engaged to defend the case on behalf of HUDA. The Hon'ble Forum is pressing hard to implement the order at the earliest.

It is therefore requested that necessary decision may kindly be taken to avoid any legal complication in the matter.

Sd/-
Estate Officer,
HUDA,

Gurgaon.

24

Follow up of the Case at District Consumer Disputes Redressal Forum, Gurgaon

The Complainant appeared before the President, District Forum on 31.1.2002 to know the progress of the case. The President showed him the copy of said letter which was given to the President, by the Estate Officer dated 30.1.2002. The President informed the complainant that the Estate Officer had complied with the orders by issue of letter dated 30..1.2002 to the Chief Administrator, HUDA, Panchkula, as per the instructions given in the previous order dated 14.12.2001 and that he was in the process of getting approval from the Chief Administrator but the complainant said that such excuses are being made from time to time. There is no rule under which this could be entertained. They must refund the money or action could be taken under Section 27 of the C.P. Act, 1986.

The complainant was not satisfied with the reply of Estate Officer and requested the Hon'ble President of the District Court that the case was being delayed intentionally on frivolous ground. It would be only appropriate, if action could be taken as per the provisions of the Act without further delay. On that the President got prepared the bailable warrant and signed on 31.1.2001. The same was issued on 1.2.2002 to the Estate Officer with the direction to appear on 20.2.2002 at 10.00. A copy of it was also obtained by the Complainant next day i.e. on 1.2.2002.

25

Again Before National Consumer Disputes Redressal Commission Regarding Revision Petition No. 491 of 1999 of HUDA

If a party is aggrieved by the order passed by the State Consumer Disputes Redressal Commission, the remedy is to approach the National Consumer Disputes Redressal Commission and not to invoke the jurisdiction of the court under Article 227 of the Constitution, *P. Subramanian V. Oriental Insurance Co. Ltd., AIR 2004 Mad. 494.*

In the meantime the Respondent appeared before the National Consumer Disputes Redressal Commission, New Delhi on 21.12.2001 regarding Revision Petition No. 491 of 1999 of HUDA.

26

Decision of National Consumer Disputes Redressal Commission, New Delhi dated 21.12.2001

The copy of the decision dated 21.12.2001 of the National Consumer Disputes Redressal Commission, New Delhi is reproduced below and also given at Annexure XXVIII.

Revision Petition No. 491 of 1999 (From the Order dated 24.7.98 in f.a.No.837/98 of the State Commission, Haryana) H.U.D.A. Vs. H.R. Bangia came up for hearing on 21.12.2001..

The case came before :	Hon'ble Mr. Justice D.P. Wadhwa, President, Hon'ble Mr. Justice J.K. Mehra, Member Mrs. Rajyalakshmi Rao, Member Mr. B.K. Taimni, Member
For the Appellant	Mr. Ravindra Bana, Advocate
For the Respondent	Mr. G.L. Malik, Advocate

21.12.2001

ORDER

J.K. MEHRA J MEMBER

In this case the Respondent/Complainant had purchased a plot at an open auction and as per the terms deposited 10% of the price. Thereafter, he went to seek an inspection of the plot and was shown the plot and discovered to his dismay that the plot had a high-tension wire passing over it, apart from that it had a depression where water had collected which need to be reclaimed. He approached the Petitioner for cancellation of his plot in view of the above serious deficiencies on the plea that he had made his bid for a developed plot free from any such problems

The Petitioner took up the stand that as per the terms of the auction if the bidder does not pay the 15% further amount within 30 days, the HUDA administration was within its rights to forfeit the 10% amount deposited. The Complainant filed a complaint alleging that HUDA could do so only if it had offered an inspection of the site before the auction. Since no inspection was offered at the time or before the auction before the bids, no such plea would come to its avail and it was liable to refund the amount which had been deposited on his successful bidding. The District Forum upheld the contention of the Respondent and decided in his favour, directing the Petitioner to refund the amount with interest at the rate of 15% p..a. The State Commission also agreed with the District and sustained that order. We see no jurisdictional error or infirmity in the concurrent findings of the two for a below which would merit our interference under Sec. 21(b) of the Consumer Protection Act, 1986.

The Revision Petition is dismissed

Sd/-

(D.P. WADHWA)
PRESIDENT

Sd/-

(J.K. MEHRA)
MEMBER

Sd/-

RAJYALAKSHMI RAO)
MEMBER

Sd/-

(B.K. TAIMNI)
MEMBER

Note:

In connection with the above it may be recorded that Shri G.L. Malik, the Counsel did not appear but the Defendant i.e. H.R Bangia. appeared. Shri Malik had given him the following letter requesting for adjournment of the case for 4 weeks. H.R. Bangia himself contested though the name of the Counsel i.e. Shri G.L. Malik is given in the Order.This could not be brought to the notice of the Commission because the orders were issued later on

————

G.L. Malik, Advocate Ph. 6332927(O), 6323387®
Chamber number 90, Gurgaon Pager number 9632-150613

Respected Mr. Bangia,

I have developed acute/shooting pain in my left leg. I have been advised by my doctor not to strain my left leg which renders me unfit to stand and argue your case on 10th instant before Hon'ble National Commission.

Please pray for an adjournment for 4 weeks.

Regards,

Yours

Sd/- G,L. Malik
4/XII/2K1

Clarification about the above letter

When the above letter was handed over to H.R. Bangia, Mr. Malik was found running about in the District Court, Gurgaon and attending his cases. Moreover, the case was first fixed for 10.12.2002. Mr. Malik was informed that it had been adjourned to 21.12.2001. He was informed specifically that in case he would not attend the case on 21.12.2002, the rest of the amount i.e. Rs. 5000/- will be not paid to him, as an amount of Rs.3,300/- was paid in advance to prepare the reply for the National Commission. Rest of the amount was agreed to be paid on the condition that the decision would be in favour of the applicant and the advocate pleads the case. Since the Advocate did not turn up to defend the case no payment was made to him.

27

Regarding Rate of Interest Payable by HUDA

As recorded in the Revision Petition No. 36 HUDA counsel pointed out that the rate of interest being charged was too much and it should had been 10%. Keeping that in mind HUDA started negotiations about the rate of interest on the amount of E.M. of Rs. 1,00,000/-.to be refunded with interest from the date of deposit. It was informed that if we could agree to claim 12% instead of 15% ordered by the Fora, they would release the amount of Rs. 1 lac. In that case we agreed with the condition that HUDA may not go in for S.L.P. before the Hon'ble Supreme Court. As such an Affidavit dated 6.2.2002 was furnished by us to HUDA on Rs. 10/- Non-Judicial Stamp Paper. Accordingly, the Affidavit was Faxed on 6.2.2002 to Ph.0091 172566381 at 1:31PM and the original Affidavit was sent by First Flight Courier No.*D 26342980* on 6. 2. 2002. to HUDA Office, Panchkula.

The purpose of brining the above fact in the case study is that how big business organizations pressurize the individuals even after the decision was given by all the Fora for repayment of the amount with interest @ 15% from the date of payment to the date of repayment by HUDA. It also shows how transparent such big organizations are!

28

Back to District Consumer Disputes Redressal Forum, Gurgaon

Final date of appearance

As the case was fixed on 20.2.2002 at 10 a.m. no one from HUDA had turned up by 1.00 p.m. It was submitted to the President District Consumer Disputes Redressal Forum, Gurgaon that non-bailable warrants could be issued under such circumstances. The President was busy in disposal of cases which were over 100 on that day and he told the Complainant (H.R. Bangia) that he should wait for some time more and thereafter he would take the proper view. A few minutes after Mr. Pradeep Kumar, Estate Officer, HUDA appeared.

The matter was taken up and recorded in the File that for disposal of the case an amount of Rs. 1,50,000/- vide Cheque No. 425817 dated 20.2.2002 drawn on Oriental Bank of Commerce, Extn. Counter, HUDA Office, Sector-14, Gurgaon-122001 in favour of Sh. H.R. Bangia against the EM of Rs. 1,00,000/- plus interest was being handed over in the presence of the President, District Forum, Gurgaon.

THUS THE ABOVE CASE WAS DECIDED ON 20.2.2002 WHICH WAS TAKEN UP ON 3.3.1998 FOR WHICH THE ORDERS BY THE DISTRICT FORUM, GURGAON WERE ISSUED ON 15.6.1998 WHICH WERE CHALLENGED IN STATE COMMISSION, HARYANA AND THEREAFTER IN NATIONAL COMMISSION TO WHICH BOTH THE COMMISSIONS AGREED WITH THE ORDERS OF THE DISTRICT FORUM, GURGAON.

29

Dates of Events (Chronological Order)

1.	Application filed	3.3.1998
2.	First Date of hearing	15.4.1998
3.	Letter to E.O. for repayment	20.7.1998
4.	Reminder again sent to EO	9.9.1998
5.	Attended	9 11.98
6.	Attended	23.12.98
7.	Attended	7/7/99
8.	Attended	14.9.99
9.	Attended	12.10.99
10.	Application u/s 25/27 filed	9.11.1999
11.	Orders of above application issued	10.12.99
12.	Appeared in DCF S.No.1	26.11.1999
13.	Appeared at S.No.22 in DCF	28.12.99
14.	Appeared at S.No.11	18.1.2000
15.	Appeared to come on 15.2.2000	14.2.2000
16.	Listed at S.No. 1	15.2.2000
17.	Listed at S.No. 1	6.3.2000
18.	Order issued under section 25 & 27 of CP Act	7.3.2000
19.	Appeal to National Commission against Revision Petition No.491 of 1999 of HUDA	22.8.2000

20.	Received Dasti of E.O. HUDA dt.6.9.2000 with RP 36 of 2000 to appear State Commission	11.9.2000
21.	Appeared before State Commission, Chandigarh	13.9.2000
22.	Application u/s 25 & 27 filed	20.6.2001
23.	Application for replacement of page No. 7 filed	23.8.2001
24.	Order issued for placement of page No.7	6.9.2001
25.	Defendant objection letter against order appeal handed over through the Counsel to Complainant in Court without knowledge of the Court.	8.10.2001
26.	Dasti to EO to appear on 8.11.2001.	23.10.2001
27.	E.O. could not attend	8.11.2001
28.	E.O. HUDA, Gurgaon appeared in person	9.11.2001
29.	Order of above issued by DCF	14.12.01
30.	E.O. HUDA Gurgaon gave copy of letter issued by him to Chief Administrator, Chandigarh to inform that he was taking action to comply with orders of the DCF.	30.1.2002
31.	At the instance of the complainant DCF issued Bailable Warrant to E.O. to appear in Person on 20.2.20002	31.1.2002
32.	Dasti issued by DCF for compliance by EO HUDA	1.2.2002
33.	E.O. appeared in person and handed over the cheque of Rs.1,50,000/- (which includes Interest and E.M. amount of Rs. 1 lac.)	20.2.2002

30

Cases Attended at State and National Commissions

In the meantime CASES Attended at State Commission and at National Commission.

34.	State Commission, Chandigarh	4.12.2000
35.	State Commission, Chandigarh	21.12.2000
36.	Case decided at State Commission, Chandigarh	15.2.2001
37.	Case Decided at National Commission, New Delhi (Previously date was fixed to appear on 10.12.2001, which was adjourned to 21.12.2001)	21.12.2001
39.	Order dated 21.12.2001 issued by National Commission for refund of amount of Rs. 1 lac with interest @ 15% per annum from the date of payment.	11.1.2002

31

Constraints/Observations

1. Application for amendment of complaint can be entertained by the District Forum, though there is no specific provision for amendment, there is also no bar in allowing amendment: *Manimalam v. K. Subrayan, AIR 2004 Mad. 446.*

2. Whereas the provisions in the Consumer Protection Act, 1986 are very clear and easy to follow even then the case was disposed of after four years of its order.

3. It is high time that individuals, institutions, NGOs, activists make the people aware about the provisions of this social legislation i.e. Consumer Protection Act, 1986 so that their grievances are given sympathetic consideration and are also decided on priority.

4. A visit to the site on 3.12.2009 it was discovered that no house had come up so far at that site of Plot No. 1578 Sector 15 II, Gurgaon.

5. The Plot adjacent to it i.e. No. 1579-P Sector 15 Part II, Gurgaon was also not accepted by the allottee Er. A.K. Rampal resident of F-26/114, Sector 7, Rohini, New Delhi. He also went for appeal for an alternate plot at the same rate and at Prime location. That plot was also still vacant and no construction had come up on that plot as yet.

6. Whereas writing a case study is not an interesting exercise but the author has described it in such a way that

it has become interesting. He has also described the case in a simple language and made it very explicit so that even the intricacies involved could also be understood by the readers. It would also facilitate in drafting the Complaints properly and to the point.

7. It is thus hoped that it will be useful for practical purposes to the common man as well. It will also be useful for the students, researchers and the activists alike.

32

Conclusion

1. Prior to filing the application, the matter was taken up for recovery of the amount under the administrative procedures; failing which the matter was filed in the District Forum, Gurgaon that too after exploring all possibilities of redressal of grievances at various levels.

2. At the outset it was not understood as to why the plot was included along with other commercial and residential plots when it did not qualify for auction for the reasons given in the appeal of the Complainant dated 3.3.98. An alluring advertisement prompted the buyers to participate in the auction.

3. HUDA's Regulation 6(2)' was mentioned at the top of the allotment letter under CC Form and at no where else the prcvisions of this Regulation 6(2) were mentioned or explained i.e. neither in the advertisement in the TOI dt. 23.11.97 nor in the pamphlets distributed widely to the public, at the auction site. It was also not explained or announced to the public at the time of auction. Whereas this regulation was evoked time and again in their appeals at all the Fora.

4. Whereas the Estate Officer, Gurgaon (Sanjay Joon) stated in the Affidavit that the contents of the affidavit were true to his knowledge and information derived from records" submitted to National Consumer Disputes Redressai Commission (copy of which was forwarded to Respondent

i.e. H.R Bangia & Anr.vide NCDRC NOTICE dated 12 July 2000) regarding HUDA Revision Petition No. 491 of 1999 (Against the Order dated 24.7.1998) even then there were the following discrepancies in their documents, which have been reproduced as they were filed:-

(a) At Annexure I of their Revision Petition No.491 of 1999 in place of Sector 15, Sector 16 was mentioned; In place of Rs. 1,00,000/-, an amount of Rs, 3,00,000/ - was mentioned, and in place of Sector (II), Sector (iII). was mentioned in their Annexure 1,which was the main and first appeal of the Complainant dated 3.3.1998.

(b) Like wise in their First Appeal.— —of 1998 in Annexure 4, in place of Rs. 7,300/- per sq meter, Rs.7900/- per sq. meter was mentioned; in place of deposited Rs. 1 lac.deposited; Rs. 2 lac was mentioned and in place of Regulation 6(2), Regulation (12) was mentioned.

(c) Statement that the plot was shown is totally baseless statement as the Complainant was never shown the plot.

(d) The date of application was not mentioned, unsigned copy furnished in I.A.No.337/1999 in RP. No.491/ 1999 was not true copy and date of filing was not indicated in the copy furnished to the defendant.

5. Since the original application of the Complainant dated 3.3.98 was decided in favour of the complainant vide order dated 15.6.98, the decision of it rests on this only and all other applications or appeals are for arguments and discussion. In order to gain time the Counsel of HUDA unnecessarily raised objections to Complainants' appeal under Sector 25/27 vide his application dated 20.6.2001 vide which Page 7 was to be replaced against which they appealed on 5.9.2001 but the District Forum allowed the complainants to replace the page vide their Order dated 6.9.2001

6. The case was decided when the Complainants filed

their third Application under Section.25/27. Whereas Section 25 of the CP.Act, 1986 clearly states that "Enforcement of orders by the Forum, the State Commission or the National Commission (Sec.25) that every order made by the District Forum, the State Commission or the National Commission may be enforced by the District, the State Commission or the National Commission, as the case may be, in the same manner as if it were decree or order made by a court in a suit pending therein and it shall be lawful for the District Forum, the State Commission or the National Commission to send, in the event of its inability to execute it, such order to the court within the local limits of whose jurisdiction "-

- *(a)* in the case of an order against a company, the registered office of the company is situated, or
- *(b)* in the case of any order against any other person, the place where the person concerned voluntarily resides or carries on business or personally works for gain, is situated, and thereupon, the court to which the order is so sent, shall execute the order as if were a decree or order sent to it for execution.

7. Under Section 27 there is provision of penalties where a traders or a person against whom a complaint is made (substituted by the Consumer Protection (Amendment) Act, 1993 (w.e.f. 18th June 1993) or the complainant) fails or omits to comply with any order made by the District Forum, the State Commission or the National Commissioner, as the case may be, such trader or person, or complainant shall be punishable with imprisonment for a term which shall not be less than one month but which may extend to three years, or with fine which shall not be less than two thousands rupees but which may extend to ten thousand rupees, or with both:

> Provided that the District Forum, the State Commission or the National Commission, as the case may be, may, if it is satisfied that the circumstances of any case so require, impose a sentence of imprison-

ment or fine, or both, for a term lesser than the minimum term and the amount lesser than the minimum amount, specified in this Section.

8. No stay order of State or National Commission was furnished by HUDA to the District Consumer disputes Redressal Forum, Gurgaon. Had the District Forum took up the matter under Section 27 at first instance of the execution application dated 9.11.98, the time taken by HUDA on frivolous grounds could be curtailed in disposing of the appeal of the complainant dated 3.3.1998 well in time. There certainly appears to be a nexus between the organizations and the judges of the District Forums that lax administration is the root cause of not getting justice quickly for which the enactment of Consumer Protection Act of 1986 was promulgated to give relief to the people within a reasonable time.

9. But where the issue involved is a legal issue, the complaint cannot be said to be frivolous, *Rasiklal Mohanlal v. Apollo Tyres Ltd., 1992(II) CPR 327.*

10. Every complaint filed under sub-section (1) of Section 12, sub-section (1) of Section 17 and Clause (a) in sub-clause (i) of Section 21 of the Act shall be accompanied by a Fee as specified (See relevant Table given in the Consumer Protection Rules, 1987) in the form of crossed demand draft drawn on a Nationalised Bank or through a crossed Indian Postal Order in favour of the President of District Forum, Registrar of the State Commission or the Registrar of the National Commission, as the case may be and payable at the respective place where the District, State Commission or the National Commission is situated.

11. **Frivolous or Vexatious complaints are also made in the Fora** merely because no court fee is payable for lodging a complaint before the Consumer Forums, parties have a tendency to misuse the provisions of the Consumer Protection Act in respect of matters not falling within its purview. This tendency must be discouraged : *Orissa Vegetable Oil Complex Ltd., v. State of Orissa, 1994 (1) CPR 32*

12.In the Revision Petition No.491/1999 HUDA under "Written Statement on behalf of Respondent" submitted the following:

> "The respondent HUDA made frivolous statements in their Revision Petition No. 491/1999 before the National Consumer Disputes Redressal Commission that the Hon'ble Forum had no jurisdiction to entertain and try the present complaint in view of Section 50 of HUDA Act; that the provisions are not applicable to the immoveable property; that the complainant is not a consumer and HUDA is not a manufacturer; that the plot in dispute does not come within the definition of goods; that the present complaint is not a complaint; that a numerous facts and law point are involved which can only be decided by a regular suit; that the complainant had not availed the remedy of arbitration as provided in terms and conditions of allotment letter; that the complaint is bad for non-joinder and mis-joinder of necessary parties; that the complainant had no locus standis to file the present complaint and that the complaint is badly time barred and the same is not maintainable in the present form."

Whereas National Commission decided in favour of the complainant but it is unfortunate that no action against HUDA was taken for making the above frivolous statement in their revision petition before the National Commission.

33

Comments on "Consumer Protection – A Classical Case Study"

Vijay Mehta
President VM Centre for Peace
97 Commercial Road London E1 1RD)

Thanks for your email and the attachment for the case study entitled "Consumer Protection - A Classical Case Study". I am pleased that a prominent figure Shri T.N. Chaturvedi has written the foreword for your book.

Your book is a good contribution and an example of governance in dealing with bureaucracy through The Consumer Protection Act 1986. Your case study highlights the obstructions and obstacles put by Haryana Urban Development Authority (HUDA) in the procurement of housing which are the rights of the citizens. This is a common disease in society which hinders progress.

Your book is an excellent study, a useful tool for information and education. It also brings forward the ways in which public can get redress from unheeding establishment. Well done for spreading consumer consciousness in the society.

G C Mathur, Convenor-Trustee Treasurer, Binty (A Voluntary Consumer Organisation)

It was a pleasure receiving your mail with an excellent experience of fighting the might's of the crooks in the public sector like that of HUDA. You deserve a thumping pat on your back for winning the case. Your intentions of educating other consumers of your experience in the consumer fora are definitely laudable and am one with you.

Prof. Srinibas Pathi, Professor and Head, Deptt of Public Admn, Mizoram (Central) University, Aizawl)

Consumer Protection - A Classical Case Study is a well thought out and well drafted work with theoretical insight and practical and empirical inputs. Urban problems including that of housing and infrastructural issues have assumed a serious turn to day. The service providers, both public and private, have a field day in the absence of consumer awareness and movement. There is an urgent need to implement all the available Acts, Rules etc in letter and spirit. The present study would definitely help other consumers and groups to take up similar steps for protecting their genuine interests

Prof. R.B. Jain, Retd Professor, DU)

Thank you for sending me the copy of your book containing Shri TNC's foreword. You are very lucky to get a Foreword from him, and he has written a very good one. Congratulations to you!

Dr. Anirban Chakraborty, IIT Kharagpur

Your entire endeavour is worthy in achieving such objective; but somehow people in our country very rarely come forward for protection of his/her rights. I hope this book will help every common citizen.

ANNEXURE I

HARYANA URBAN DEVELOPMENT AUTHORITY

Book No. Dated 27.11.97

Receipt No. 413

Received Form No. ——————from Shri/Smt. H.R. Bangia & Smt. Subhash Bangia A sum of Rupees One lac only.

In Cash/Bank Draft/Cheque No. Cash dated——— ——— 27.11.97

Drawn on——————————————————

On account of E.M. Plot 1578/15 II

Rs. 1,00,000/——————————————

Sd/-

Signature of Issuing Authority
(Official Stamp)

ANNEXURE II

The Estate Officer,
Haryana Urban Development Authority
Gurgaon (Haryana)

Attn: Shri Sanjay Joon, HCS

Dt.27.11.97

Subject: **Auction on 27.11.1997 for Plot No. 1578 in Sector 15-II** Refund of the earnest amount paid for the plot

Sir,

1. I am to state that as per the advertisement in Times of India on November 23, 1997, I was tempted to come all the way to Gurgaon as I am working in Delhi. I don't have any house/land/plot either in Delhi or in Gurgaon so I wanted to have a plot for which I came to explore the possibility of getting a plot to construct the house on urgent basis as **I am due to retire on June 30, 1998.**

2. I was the highest bidder and paid an amount of Rs.7320/-p..Meter for plot of 6 *marla* in **Sect‹ r 15-II Plot No. 1578.**

3. On going to the site of the above plot it is observed that the said plot is situated at a **live High Tension** wire over the plot and there is *'dal-dal'* on the site. I **don't know how it was cleared for auction when as per rules there should be no live HT over the plot.** I am an officer in Semi-Govt. organization of National Institute of Public Cooperation & Child Development under the Department of Women & Child Development, Ministry of Human

Resource Development, Govt. of India, New Delhi. I have been put to mental agony and tension on looking at the site of the said plot. I, therefore, request you to kindly refund me the amount of Rs. 1,00,000/-(Rupees one lac paid against receipt No. 413 dt. 27.11.1997.

Kindly help me on this mental tension and oblige.

Yours faithfully,
Sd/-
(H.R. Bangia)
ADMINISTRATIVE OFFICER,
NIPCCD
D-3, NIPCCD Campus,
Opp. Police Station, Hauz Khas,
New Delhi-110016
Ph.6960950

ANNEXURE III

H.R. Bangia

D-3 NIPCCD Campus,
Opp. Police Station,
Hauz Khas,
New Delhi-110 016

Nov. 30, 1997

Shri R.S. Verma,
Chief Secretary, Govt. of Haryana,
Chandigarh.

Refund of E.M. of Rs. 1 lac paid in auction of Plot No. 1578 in Sec. 15-II, HUDA, Gurgaon

Respected Sir,

In the auction held on 27th Nov. 1997 at Sec.14, Gurgaon, I being the highest bidder for plot No.1578/15-II paid an amount of Rs. 1 lakh as earnest money for the said plot.

Immediately after inspection of the site on 27th Nov.1997 itself it was discovered that the said plot is not at all liveable and approached the Estate Officer, HUDA, Gurgaon for refund as per copy of letter dt. 27.11.1997 enclosed for your kind perusal.

I or my family don't own any plot or house in Delhi or Gurgaon and I am due to retire in June '98. We cannot start construction on the said plot on the following grounds:

1. That the live H.T. wire which is right on the head of the adjacent preferential plot No.1579P is also passing very close to the said plot;

2. That some unauthorized construction is existing on the said plot for years together and is reported to be under litigation.
3. That the adjacent plot was also auctioned but the bidder did not deposit the E.M. after inspection of the site.
4. That because of High Tension wire on a number of plots in front of the said plot, 5 years hence possession of those plots has not been given to the allottees.
5. The roads in front are very narrow and are not approachable. All plots are dugged deep with 'dal-dal' and breeding mosquitoes for years.
6. There is no appropriate entry to this part of the area for hundreds of plots and on turnings from these narrow roads even smallest vehicle may go into 'khuds'.
7. About 20′ high mound and not less than 1 km. long by the side of the said plot has segregated this part of the area to the other side of Sector 15-II.
8. The whole area has not at all been developed and it appears as if it is not a part of the other area of Sector 15-II where a number of VIPS are allotted plots and residing also.
9. There is a colony called 'Patel Nagar' which is touching the very area of this Sector and has not been separated from that colony.

On perusal of the site it would reveal that this is not at all a part of Sector 15-II and is unfit for immediate construction.

Since I am residing at Govt. accommodation which is to be vacated after retirement, I shall be grateful if the earnest money is refunded to me at the earliest so that I may make some alternate arrangements for my abode and peacefully discharge my other liabilities of unsettled children as I have been put to mental tension on looking at the site of the said plot.

I am sure, yourgoodself shall be very benevolent and issue orders to the Administrator, HUDA, Gurgaon for refund of the earnest money paid vide receipt No.413 dt. 27.11.1997 for Rs. 1 lakh for the above said plot.

I shall be ever grateful to you for this act of kindness.

Yours faithfully,
Sd/-
H.R. Bangia

Encl: As above.

ANNEXURE IV

प्रेषक

मुख्य प्रशासक,
हरियाणा शहरी विकास प्राधिकरण,
सैक्टर-6, पंचकूला ।

सेवा में

सम्पदा अधिकारी,
हुडा, गुड़गांवा ।

यादी क्रमांक: ए-5-97/41350-57 दिनांक: 19/12/97

विषय: प्लाट न0 1578 सैक्टर-15 पार्ट-II गुड़गांवा को नीलामी में खरीद करते समय जमा करवाई गई राशि को वापिस करने बारे ।

उपरोक्त विषय के संदर्भ में ।

श्री एस.आर. बांगिया से प्राप्त प्रार्थना पत्र दिनांक 30.11.97 की प्रति आपको भेजते हुए अनुरोध है कि मामले का नीतिगत निरीक्षण कर, शीघ्र निपटान करते हुए, प्रार्थी को उचित उत्तर देने का कष्ट करें तथा इसकी सूचना इस कार्यालय को भी भेजें ।

प्रशासकीय अधिकारी,
कृते: मुख्य प्रशासक, हुडा, पंचकूला ।

पृ0 क्रमांक: ए-5-97/ दिनांक:

एक प्रति श्री एस.आर. बांगिया डी-3 NLSCP कैम्पस सामने पुलिस स्टेशन, हौजखास नई दिल्ली। उनके पत्र दिनांक 30.11.97 के संदर्भ में जो मुख्य सचिव, हरियाणा सरकार को प्रेषित था, प्रेषित करते हुए अनुरोध है कि वह उक्त विषय पर सम्पदा अधिकारी, हुडा, गुड़गांव से सम्पर्क स्थापित करें ।

प्रशासकीय अधिकारी,
कृते: मुख्य प्रशासक, हुडा, पंचकूला ।

ANNEXURE V

H.R. Bangia

D-3, NIPCCD Campus,
Opp. Police Station,
Hauz Khas,
New Delhi—110 016
Ph.6960950
December 22, 1997.

Estate Officer,
HUDA, Gurgaon

Subject: Refund for Plot No. 1578 Sector 15 Part II, Gurgaon. Paid on 27.11.1997 during auction.

Sir,

I enclose photocopy of letter No. A-5-97/41350-51 dated 19.12.1997 from the office of Chief Administrator, HUDA, Panchkula, Sector 6 vide which a copy of the representation dt. 30.11.1997 was enclosed to Estate Officer, HUDA, Gurgaon with the instructions to kindly get the matter examined and settled at your end and intimate the position to Chief Administrator's Office immediately.

2. In this connection, no such information has been received for refund of the amount of Rs. 1 lakh paid so for but the undersigned has received letter (Form 'CC") under registered cover No. 1056 dt. 19.12.1997 today the 22nd December, 1997 for demand of balance payment of Rs. 1,49,112.50 in order to make 25% price of the said plot.

3. Attention is invited to clause 24 vide which on payment of 25% price we may obtain possession on any working day Wednesday. Whereas under the said Form 'CC' clause 6, the possession of the site will be offered to me

on completion of the development works in the area. In the case of building or undeveloped land, the possession shall, however, be delivered within 90 days from the date of the said letter. It may be noted that there is no use to obtain the possession while making payment as the land is lying undeveloped and is not liveable as may be seen in my letter dt. 30.11.1997 addressed to Chief Secretary, Govt. of Haryana, Chandigarh who has forwarded the same to Chief Administrator, Sector 6, Panchkula for taking immediate action.

In view of the above, it is requested to kindly refund the amount of Rs. 1 lakh paid by us for the said plot and treat the Form 'CC' as cancelled. The position may also be intimated to the Chief Administrator, HUDA, accordingly to settle the matter pending at your end.

Thanking you,

Yours faithfully,
Sd/-
Hem Raj Bangia
Sd/=
Smt. Subhash Bangia

Encl: As above

Petitioners.

ANNEXURE VI
FORM 'CC'
(SEE REGULATION 6(2)

From the Allotment Letter, for allotment made on free-hold basis – To Be used for residential/industrial/commercial plots/building disposed of by auction only.

From –

Estate Officer,
Haryana Urban Development Authority,
Gurgaon.

To:

Shri H.R. Bangia & Smt. Subhash Bangia
D-3, NIPCCD Campus, Opp. Police Station
Hauz Khas, New Delhi-110016

Memo No. EO (G)-84/294
Dated 18.12.97

Subject: Allotment by sale of Residential Plot No. 1578 Sector 15-II at

GURGAON ON FREE-HOLD BASIS

Please refer to your bid for Plot/Building No. 1578 in Sector 15-II at Gurgaon

Your bid for Plot/Building No. 1578 in Sector 15-II at Gurgaon has been accepted and the plot/building, as detailed below has been allotted to you on free-hold basis as per the following terms and conditions and subject to the provisions of the Haryana Urban Development Authority Act, 1977 (hereafter referred to as the Act) and the rules/ regulations applicable thereunder and as amended from time to time including terms and conditions as already announced at the time of auction and accepted by you.

Sector No.	Name of Urban Area	Plot/Building No.	Appro.dimension or description As notified at the Time of auction	Area in Sq.Mtrs.	Price of the Plot/ building
15-II	Gurgaon	1578	7.5x18.20	136.5 Sq.Mtr	Rs.9996450/- @ Rs.7300/- Per Sq. mtr.

The sum of Rs. 1,00,000=00 deposited by you of bid money at the time of bid will be adjusted against the said plot/building.

You are requested to remit Rs. 1,49,112=50 in order to make the 25% price of the said plot/building with in 30 days from the date of issue of allotment letter. The payment shall be made by a bank draft payable to the Estate Officer GURGAON and drawn on any scheduled Bank at Gurgaon. In case of failure to deposit the said amount within the above specified period, the allotment shall be cancelled and the deposit of 10% bid money deposited at the time of bid shall stand forfeited to the Authority. Against which you shall have no claim for damages.

The balance amount of Rs. 7,47,337.50 of the above price of the plot/building can be paid in lump-sum without interest within 60 days from the date of issue of allotment letter or in six half yearly instalments. The first installment will fall due after the expiry of six months'one year of the date of issue of this letter . Each installment would be recoverable together with interest on the balance price at 15% interest on the remaining amount. The interest shall, however, accrue from the date of offer of possession.

The possession of the site will be offered to you on completion of the development works in the area. In the case of building of undeveloped land, the possession shall, however, be delivered within 90 days from the date of this letter.

Each instalment shall be remitted to the Estate Officer and every such remittance shall be accompanied by a letter showing the full particulars of the site i.e. the number of the plot and sector number to which the payment pertains. In the absence of these particulars the amount remitted shall not be deemed to have been received

In case the instalment is not paid by the 10th of month following the month in which it falls due the Estate Officer shall proceed to take action for imposition of penalty and resumption of plot in accordance with the provisions of section 17 of the said Act.

In the event of breach of any other condition of transfer. The Estate Officer may resume the land in accordance with the provision of section 17 of the Act.

The land/building shall continue to belong to the Authority until the entire consideration money together with interest and other amounts, if any due to the Authority on account of sale of such land or building or both is paid. You shall have no right to transfer by way of sale, gift, mortgage or otherwise the plot building or any right, title or interest there in till the full price is paid to the Authority, except with the prior permission of the competent Authority.

On payment of 100% of the price of the plot/building. You shall execute the Deed of Conveyance in the prescribed form and in such manner as may be directed by the Estate Officer. The charges for registration and stamp duty will be paid by you.

The plot/building shall not be used for any purpose other than that for which it has been allotted in accordance with the plans approved by the competent authority. No obnoxious trade shall be carried out in or on any land/building.

You shall have to pay all general and local taxes, rates or cesses imposed or assessed on the said land building by the competent authority.

You shall have to pay separately for any constructions material, trees, structure and compound wall existing in your plot at the time of allotment of which compensation has been assessed and paid by the authority if you want to make use of the same.

The Authority will not be responsible for leveling the uneven sites.

You will have to complete the construction within two years of the date of offer of possession, after getting the plans of the proposed building approved from the competent authority in accordance with the regulations governing the erection of building. This time limit is extendable by the Estate Officer if he is satisfied that non-construction of the building was due to reasons beyond your control, otherwise this plot is liable to be resumed and the whole or part of the money paid, if any in respect of it forfeited in accordance with the provision of the said Act. You shall not erect any building or make any alteration, addition without prior permission of the Estate Officer. No fragmentation of any land or building shall be permitted.

The Authority reserves to itself all mines and minerals whatsoever in or under the said site with all such rights and powers as may be necessary or expedient for the purpose of searching or, working, obtaining, removing and enjoying the same at all such times and in such manner as the Authority shall think fit, with power to carry out any surface of any under ground working and to let down the surface of all or any part of the said site and to sink pits erect building, construct lines and generally appropriate and use surface of the said site for the purpose of doing all such things as may be convenient or necessary for the full enjoyment of the exceptions and reservations herein contained.

Provided that the allottee shall be entitled to receive from the Authority such payment for the occupation by him of the surface and for the damage done to the surface or building on the said land by such works or working or letting down as may be agreed upon between the Authority and the allottee or failing such agreement as shall be ascertained by reference to arbitration.

The Authority may be its officers and servants at all reasonable time and reasonable manners after 24 hours notice in writing enter in and upon any part of the said land building erected thereon for the purpose of ascertaining that the allottee has duly performed and observed the conditions to be observed under the Rules/Regulations applicable under the said Act.

The Authority shall have full right power and authority at all times to do through its officers or servants, all facts and things which may be necessary or expendient for the purpose of enforcing compliance with all or any of the terms, conditions and reservations imposed and to recover from you as first charge upon the said land/building, the cost of doing all or any such act and things and all cost incurred in connection there with or any way relating therein.

All disputes and differences arising out of or in any way touching or concerning this allotment whatsoever shall be referred to the sale arbitration of the Chief Administrator or any other officer appointed by him. It will not an objection to such appointment that the arbitrator so appointed is a Govt. servant or any officer of the Authority that he had to deal with the matter to which this allotment relates and in the course of his duties as such Government servant or officer as the case may be, he has expressed his views on all or any of the matters in disputes or difference. The decision of such arbitrator shall be final and binding on the concerned parties.

All payment shall be made by means of a demand draft payable to the Estate Officer, Haryana Urban Development Authority, GURGAON drawn on any scheduled bank at Gurgaon.

No separate notice will be sent for the payment of the yearly installments. However, the information regadrding the instalment, the due etc. may be sent as a matter of courtesy.

On payment of 25% price you may obtained possession

on any working Wednesday...........(any other condition not incorporated above but announced at the time of auction to be indicated.....)

Interest @ 18% p.a. will be charged for the delay period of instalments.

Sd/-	Sd/-	Sd/-	Sd/-
Asstt.	H.C.	Acctt.	A.O.

Sd/-Sanjay Joon
ESTATE OFFIER
Haryana Urban Development Authority
GURGAON

Note: (i) any change in address must be notified by registered A.D. Post.
(ii) Strike out whichever is not applicab

ANNEXURE VII

H.R. Bangia

D-3 NIPCCD Campus,
Opp. Police Station,
Hauz Khas,
New Delhi-110 016
Speed Post
January 21, 1998

The Administrator,
Haryana Urban Development Authority,
HUDA Office Complex, Sector 14,
Gurgaon (Haryana)

Subject: Refund for plot No.1578 Sector 15-II, Gurgaon paid in auction held on 27.11.1997.

1. Reference my letter dated 27.11.1997 submitted immediately on inspection of said plot.
2. My letter dated 30.11.1997 addressed to Shri R.S. Verma, Chief Secretary, Govt. of Haryana, Chandigarh
3. Letter No.A-5-97/41350-51 dt. 19.12.97 from the office of Chief Administrator with the request to kindly get the matter disposed of after inspection and inform the applicant under intimation to him wrt my letter dt. 30.11.1997.
4. Estate Officer, HUDA, Gurgaon Memo.No.EO(G)-84/294 dt.18.12.1997 in form 'CC' regarding allotment by sale of residential plot No.1578 Sector 15/II Gurgaon to the Petitioner (Received on 22.12.1997)
5. Petition on the above subject dt. 22.12.97 addressed to the Estate Officer, HUDA, Gurgaon.
6. Telegram to Estate Officer, HUDA, Gurgaon dt.

31.12.1997 with a copy by post in confirmation with the request to kindly convey orders for refund and send copy of reply if any sent to the Chief Administrator wrt my letter dt. 30.11.1997 referred to above.

Sir,

It is humbly requested to kindly get the facts ascertained as per details given in the above references and refund the amount paid on 27.11.1997 in auction for plot No.1578 Sector 15 Part II, Gurgaon in view of the following:

- The said plot is not free from encumbrances.
- The said plot does not meet the specifications as set in Auction as per pamphlet distributed widely to the public and is not Prime residential plot in Sector 15 Part II Gurgaon
- Even on payment of 25% price, HUDA cannot give possession as it is not free from encumbrances.
- I or my family do not own any plot/house in Gurgaon or in Delhi.
- I am residing in NIPCCD accommodation and have to vacate after I retire on June 30, 1998; failing which I shall have to pay market rent apart from action which may be taken by the Institute as per Govt. of India rules.
- Both my children are not yet settled for whom I have to make arrangements before I retire on June 30, 1998.
- I am to arrange the marriage of my daughter in April, 1998.

It is once again requested to kindly look into the above and favour me with your orders for refund of the amount of Rs. 1 lakh paid against the said plot so that I may not be put to mental tension which is persistent since I paid the amount in auction on 27.11.1997 and making frequent requests to the Estate Officer, HUDA, Gurgaon.

An early action in the matter may kindly be taken to avoid further harassment to me as I have not heard wrt my repeated requests.

Thanking you,

Yours faithfully,
Sd/-
Hem Raj Bangia
D-3, NIPCCD Campus,
Opp. Police Station,
Hauz Khas,
New Delhi-110016

P.S.: I have already sent the above referred papers in confirmation to all concerned.

ANNEXURE VIII

BEFORE THE DISTRICT CONSUMER DISPUTES REDRESSAL FORUM GURGAON

I, H.R. Bangia **2. Smt. Subhash Bangia,** both residents of D-3. NIPCCD Campus, Opp. Police Station, Hauz Khas, New Delhi-110016

... **Complainant**

VERSUS

Haryana Urban Development Authority, Sector – 14, Gurgaon through the Estate Officer

... Respondent

COMPLAINT UNDER CONSUMER PROTECTION ACT, 1986

Sir,

The complainants submit as under: -

1. That the complainant No. 1 is an officer in Semi-Govt. Organisation of National Institute of Public Cooperation and Child Development under the Department of Women & Child Development, Ministry of Human Resource & Development Govt. of India, New Delhi. The complainants were not having any house/land/plot to construct their house on urgent basis as the complainant No. 1 is due to retire on June 30, 1998.

2. That the respondent advertised for the auction of **prime residential plot in Sector 15 II, Gurgaon** through advertisement in **Times of India News Paper** as well as

through hand pamphlet containing terms and conditions. One of such pamphlet and Photostat copy of Times of India advertisement dated 23.11.97 is attached herewith at (Annexure XXIX).

3. That the venue of auction on dated 27.11.97 at 11 A.M. was Estate Officer HUDA Sector-14, Delhi Road, Gurgaon. The complainants were tempted to come all the way to Gurgaon and they participated in the auction for residential plots and being the highest bidder at the rate of Rs. 7300/-per sq. mtrs. For plot of six marla in Sector 15-II bearing No.1578. A sum of Rs. 1,00,000/- was deposited on the same day by the complainants in cash as an earnest money for the said plot. Photostat copy of the receipt is attached herewith.

4. That immediately after the completion of the bid the complainants went to the spot and found that the said plot was lying undeveloped and was situated at a live high tension wire over the plot and there was '*dal*-dal' on the site and was not at all fit for raising construction over it for residential purposes. There were encroachments over that plot by the houses of an already existing unauthorized colony inhabitants and the said plot was not qualifying for adjective **'Prime'** plot. The length of the plot was also not 18.2 mtrs. as specified in the auction and the pamphlet distributed to the public. It was also not two side open as was declared at the time of auction. A lay out plan would clarify the exact position of the plot in question which is attached herewith (Annexure XXX).

It caused a great mental agony and tension to the complainants and thus a letter for cancellation of the auction and for the refund of earnest money of Rs.1,00,000/- was given to the Estate Officer HUDA by the complainants on the same day i.e. 27.11.97. Photostat copy of the same is attached herewith. (Annexure II)

5. That the complainant No. 1 therefore sent a letter to Sh. R.K. Verma, Chief Secretary Govt. of Haryana Chandigarh for the refund of earnest money of the plot in question on 30.11.97 stating therein the full facts about the

highhandedness and deficiency in service on the part of the respondent. Photostat copy of same is attached herewith. (Annexure III)

6. That a letter dated 19.12.97 was written by Chief Administrator HUDA Panchkula to Estate Officer HUDA Gurgaon for the early disposal of the case of the complainant and a copy of the same was received by complainant No. 1 which is attached herewith. (Annexure IV)

Thereafter the complainant No. 1 wrote a letter on 22.12.97 to Estate Officer HUDA (Annexure V) and requested him to refund the amount of Rs.1,00,000/- but no action was taken by him in spite of a telegram dated 31.12.97. Photostat copy of which is attached herewith.

Another letter dated 21.1.98 was written by the complainant No. 1 to the Administrator HUDA Gurgaon stating therein full facts for the refund of the earnest money amount in respect of the plot in question but nothing has been done by the respondent till today. Photostat copy of the said letter is attached herewith. (Annexure VII)

7. That the plot in question was not free from encumbrances and did not meet the specification as set in auction as per pamphlet distributed widely to the public and was not a prime residential plot and the complainant have been duped by the respondent and was tempted to part with his hard-earned money in order to dump it in the mud which is altogether a great deficiency in service on the part of the respondent and hence the complainants have become entitled to file the present complaint before this Hon'ble Forum for the refund of the earnest money of Rs.1,00,000/- along with interest @ 18% and also for damages for mental agony and harassment.

It is therefore prayed that the respondent be directed to refund the amount of Rs.1,00,000/- deposited by the complainant on 27.11.97 as an earnest money to the plot No.1578 Sector 15-II, Gurgaon along with interest @ 18% PA from the date of deposit till final payment. The complainants be also **awarded damages** for mental agony

and harassment to the tune of Rs. 10,000/- besides costs of the present proceedings.

VERIFICATION: -	COMPLAINTANTS :
Verified that the contents	H.R. Bangia,
of above complaint	Smt. Subhash Bangia
are true and correct to the	rs/o D-3, NIPCCD Campus,
best of my	Opp. Police Station,
knowledge and belief.	Hauz Khas-110016
Verified at Gurgaon	through Sd/-
on 3.3.98	**Sh.Sunder Lal Garg,**
	Advocate, Gurgaon

ANNEXURE IX
BEFORE THE DISTRICT CONSUMER DISPUTES REDRESSAL FORUM GURGAON

C.P.A. No.287/3.3.98

1. H.R. Bangia **2. Smt. Subhash Bangia,**
both residents of D-3. NIPCCD Campus, Opp. Police Station, Hauz Khas, New Delhi-110016

... **Complainant**

VERSUS

Haryana Urban Development Authority, Sector - 14, Gurgaon through the Estate Officer

— Respondent

Present : Sh. S.L. Garg, Counsel for the complainant
Sh. Randhir Singh, DDA for the respondent

ORDER:

1. The complainant filed this complaint under consumer jurisdiction for directing the respondent to refund him the amount of Rs.1,00,000/- deposited by him with the respondent on 27.11.97.

2. Briefly stated the facts of the case are that the complainant bid the auction of a plot in Sector 15-II and he turned out to be the highest bidder for plot bearing No.1578 so he deposited Rs.1,00,000/- as earnest money. But soon thereafter he visited the plot and found that there was a live High tension electricity wire passing over the plot

and the plot was full of dirty water. He at once changed the idea of purchasing the plot and applied for the refund. But the respondent has not taken any action as yet. Hence he filed this complaint.

The respondent contested the complaint on the grounds that the complainant himself offered the bid for the highest amount and deposited Rs.1 lac as 10% of the tentative price. That he filed an application for the refund of this money. As the money was not refundable, he was issued the allotment letter.

We have heard the parties and have gone through the documentary evidence on the file. Even in the case of draw of lot a period of one month is given to the applicant whether he accepts the plot or not. So in the case of open auction that option should be available as the plots are not shown before the auction. When the complainant saw the plot it was found not worth the auction. No house could be built at that plot. So he immediately applied for the refund of his earnest money. Thus it is ordered that the amount of Rs.1,00,000/- be refunded to the complainant with interest at the rate of 15% per annum from the date of deposit till the date of repayment.

Announced.
15.6.98

Sd/-
D.D. Yadav,
President,
District Consumer Disputes
Redressal Forum, Gurgaon

Sd/-
Veena Kumari Sharma, Member

Sd/-
Manohar Lal Dhingra, Member

Date of application for certified
copy 6274/ 18.6.98
Sd/-
Certified to be True Copy

ANNEXURE X

H.R. Bangia

D-3 NIPCCD Campus,
Opp. Police Station
Hauz Khas,
New Delhi-110016
July 20, 1998

Estate Officer,
Haryana Urban development Authority,
Sector 14,
Gurgaon (Haryana)

Subject: C.P.A No.287/3.3.98 Decided on 15.6.98 for refund of Rs. 1 lakh deposited against Plot No. 1578 Part II, Gurgaon.

Sir,

Kindly refer to the above case before the District Consumer Disputes Redressal Forum; Gurgaon decided on 15.6.98 for CPA No.287/3.3.98. I enclose photocopy of the order issued on 18.6.98 vide No.6274, which is self-explanatory.

2. It has been ordered in the above case to the complainant with interest at the rate o 15% per annum from the date of deposit till the date of repayment.

3. In view of the above, it is requested to kindly be informed to take appropriate action to refund the amount of Rs. 1,00,000/- paid as earnest money for the auctioned

plot No. 1578, Part II, Gurgaon dated 27.11.1997 since the said payment has not been made to me since the order was issued on 18.6.1998 as decided on 15.6.1998.

An early action may please be taken to comply with the orders of the Forum.

Thanking you,

Yours faithfully,

Sd/-
Hem Raj Bangia

Sd/-
Smt. Subhash Bangia

Encl: As above

ANNEXURE XI

REGISTERED September 09, 1998

The Estate Officer,
Haryana Urban Development Authority,
Sector-14,
Gurgaon (Haryana)

Subject: C.P.A. No.287/3.3.98 decided on 15.6.98 for refund of Rs. 1.00 Lakh deposited against plot No.1578, Sector 15, Part II, Gurgaon

Sir,

Kindly find enclosed a copy of my Petition dated July 20, 1998 on the above subject for refund of Rs. One lakh which was paid as Earnest Money for the auctioned Plot No.1578 Part II, Sector 15, Gurgaon dated 27.11.1997.

The details are already given in the Petition dated July 20, 1998 based on the case decided on 15.6.98 (CPA No.287/ 3.3.98).

An early action is requested to comply with the orders of the Forum as I retired from Government service on 30.6.1998 and I am finding it financially very difficult to make alternate arrangement for my stay from the present Government accommodation which is to be vacated within four months of retirement.

Yours faithfully,

Sd/-
Hem Raj Bangia
Petitioner
D-3, NIPCCD Campus,
Opp. Police Station,
New Delhi-110016

Encl: As above.

ANNEXURE XII

(Contempt of Court)
BEFORE THE DISTRICT CONSUMER DISPUTESD REDRESSAL FORUM GURGAON

I, H.R. Bangia 2. Smt. Subhash Bangia, both residents of D-3. NIPCCD Campus, Opp. Police Station, Hauz Khas, New Delhi-110016

... **Complainant**

VERSUS

Haryana Urban Development Authority, Sector - 14, Gurgaon through its Estate Officer

— Respondent

COMPLAINT UNDER CONSUMER PROTECTION ACT, 1986 SECTON 25 AND SECTION 27

Sir,

The complainants submit as under: -

1. That the complainant No. 1 was an officer in Semi-Govt. Organisation of National Institute of Public Cooperation and Child Development under the Department of Women & Child Development, Ministry of Human Resource & Development Govt. of India, New Delhi. That the complainants were not having any house/land/plot to construct their house on urgent basis as the complainant No. 1 was due to retire on June 30, 1998. The complainant No. 1 has since retired on June 30, 1998.
2. That the respondent advertised for the auction of **prime residential plot in Sector 15 II, Gurgaon** through advertisement in **Times of India News Paper** as well as through hand pamphlet about it containing terms and

conditions. One of such pamphlets and Photostat copy of Times of India advertisement dated 23.11.97 are attached herewith.

3. That the venue of auction on dated 27.11.97 at 11 A.M. was Estate Officer HUDA Sector-14, Delhi Road, Gurgaon. The complainants were tempted to come all the way to Gurgaon and they participated in the auction for prime residential plots and being the highest bidder at the rate of Rs.7300/-per sq. mtrs. for plot of six marla in Sector 15-II bearing No.1578. A sum of Rs. 1,00,000/- (Rupees one lac only) was deposited vide Cash Receipt No. 413 (Book No. nil) dated 27.11.1997 (Photocopy at Annexure II).

4. That immediately after the completion of the bid the complainants went to the spot and found that the said plot was lying undeveloped and was situated at a live high tension wire passing near the plot and there was '*dal*-dal' on the site and was not at all fit for raising construction over it for residential purposes and there was encroachment over this plot by the houses of an already existing unauthorized colony inhabitants and as such the said plot was not qualifying for adjective **'Prime'** plot as advertised in the pamphlets widely distributed at the time of auction and also in the Times of India dt. 23.11.1997 newspapers (as mentioned at para 2 above). There was no construction on the left and right side of the said plot. Since the live high tension wire was passing by the side of this plot, all the plots opposite this plot though allotted for more than five years were not given possession to the allottees. The length of the plot was also not 18.2 mtrs. as specified in the auction and the pamphlet distributed to the public. It was also not two side open as was declared at the time of auction. The said facts were reported in my Petition dated 3.3.1998. (Photocopy of Petition dt. 3.3.1998 At Annexure VIII.) It caused a great mental agony and tension to the complainants and he suffered a heart-attack on 4.3.1998 (on the night of 3.3.1998) and he was admitted to the St. Stephen's Hospital, Tis Hazari, Delhi. I was advised bed rest for two months by the Attending Medical Expert Dr. Madhukar Shahi, MD DM DNB,

Consultant, and Cardiologist. I have been advised not to undergo any mental or physical stress for another period of six months vide his Certificate dt. 22.10.98 . Thus a letter for cancellation of the auction and for the refund of earnest money of Rs. 1,00,000/- was given to the Estate Officer HUDA, Gurgaon by the complainants on the same day i.e. 27.11.1997. (Annexure II).

5. That the complainant No. 1 thereafter sent a letter dt.30.11.1997 to Sh. R.K. Verma, Chief Secretary Govt. of Haryana Chandigarh for the refund of earnest money of the plot in question on 30.11.97 stating therein the full facts about the highhandedness and deficiency in service on the part of the respondent. (Photostat copy furnished with Petition dt. 3.3.1998).

6. That a letter dated 19.12.97 was written by the office of the Chief Administrator HUDA Panchkula to the Estate Officer HUDA Gurgaon for the early disposal of the case of the complainant No. 1 (Photo copy already furnished with Petition dt. 3.3.1998). Thereafter the complainant No. 1 wrote a letter on 22.12.97 to Estate Officer, Gurgaon HUDA and requested him to refund the amount of Rs.1,00,000/- but no action was taken by him in spite of a telegram dated 31.12.97. (Photostat copy furnished with Petition dt. 3.3.1998). Another letter dated 21.1.98 was written by the complainant No. 1 to the Administrator HUDA Gurgaon stating therein full facts for the refund of the earnest money of Rs.1,00,000/- in respect of the plot No.1578 Part II, Gurgaon but nothing had been done by the respondent till today. (Photostat copy furnished with Petition dt. 3.3.1998).

7. That the plot in question was not free from encumbrances and did not meet the specification as set in auction as per pamphlet distributed widely to the public and was not a prime residential plot as advertised in Times of India dt. 23.11.1997 (Annexure XXIX) and the complainants have been duped by the respondent and was tempted to part with his hard-earned money in order to dump it in the mud which is altogether a great deficiency in service on the part of the respondent and hence the complainants

became entitled to file the suit on 3.3.1998 for refund of the earnest money of Rs.1 lac along with interest @ 18% and also for damages for mental agony and harassment.

8. That the Complainant No. 1 and Complainant No. 2 prayed vide their Petition dated 3.3.1998 (Annexure VIII) that the Respondent be directed to refund the amount of Rs. 1,00,000/- (Rupees one lac only) deposited by the Complainants on 27.11.1997 as an earnest money to the Plot No. 1578 Sector 15 Part II, Gurgaon along with interest @ 18% p.a. from the date of deposit till final payment. It was also prayed to award damages for mental agony and harassment to the tune of Rs.10,000/- besides costs of the proceedings

9. That the Petition dated 3.3.1998 before the District Consumer Dispute Redressal Forum, Gurgaon was heard vide C.P.A. No.287/3.3.98 from time to time every month and the respondent did not even furnish the reply to Petition dt. 3.3.1998 to the learned President Shri D.D. Yadav and the Members present in the Forum. The Forum vide their decision dt 15.6.1998 ordered that the amount of Rs. 1,00,000/- be refunded to the complainants with interest at the rate of 15% per annum from the date of deposit till the date of repayment. (Photo copy at Annexure IX)

10. That the Complainants vide their letter dated July 20, 1998 handed over the orders dt. 15.6.1998 personally at the office of Estate Officer, HUDA, Gurgaon on 20.7.1998 itself and obtained the receipt from his office. Another request dt. 9.9.1998 as a reminder was also sent by Regd. Post for refund as per decision dt. 15.6.1998 and to comply with the orders of the Forum.

11. That since then neither the said amount with interest nor any reply has been furnished to the complainants **which amounts to contempt of the Forum vide Section 25 of the Consumer Protection Act, 1986** since every order made by the District Forum may be enforced by the District Forum, in the same manner as if it were a decree or order made by a Court in a suit pending therein and it shall be lawful for the District Forum to send, in the event of its inability

to execute it, such order to the court within the local limits of whose jurisdiction -

(i) in the case of an order against a company, the registered office of the company is situated; or
(ii) in the case of an order against any other person, the place where the person concerned voluntarily resides or carries on business or personally works for gain, is situated,

and thereupon, the court to which the order is so sent, shall execute the order as if it were a decree or order sent to it for execution.

That it is prayed that the Respondent be directed to refund the amount of Rs. 1,00,000/- to the complainants with interest at the rate of 15% per annum from the date of deposit i.e. 27.11.1997 till the date of repayment and further order to the Respondent be given as per Section 25 of the Consumer Protection Act, 1986 for non-compliance of the order of the Hon'ble District Forum dt. 15.6.1998 till the date of the present petition besides costs of the present proceedings which may be deemed fit by the Honourable Forum.

VERIFICATION

Verified that the contents of the above complaint are true and correct to the best of our knowledge and belief.

Sd/-
(Smt. Subhash Bangia)
Complaintant No. 2

Sd/-
(H.R. Bangia)
Complainant No. 1

Both resident of D-3, NIPCCD Campus, Opp. Police Station, Hauz Khas, New Delhi-110016

Verified at Gurgaon
dt. 9.11.1998

ANNEXURE XIII
BEFORE THE DISTRICT CONSUMER DISPUTES REDRESSAL FORUM GURGAON

CPA NO. 3899/9.11.98
Date of decision 12.10.99

1. H.R. Bangia **2. Smt. Subhash Bangia,**
both residents of D-3 NIPCCD Opp. Police Station, Hauz Khas, New Delhi-110016

... **Complainants**

VERSUS

Haryana Urban Development Authority, Sector - 14, Gurgaon through its Estate Officer

— Respondent (Opposite Party)

CONSUMER COMPLAINT U/ss 25&27 CPACT

Present : Complainant in person
Counsel for the Opposite party.

ORDER

The complainants have invoked jurisdiction of this Forum for a direction to HUDA for refund of Rs.One Lac with interest and costs of proceedings alleging that they had purchased plot No.1578 Sector 15 Part II in a public auction held on 27.11.97 and had deposited Rs. One Lac against receipt No.413 that on inspection the said plot was found unfit to raise construction of a house due to live high tension wire and other defects, including having encroachment; that the said plot was not prime or having length and breadth as advertised by HUDA; that as a result of depression and mental agony complainant No. 1 suffered heart attack on 3.3.98, and that in fact they had delivered the letter of non

-acceptance on 27.11.97 itself and for refund of earnest money of Rs. One Lac. It is further alleged that since then the complainants have been trying for the refund of the amount deposited by them but no heed has been paid by the functionaries of the state and HUDA bringing the cause within the Consumers' Jurisdiction and hence they had filed complaint, before this Forum on 3.3.98 which was disposed of on 15.6.98 ordering the respondent HUDA to refund the amount of Rs. One Lac with interest @ 15% p.a. It is now alleged that despite delivery of copy of the said order to the Opposite party the same remained un-complied with and hence this application under sections 25/27 of the CP Act for a further direction to HUDA to make refund with interest and costs as also punishing the respondent HUDA as per provisions.

2. On notice the ADA of HUDA put in appearance on 23.12.98 but till this day no reply has been filed. Rightly so because they have no excuse to make. Hence they did not file any reply. In this view of the matter the respondent & HUDA is afforded another opportunity to refund the amount of Rs. One Lac with interest @ 15% p.a. from the date of deposit till payment within 25 days of the order of this case; failing which the HUDA and its concerned functionaries will be proceeded against as per provisions of Sections 25/27 CP Act.

Announced in open court
12.10.99

Sd/-
(B.S. Indora)
President
Distt.. Consumer
Dis. Red. Forum,
Gurgaon

We Agree

Sd/-
(M.L. Dhingra) Member

Sd/-
(Mrs. Asha Barak) Member

302/20.10.99
Certified to be True Copy

ANNEXURE XIV

D-3, NIPCCD Campus,
Opp. Police Station,
Hauz Khas,
New Delhi – 110 016
Ph.6960950

19th November, 1998

The Editor,
The Times of India,
7, Bahadur Shah Zafar Marg,
New Delhi-110002

Subject: Article on "HUDA and the Role of M.R.T.P.C."

I have made a Case Study of the activities of HUDA, Gurgaon and discovered that while HUDA is minting money the allottees are put to financial loss. The confusion created by HUDA should be corrected by MRTPC as HUDA does not honour the decisions of the District Consumer Disputes Redressal Forum in many cases. *

I am thus enclosing the article on "**HUDA and the Role of MRTPC**", with the clippings of two Advertisements of India of India dated 23.11.97 and 5.11.97 in support of my comparative study made.

Kindly publish it at the earliest and acknowledge the receipt of this article.

Thanking you,

Yours faithfully,

Sd/-
(H.R. Bangia)

Encl: As above

* See Annexure XXXI
Copy for action to : Chairman,
M.R.T.P.C.
Kota Annexe,
Shahjahan Road,
New Delhi-110011

ANNEXURE XV

In the Court of Hon'ble Consumer Disputes Redressal Forum, Gurgaon.

H.R. Bangia 2. Smt. Subhash Bangia residents of G-50 B (FF), Kalkaji, New Delhi

Versus

Haryana Urban Development Authority Sector 14, Gurgaon through its Estate Officer

CPA Number .287/3.3.98
Decided on 15.6.98

CPA number 1899/9.11.98
Decided on 12.10.99

Contempt Petition cum Petition U/Ss. 25 & 27 of C.P. Act.

Petitioners submit:

1. That vide CPA number 287 of 98 respondent had been directed to refund Rs.1,00,000/- with interest @ 15% from the date of deposit to complainant about was not bothered about by respondent which resulted in filing CPA number 1899 of 98.

2. That to exact obedience to its order dated 15.6.98, this Hon'ble court had afforded another opportunity to respondent to pay the amount in question within 25 days about which too respondent has not cared.

It is prayed that the Estate Officer and concerned officials of respondent may be punished as per law for said disobedience.

Sd/-
Petitioners No. 1
12.11.1999

ANNEXURE XVI
BEFORE THE DISTRICT CONSUMER DISPUTES REDRESSAL FORUM GURGAON

Execution Appl. No. 207/12.11.99

Date of decision 7.3.2000

H.R. Bangia **2. Smt. Subhash Bangia**
Residents of G 50 B (FF) Kalkaji, New Delhi
... **Complainants**

VERSUS

Haryana Urban Development Authority, Sector - 14, Gurgaon through its Estate Officer
— Respondent

Present : Complainant in person
Sh. Dharmesh Sharma, Counsel /ADA for the respondent.

ORDER:

By this order we are going to dispose of this execution application filed by the applicant under section 27 of Consumer Protection Act for due execution of our order dated 15.6.98 in CPA No. 207 of 1998.

2. Brief facts of the case are that the complainant filed a complaint before this Forum against the respondent which was decided on 15.6.98 ordering the respondent to refund

Rs. One lac with interest @ 15% to the complainant but the respondent has not made the compliance of the order. So the complainant filed execution application which was decided on 12.10.99 and the following order was passed.

> "In this view of the matter the respondent-HUDA is afforded another opportunity to refund the amount of Rs. One Lac with interest @ 15% per annum from the date of deposit till the payment within 25 days of the order of this case ; failing which the HUDA and its concerned functionaries will be proceeded against as per provisions of Section 25/27 of CP Act".

But when the compliance was not made, the applicant filed this 2nd execution application.

3. Notice of the application was given to the respondent and the respondent appeared through their ADA and filed reply taking the plea that that the complainant gave highest bid for plot No. 1578/15 II, Gurgaon and also deposited Rs. 1 lac being 10% of the total cost at the time of auction. The complainant had given bid in open auction so he is not a consumer as per settled law. The orders passed by Hon'ble DCF, Gurgaon have been **challenged in the Hon'ble National Commission, New Delhi** through Sh. Ravindera Rana, Advocate. It is submitted that the orders of the DCF Gurgaon shall be complied with the prior approval of the competent authority.

4. We have heard the complainant in person and the counsel for the respondent and have gone through the evidence and record on the file. The complainant had purchased plot Number 1578 Sector 15-II in a public auction held on 27.11.97. He had deposited Rs. One lac but the said plot was not fit for construction. So the complainant approached the respondent for the refund of Rs. One lac but the respondent failed to do so so far. So the complainant filed C.P.A. No.287/3.3.98 decided on 15.6.98 but all in vain. The complainant again filed execution application under Section 25 & 27 C.P.Act in which it was ordered that the

respondent shall refund the amount of Rs. One lac with interest @ 15% from date of deposit till the date of payment within 25 days of the order dated 12.10.99. HUDA again failed to comply with the order passed by this Forum.

So the applicant again filed an execution application against the order dated 12.10.99. Several show cause notices were given to the respondent for comply with the order but the respondent stated that the **order passed by this Forum have been challenged in the Hon'ble National Commission but no copy of stay order has been placed on the file. No copy of complaint has been placed on the file. No any proceedings of Hon'ble National Commission in respect of the complaint has been filed by the respondent-HUDA. No affidavit in this regard has been filed by the HUDA.**

So in these circumstances, the respondent is directed to refund the amount of Rs. One lac to the complainant with interest @ 15% per annum from the date of deposit till the date of payment within 25 days from today; failing which HUDA shall pay Rs. 100/- per day to the complainant and strict action will be taken.

No order as to costs

Announced:
7.3.2000

Sd/-
B.S. Indora
President.
Distt. Consumer Disputes
Redressal Forum, Gurgaon

Sd/-
Mrs. Asha Barak, Member

ANNEXURE XVII

National Consumer Disputes Redressal Commission
Under Consumer Protection Act, 1986

Telephone **No.3712109**

JANPATH BHAWAN
(Old Indian Oil Bhavan)
5th Floor, 'A' Wing,
Janpath,
NEW DELHI-110001

REVISION PETITION NO. 491 OF 1999

(Against the Order dated: 24.7.1998 in Appeal No. 837/98 of the State Commission, Haryana)

HUDA - Petitioners

Versus

H.R. Bangia & Anr. - Respondents

To

H.R. Bangia & Smt. Subhash Bangia,
Both R/o D-3, NIPCCD Campus,
Opp: Police Station,
Hauz Khas,,
NEW DELHI-110 016

NOTICE

WHEREAS THE Revision Petition above-mentioned has been filed in the National Commission by the Petitioners above-named from the Order dated a/m in Appeal No. a/

m of the State Commission, Haryana) Copy where of is enclosed).

AND WHEREAS THE Petition came up for hearing on 5.7.2000 for directions whether notice be issued to the Respondents when the National Commission directed issue of Notice to the Respondents returnable in one month.

NOW, THEREFORE, TAKE NOTICE that you may file your version of the case, if any, in the matter in English (with six sets of spare copies) within thirty days from the date of receipt of this Notice. A copy of your version of the case may be served on the Petitioners at the address given hereunder.

Mr. Ravinder Bana,
Advocate,
118, Lawyers Chambers,
Supreme Court of India,
New DELHI-110 001

TAKE FURTHER NOTICE that in default of appearance the matter will be heard and determined ex-parte.

Dated New Delhi, the 12th July, 2000

Sd/-
Assistant Registrar

BEFORE THE HON'BLE NATIONAL CONSUMER DISPUTES REDRESSAL COMMISSION, NEW DELHI

REVISION PETITION NO. 491 /1999

IN THE MATTER OF :"

Revision Petition under Section 21(B) of the Consumer Protection Act, 1986 against order dated 24.7.1998 passed in First Appeal No. 837/98 by the

Hon'ble State Consumer Disputes Redressal Commission, Haryana, Chandigarh

A N D

IN THE MATTER OF :

H.U.D.A. —Petitioner

H.R. Bangia & Anr. —Respondent

I.A. No. 337/1999
(Application for Stay)

PAPER BOOK
(For Index, Please see inside)

Advocate for the Petitioner: Mr. Ravindra Bana
118, Lawyers' Chamber,
Supreme Court
New Delhi - 11001

I N D E X

S. No.	Particulars	Page Nos.
4.	Revision Petiton No. 491/1999 with Affidavit	5 - 14
5.	Annexure - 1 Copy of complaint dated 3.3.1998 filed by Complainants before District Forum, Gurgaon	15 - 19
6.	Annexure - 2 Copy of the reply filed by HUDA before District Forum	20 - 21
7.	Annexure - 3 (Pl. see Sl.No. 2 above)	–
8.	Annexure - 4 Copy of Memo of Appeal filed by petitioner before the Hon'ble State Commission, Haryana	22 - 26
9.	I.A. No. 337/1999 (Application for Stay)	27 - 29

SYNOPSIS & LIST OF DATES IN CHRONOLOGICAL ORDER

The petitioner is filing the present Revision Petition before this Hon'ble Commission against the judgment and order dated 24th July, 1998 passed by the Hon'ble State Consumer Disputes Redressal Commission, Haryana, Chandigarh in First Appeal No. 837/98, whereby the Hon'ble State Commission while dismissing the said appeal of the petitioner, has affirmed the order of the District Consumer Disputes Redressal Forum, Gurgaon dated 15th June 1998 by which the District Forum directed the present petitioner to refund the amount of Rs. 1 lakh deposited by the Complainant as Earnest Money notwithstanding that the terms of the auction under which the complainant had made the bid in respect of the plot had clearly provided that the highest bidder was bound to deposit 15% of the bid within 30 days of the date of allotment letter conveying the acceptance of the bid, failing which 10% amount already deposited would stand forfeited to the Authority. The chronological sequence of events is narrated hereinbelow:

27.11.1997 The complainant/respondent made a bid and he turned out to be the highest bidder for the plot and he deposited Rs. 1 lakh (One lakh) as Earnest Money. That Regulation No. 6, Sub-Clause 2 of the Urban Development (Disposal of Land and Buildings) Regulation, 1978 reads as under:'

"6. SALE OR LEASE OF LAND OR BUILDING BY AUCTION:-

10 percent of the highest bid shall be paid on the spot by the highest bidder in cash or by means of a Demand Draft in the manner specified in sub-regulation (2) of Regulation 5. The successful bidder shall be issued allotment letter in form 'cc' or 'c-II' by registered post and another 15% per cent of bid accepted shall be payable by the successful bidder. In the manner indicated, 'within 30 days of the date of allotment letter conveying acceptance of the bid by the Chief Administrator, failing which the 10% amount already deposited shall stand forfeited to the Authority and the successful bidder shall have no claim to the land or building auctioned'

The respondent failed to comply with the requirement of depositing another 15% of the bid within 30 days of the allotment letter and as such, he was not entitled to the refund of 18% of the Earnest Money made by him at the time of participating in the bid.

3.3.1998	Feeling aggrieved by the refusal of the request for the refund, the complainant filed a complaint before the Hon'ble District Consumer Disputes Redressal Forum, Gurgaon claiming the refund of the Earnest Money. In response to the notice issued by the Hon'ble District Forum, the petitioner Authority contested the claim and claimed that the claimant was not entitled for the refund of the amount and interest or damages as claimed, as admittedly he was the highest bidder and after depositing the Earnest Money, had failed to deposit the further amount.
15.6.1998	Hon'ble District Consumer Disputes Redressal Forum, Gurgaon vide its order dated 15.6.1998 accepting the contentions of the complainant, directed the amount of Rs. 1 lakh to be refunded to the complainant with interest @ 15% per annum from the date of deposit till the date of repayment.
July '98	Aggrieved by the order of the Hon'ble District Forum, the present petitioner filed an appeal, being first Appeal No. 837 of 1998 before the Hon'ble State Consumer Disputes Redressal Commission, Haryana, Chandigarh contending, inter-alia, that the order of the District Forum directing refund of the amount deposited by the complainants was in violation of Regulation 6(2) of the Regulation inasmuch as the complainant had failed to deposit the additional amount. It was also contended that there was no deficiency on the part of the petitioner as the complainant was well aware of the situation of the plot

at the time of the auction and that awarding of interest @ 15% was clearly erroneous.

24.7.1998 The Hon'ble State Consumer Disputes Redressal Commission, Haryana, Chandigarh vide its order dated 24th July 1998 was pleased to dismiss the appeal of the present petitioner and affirmed the order of the Hon'ble District Forum.

Dec..1998 Hence the instant Revision Petiton filed before this Hon'ble Commission.

It is respectfully submitted that the order of the Hon'ble State Consumer Disputes Redressal Commission and the Hon'ble District Forum are clearly contrary to Regulation 6(2) which governs the auction and provisions for that in case the highest bidder fails to deposit the 15% of the cost of the plot within 30 days of the date of the auction, the Earnest Money being 10% deposited at the time of the bid would stand forfeited.

It is respectfully submitted that the State Commission and the District Forum ought to have noticed that the situation of the plot for which the complainant had made the bid was in his full knowledge and knowing fully well he had made the bid and after making the bid, he cannot be allowed to withdraw in view of the Regulation 6(2) governing the auction.

It is respectfully submitted that the State Commission and the District Forum have erred in directing the present petitioner to refund the amount deposited by the respondents as the same is in violation of Regulation 6(2) of the Regulation. From the perusal of the Regulation, reproduced above, it is clear that the respondents were bound to deposit another 15% of the bid accepted by the successful bidder/respondents within 30 days of the allotment letter conveying the acceptance of the bid by the Chief Administrator, failing which 10% amount already deposited shall stand forfeited to the Authority. As the respondents failed to deposit the another 15% of the bid, so they are not entitled for the refund of the amount, as the same stand forfeited as per the Regulation 6(2) of the Regulations.

It is respectfully submitted that the State Commission and the District Forum have erred in not considering the fact that there is no deficiency on the part of the petitioner and the respondents were well aware of the situation of the plot at the time of auction, even the complaint filed by the respondents was not maintainable as the impugned order is not an appealable order.

It is respectfully submitted that the State Commission and the District Forum have erred in directing the appellant/ petitioner herein to refund the amount of Rs. 1 lakh with 15% interest per annum from the date of deposit till the date of repayment. As per Regulation 6(2) of the Regulations, the 10% amount of the bid deposited by the respondents stood forfeited as the respondents did not deposit the another 15% of the amount of bid. As such, the respondents are not entitled to the refund of 10% amount of bid and interest thereon.

ANNEXURE - 3
BEFORE THE DISTRICT CONSUMER DISPUTES REDRESSAL FORUM GURGAON

C.P.A. No.287
Decided on 15.6.98

1. H.R. Bangia **2. Smt. Subhash Bangia,**
both residents of D-3. NIPCCD Campus, Opp. Police Station, Hauz Khas, New Delhi-110016

... **Complainant**

VERSUS

Haryana Urban Development Authority, Sector - 14, Gurgaon through the Estate Officer

— Respondent

Present : Sh. S.L. Garg, Counsel for the complainant
Sh. Randhir Singh, DDA for the respondent

ORDER ;

1. The complainant filed this complaint under consumer jurisdiction for directing the respondent to refund him the amount of Rs.1,00,000/- deposited by him with the respondent on 27.11.97.

Briefly stated the facts of the case are that the complainant bid the auction of a plot in Sector 15-II and he turned out to be the highest bidder for plot bearing No.1578 so he deposited Rs.1,00,000/- as earnest money. But soon thereafter he visited the plot and found that there was a live High tension electricity wire passing over the plot and the plot was full of dirty water. He at once changed the idea of purchasing the plot and applied for the refund. But the respondent has not taken any action as yet. Hence he filed this complaint.

The respondent contested the complaint on the grounds that the complainant himself offered the bid for the highest amount and deposited Rs.1 lac as 10%of the tentative price. That he filed an application for the refund of this money. as the money was not refundable, he was issued the allotment letter.

We have heard the parties and have gone through the documentary evidence on the file. Even in the case of draw of lot a period of one month is given to the applicant whether he accepts the plot or not. So in the case of op^n auction that option should be available as the plots are not shown before the auction. When the complainant saw the plot it was found not worth the auction. No house could be built at that plot. So he immediately applied for the refund of his earnest money. Thus it is ordered that the amount of Rs.1,00,000/- be refunded to the complainant with interest at the rate of 15% per annum from the date of deposit till the date of repayment.

Announced.
15.6.98

Sd/-
D.D. Yadav,
President,
District Consumer Disputes
Redressal Forum, Gurgaon

Sd/-
Veena Kumari Sharma, Member

Sd/-
Manohar Lal Dhingra, Member

/ True Copy /

STATE CONSUMER DISPUTES REDRESSAL COMMISSION, HARYANA, CHANDIGARH

First Appeal No.837 of 1998

Date of Decision: 24.7.98

Estate Officer, Haryana Urban Development Authority, Gurgaon ——Appellant (s)

Versus

H.R. Bangia and Smt. Subhash Bangia, resident of D-3, NIPCCD ———————Respondent(s)
Campus, Opp. Police Station, Hauz Khas, New Delhi-110016.

Present: Mr. O.P. Sharma, Advocate with Mr. Rajiv Sharma, Advocate, for the appellant

BEFORE:

Hon'ble Mr. Justice M.R. Agnihotri, President
Smt. Sushil Paul, Member.

ORDER

M.R. Agnihotri, J.

In this appeal filed by the Haryana Urban Development Authority against the order dated 15.6.98 passed by the learned District Consumer Forum, Gurgaon, the short point involved is, as to whether the complainant was entitled to the refund of the amount deposited by him at the time of bidding for the plot when HUDA failed to deliver the possession of the plot.

The learned District Consumer Forum, after examiningg the evidence in detail, came to the conclusion that the complainant, who was the highest bidder for plot No. 1578 in Sector 15-II, Gurgaon had deposited rupees one lac as earnest money, but soon thereafter when it transpired that a live high tension electric wire was passing over the plot and otherwise also due to some depression it was full of dirty water, he applied for the refund of the earnest money. When HUDA refused to refund the amount, the learned District Consumer forum allowed the complaint by recording the following direction:-

'Even in the case of draw of lots a period of one month is given to the applicant whether he accepts the plot or not. So, in the case of open auction that option should be available as the plots are not shown before the auction. When the complainant saw the plot it was found not worth the auction. No house could be built at that plot. So, he immediately applied for the refund of his earnest money. Thus, it is ordered that the amount of Rs. 1,00,000/- be refunded to the complainant with interest at the rate of 15% per annum, from the date of deposit till the date of repayment."

We have heard the learned counsel for the appellant at length but we do not find any legal infirmity in the direction issued by the learned District Forum. Obviously when the complainant was not bound in law to accept the allotment of a plot over which a high tension electric wire was passing,

HUDA was bound to refund the earnest money. Consequently, the appeal is dismissed with no order as to costs.

Announced in open Court.

Sd/-
M.R. Agnihotri
President

July 24, 1998.

Sd/-
Sushila Pal
Member

BEFORE THE HON'BLE NATIONAL CONSUMER DISPUTES REDRESSAL COMMISSION: NEW DELHI

REVISION PETITION NO. 491/1999

IN THE MATTER OF :

Revision Petition under Section 21(B) of the Consumer Protection Act, 1986 against order dated 24.7.1998 passed in First Appeal No.837 of 1998 by the Hon'ble State Consumer Disputes Redressal Commission, Haryana, Chandigarh;

A N D

IN THE MATTER OF :

Estate Officer,
Haryana Urban Development
Authority, Gurgaon
Haryana

.. Petitioner

Vs.

H.R. Bangia and
Smt. Subhash Bangia,
Both r/o D-3

Nipccd Campus,
Opp. Police Station,
Hauz Khas, New Delhi-16

.. Respondents

The humble petition of
The Petitioner above-named

MOST RESPECTFULLY SHOWETH:

The petitioner is filing the instant Revision Petition before this Hon'ble Commission against the judgment and order dated 24th July, 1998 passed by the Hon'ble State Consumer Disputes Redressal Commission, Haryana, Chandigarh in First Appeal No.837/98, whereby the Hon'ble State Commission while dismissing the said appeal of the petitioner, has affirmed the order of the District Consumer Disputes Redressal Forum, Gurgaon dated 15th June, 1998, by which the District Forum directed the present petitioner to refund the amount of Rs. 1 lakh deposited by the Complainant as Earnest Money notwithstanding that the terms of the auction under which the Complainant had made the bid in respect of the plot had clearly provided that the highest bidder was bound to deposit 15% of the bid within 30 days of the date of allotment letter conveying the acceptance of the bid, failing which 10% of the bid within 30 days of the date of allotment letter conveying the acceptance of the bid, failing which 10% amount already deposited would stand forfeited to the Authority.

That the brief facts of the case giving rise to the present petition are that the complainant/respondent made a bid and he turned out to be the highest bidder for the plot and he deposited Rs.1 lakh (Rs.One Lakh) as Earnest Money.

That Regulation No. 6, Sub-Clause 2 of the Urban Development (Disposal of Land and Buildings) Regulation, 1978 reads as under:-

"6. SALE OR LEASE OF LAND ON BUILDING BY AUCTION:-

(2) 10 PERCENT OF THE HIGHEST BID SHALL BE PAID ON THE SPOT BY THE HIGHEST BIDDER IN CASH OR BY MEANS OF A DEMAND DRAFT IN THE MANNER SPECIFIED IN SUB-REGULATION (2) OF Regulation 5. The successful bidder shall be issued allotment letter in form 'CC' or 'C-II' by registered post and another 15 percent of bid accepted shall be payable by the successful bidder in the manner indicated, within 30 days of the date of allotment letter conveying acceptance of the bid by the Chief Administrator, failing which the 10% amount already deposited shall stand forfeited to the Authority and the successful bidder shall have no claim to the land or building auctioned."

That the respondent failed to comply with the requirement of depositing another 15% of the bid within 30 days of the allotment letter and as such, was not entitled to the refund of the 10% of the Earnest Money made by him at the time of participating in the bid.

That feeling aggrieved by the refusal of the request for the refund, the complainant filed a complaint before the Hon'ble District Consumer Disputes Redressal Forum, Gurgaon claiming the refund of the Earnest Money. A copy of the complaint filed by the complainant before the Hon'ble District Forum, Gurgaon dated 3.3.98 is filed herewith as Annexure-1.

That in response to the notice issued by the Hon'ble District Forum, the petitioner Authority contested the claim and claimed that the claimant was not entitled for the refund of the amount and interest or damages as claimed, as admittedly, he was the highest bidder and after depositing the Earnest Money, had failed to deposit the further amount. A copy of thereply filed by the present petitioner before the District Forum, Gurgaon, is filed herewith and marked Annexure-2.

That the Hon'Ble District Consumer Disputes Redressal Forum, Gurgaon vide its order dated 15th June, 1998, accepted the contentions of the complainant and directed the amount of Rs. 1 lakh to be refunded to the complainant with interest @ 15% per annum from the date of deposit till the date cf repayment. A true copy of the order dated 15.6.1998 passed by the District Forum is filedherewith and marked Annexure-3.

That aggrieved by the order of the Hon'ble District Forum, the petitioner filed an appeal, being First Appeal No.837 of 1998 before the Hon'ble State Consumer Disputes Redressal Commission, Haryana, Chandigarh contending, inter-alia, that the order of the District Forum directing refund of the amount deposited by the complainants was in violation of Regulation 6(2) of the Regulations inasmuchas the complainant had failed to deposit the additional amount. It was also contended that there was no deficiency on the part of the petitioner as the Complainant was well aware of the situation of the plot at the time of the auction and that awarding of interest @ 15% was clearly erroneous. Copy of the Memo of Appeal filed by the petitioner before the State Commission is filed herewith and marked Annexure-4 to this petition.

That the Hon'ble State Consumer Disputes Redressal Commission,Haryana, Chandigarh vide its order dated 24th July 1998 was pleased to dismiss the appeal of the present petitioner and affirmed the order of the Hon'ble State Forum, Gurgaon. Certified copy of the order dated 24th July '98 passed by the State Commission is filed herewith.

That the annexure filed with this petition are true copies of their respective originals;

That the petitioner has not filed any other petition earlier in this Hon'ble Commission or elsewhere against the order dated 24.7.1998 passed by the State Commission, which is under appeal, and that the petitioner is filing the instant revision petition before this Hon'ble Commission on the following, amongst other.

G R O U N D S

I. It is respectfully submitted that the State Commission

has erred in law and in the facts of the present case in dismissing the appeal of the petitioner.

II. It is respectfully submitted that the order of the State Commission and the District Forum are clearly contrary to Regulation 6(2) which governs the auction and provide for that in case the highest bidder fails to deposit the 15% of the cost of the plot within 30 days of the date of the auction, the Earnest Money being 10% deposited at the time of the bid would stand forfeited.

III. It is respectfully submitted that the State Commission and the District Forum sought to have noticed that the situation of the plot for which the complainant had made the bid was in his full knowledge and knowing fully well he had made the bid and after making the bid, he cannot be allowed to withdraw in view of Regulation 6(2) governing the auction.

IV. That the State Commission and the District Forum have erred in directing the present petitioner to refund the amount deposited by the respondents as the same is in violation of the Regulation 6(2) of the Regulation. From the perusal of the Regulation, reproduced above, it is clear that the respondents were bound to deposit another 15% of the bid accepted by the successful bidder/respondents within 30 days of the allotment letter conveying the acceptance of the bid by the Chief Administrator, failing which 10% amount already deposited shall stand forfeited to the Authority. As the respondents failed to deposit the another 15% of the bid, so they are not entitled for the refund of the amount, as the same stand forfeited as per Regulation 6(2) of the Regulations.

V. It is respectfully submitted that the State Commission and the District Forum have erred in directing the appellant/petitioner herein to refund the amount of Rs. 1 lac with 15% interest per annum from the date of the deposit till the date of repayment. As per the Regulation 6(2) of the Regulation, the 10% amount of the bid deposited by the respondents stood forfeited as the respondents did not deposit the another 15% of the amount of bid. As such, the respondents are not entitled to the refund of 10% amount of bid and the interest thereon.

VI. It is respectfully submitted that the State Commission and the District Forum have erred in not considering the fact that there is no deficiency on the part of the petitioner and the respondents were well aware of the situation of the plot at the time of auction. Even the complaint filed by the respondents was not maintainable as the impugned order is not appealable order.

PRAYER

For the reaons mentioned above and in the interest of justice, this Hon'ble Commission may be pleased to :-

(a) admit and allow the instant revision petition filed by the petitioner and set aside the judgment and order dated 24.7.1998 of the State Commission passed in F.A. No.837 of 1998; and

(b) pass such other and further order as deemed just and proper in the facts and circumstances of the case.

Drawn & Filed by,

(Ravindra Bana)

Advocate for the Petitioner

Place: New Delhi

Dated: December, 1998.

BEFORE THE HON'BLE NATIONAL CONSUMER DISPUTES REDRESSAL COMMISSION, NEW DELHI

REVISION PETITION NO.----------/1998

IN THE MATTER OF :

H.U.D.A. ... Petitioner

Vs.

H.R. Bangia ...Respondent

AFFIDAVIT

I, Sanjay Joon, Estate Officer, HUDA, Gurgaon do hereby solemnly affirm the state as under:-

1. That I am Estate Officer of the petitioner Authority and as such, am conversant with the facts of the case and competent to swear this Affidavit.
2. That I have read and understood the contents of the Revision Petition and the I.A.s and I state that the same are true and correct as per the records available to the office of the petitioner, no part of it is false and nothing material has been concealed therefrom.
3. That the annexures filed with the petition are true copies of their respective originals.

Verified at Gurgaon on this the day of

November, 1998 that the contents of my above Affidavit are true to my knowledge and the information derived from records.

Attested

Sd/-
Sanjay Joon
2/12/98

DEPONENT
Sd/-
Sanjay Joon

Annexure -1

Before the District Consumer Disputes Redressal Forum, Gurgaon

H.R. Bangia. 2. Smt. Subhash Bangia, both residents of D-3, NJPCCD Campus, Opp. Police Station, Hauz Khas, New Delhi-110016

....Complainants.

Versus

Haryana State Urban Development Authority, Sector-14, Gurgaon through its Estate Officer.

....Respondent.

Complaint Order Consumer Protection Act..

Sir,

The Complainants submits as under:-

1. That the complainant No. 1 is an officer in Semi-Govt. Organisation of National Institute of Public Corporation and Child Development under the Department of Women & Child Development, Ministry of Human Resource & Development Govt. of India New Delhi. The complainants were not having any house/land/plot either in Delhi or in Gurgaon so they wanted to have a plot to construct their house on urgents basis as the complainant no.1 is due to retire on June 30, 1998.
2. That the respondent advertised for the auction of Prime residential plot in Sector-16 II, Gurgaon through advertisement in Times of India News Paper as well as through hand pamphlet containing terms and conditions. One of such pamphlet and Photostat copy of Times of India advertisement dated 23.11.97 is attached herewith.

3. That the Venue of auction on dated 27.11.97 at 11 a.m. was Estate Office HUDA Sector-14, Delhi Road, Gurgaon. The complainants was tempted to come all the way to Gurgaon and they participated in the auction for residential plots and being the highest bid at the rate of Rs. 7300/- per sq-mtr. For plot of six marla in Sector-15-II bearing No.1578. A sum of Rs.1,00,000/- was depositing on the same day by the complainants in cash as an earnest money for the said plot. Photostate copy of the receipt in attached herewith.
4. That immediately after the completion of the bid the complainants went to the plot and found that the said plot was lying under-developed and was situated at a live high tension wire hear plot and there was *Dal-Dal* on the plot and was not at all fit for raising construction over it for residential purposes. There were endroachment over those plot by the houses of an already existing unauthorized colony inhabitants and the said plot was not qualifying for adjective 'Prime - plot.. The length of the plot was also not 18.2. mtrs as specified in the auction and the pamphlet distributed to the public. It was also not two side open as was declared at the time of auction. A lay out plant would clarify the exact position of the plot in question which is attached herewith. It caused a great mental agony and tension to the complainants and thus a letter for cancellation of the auction and for the refund of earnest money of Rs. 3,00,000/- was given to the Estate Officer HUDA by the complainants on the same day i.e. 27.11.97. Photosate copy of the same is attached herewith.
5. That the complainants no.1 thereafter sent a letter to Sh. R.S. Verma, Chief Secretary Govt. of Haryana Chandigarh for the refund of earnest money of the plot in question on 30.11.97 stating there in the full facts about the high headness and deficiency in

service on the part of the respondent. Photostat copy of the same is attached herewith. .

6. That a letter dated 19.12.97 was written by Chief Administrator HUDA Panchkula to Estate Officer HUDA Gurgaon for the early disposal of the case of the complainant and a copy of the same was received by the complainant no. 1 which is attached herewith. Thereafter the complainant no. 1 wrote a letter on 22.12.97 to Estate Officer HUDA and requested him to refund the amount of Rs. 1,00,000/- but no action was taken by him in spite of a telegram dated 31.12.97. Photostate copy of which is attached herewith Another letter dated 21.1.98 was written by the complainant no. 1 to the Administrator HUDA Gurgaon making there in full facts for the refund of the earnest money amount in respect of the plot in question but nothing has been done by the respondents till today. Photostate copy of the said letter is attached herewith.
7. That the plot in question was not free from encumbrances and did not meet the specifications as set in auction as per pamphlet distributed to the public and was not a residential plot and the complainant have been duped by the respondent and was tempted to part with his hard earned money in order to dump it in the mud which is altogether a great deficiency in service to the part of the respondent and hence the complainants have become entitled to file the present complaint before this Hon'ble Forum for the refund of the earnest money of Rs. 1,00,000/- along with interest @ 18% and also for damages for mental agony and harassment.

It is, therefore, prayed that the respondent be directed to refund the amount of Rs. 1,00,000/- deposited by the complainant on 27.11.97 as an earnest money to the plot No. 1578 Sector (III.) Gurgaon along with interest @ 18% P.A. from the date of deposit till final payment. The complainants be also awarded damages for mental agony and harassment to the tune of Rs. 10,000/- besides costs of the present proceedings.

Complainants
H.R. Bangia Smt Subhash Bangia
r/o D-3, NIPCCD Campus, Opp.
Police Station, Hauz Khas,
New Delhi.

Verification:
Verified that the contents of above
Complaint are true & correct to the best of my
Knowledge and belief.

Verified at
Gurgaon
On 3.3.98

/ True Copy/

Annexure -2

Before the President, District. Consumer Disputes Redressal Forum, Gurgaon

H.R. Bangia Vs. H.U.D.A.

Written Statement onbehalf of respondent.

Sir,

It is humbly submitted as under:-

PRELIMINARY OBJECIONS

1. That Hon'ble Forum has no jurisdiction to entertain and try the present complaint in view of section 50 of HUDA Act.

2. That provisions of Consumer Protection Act 1989 are not applicable to the immovable property, hence the complaint may be dismissed.
3. That the complainant is not a consumer and HUDA is not a manufacturer as defined in Consumer Protection Act, 1955.
4. That plot in dispute does not come within the definition of goods as defined in sales of goods act.
5. That present complaint is not a complaint as defined in Consumer Protection Act and the same may be dismissed.
6. That in this complaint a numerous facts and law point are involved which can only be decided by a regular suit, hence the complaint may be dismissed.
7. That the complainant has not availed the remedy of arbitration as provided in terms and conditions of allotment letter.
8. That complaint is bad for non-joinder and mis-joinder of necessary parties.
9. That complainant has no locus standis to file the present complaint.
10. That complaint is badly time barred and the same is not maintainable in the present form.

ON MERIT:

That para 1 is denied for want of knowledge.

That para No. 2 is informative one.

That in reply to para-3 of the complaint, it is submitted that the complainant gave highest bid for plot No. 1578, Sector-15, Part-II at Rs.7300/- per sq.mtr. and deposited a sum of Rs. One Lac being 10% of the total costs.

That in reply to para 4 it is submitted that the complainant filed an application for refund of the amount deposited by him. However, allotment letter of this plot was issued vide Memo No.294 dated 18.12.97.

That para No. 5 is informative one.

That para No. 6 of the complaint is informative.

That para No. 7 of the complaint is wrong and hence denifed. The complainant is not entitled for the refund of the amount and interest and damages.

It is, therefore, prayed that this complaint may be dismissed with costs. There is no deficiency of service on the part of the respondent in any manner. The complaint is not entitled for the refund of the amount deposited by him as allotment letter of this plot was issued in the name of the complainant on dt. 18.12.97.

RESPONDENT
Sd/-
Haryana Urban Dev. Authority-
Thru' Estate Officer, Gurgaon.

Dated.: 15.6.98

/ True Copy/

Annexure 4

BEFORE THE STATE CONSUMER DISPUTES REDRESSAL COMMISSION HARYANA AT CHANDIGARH

First Appeal No.– – – – – – –of 1998

Haryana Urban Development Authority, Sector - 14, Gurgaon through its Estate Officers

– – –Appellant

Versus

H.R. Bangia,
Smt. Subhash Bangia

Both residents of D-3, NIPCCD Campus, Opposite Police Station, Hauz Khas, New Delhi-110016

– – –Respondents

Appeal under Section 15 of the Consumer Protection Act 1986 against the order dated 15.6.1996 passed by the learned District Forum, Gurgaon, with view to the acceptance of the appeal and setting aside the said Order

RESPECTFULLY SHOWTH :

That the Order dated 15.6.1998 passed by the learned District Forum Gurgaon is against law, facts and evidence on record and is liable to set aside keeping in view the facts and circumstances of the case.

That the respondents being the highest bidder for the plot No. 1578, Sector-15,Part-II @ Rs.7900/- per sq. Meter, deposited Rs. 2 lac being the 10% of the total costs of the plot at the time of the auction the respondents were well aware of the position of the plot and it is only after that respondents gave the highest bid. Keeping in view the auction of the plot a allotment letter of the plot was issued vide Memo. No.294 dated 18.12.1997. As per Regulations No.6 sub-clause (2) of the Urban Development (Disposal of Land & Buildings), Regulations 1978 (hereinafter called the Regulation), the respondents were bound to deposit 15% of the bid within 30 days of the date of the allotment letter conveying the acceptance of the bid by the Chief Administrator failing which 10% amount already deposited shall stand forfeited to the authority. Regulation (12) of the Regulation is being reproduced for the kind perusal of this Hon'ble Court:-

"6. SALE OR LEASE OF LAND OR BUILDING BY AUCTION:-

(2) 10 percent of the highest bid shall be paid on the spot by the highest bidder in cash or by means of a Demand Draft in the manner specified in sub-regulation (2) of Regulation 5. The successful bidder shall be issued allotment letter in form 'cc' or 'c-II' by registered post and another 15% per cent of bid accepted shall be payable

by the successful bidder. In the manner indicated, 'within 30 days of the date of allotment letter conveying acceptance of the bid by the Chief Administrator, failing which the 10% amount already deposited shall stand forfeited to the Authority and the successful bidder shall have no claim to the land or building auctioned'.

That the learned District Forum erred in directing the appellant to refund the amount deposited by the respondents as the same is in violation of Regulation 6(2) of the Regulations. From the perusal of the Regulation reproduced above, it is clear that the respondents were bound to deposit another 15% of the bid accepted by the successful bidder/ respondents, within 30 days of the allotment letter conveying the acceptance of the bid by the Chief Administrator, failing which 10% amount already deposited still stand forfeited to the Authority. As the respondents failed to deposit the another 15% of the bid so they are not entitled for the refund of the amount, as the same stand forfeited as per regulation 6(2) of the Regulation.

That the learned District Forum erred in directing the appellant to refund the amount of Rs. 1 lac within 15% interest per annum from the date of the deposit till the date of repayment. As per the Regulation 6(2) of the Regulations of 10% of the Regulations of 10% amount of bid deposited by the respondents stood forfeited as the respondents did not deposit the another 15% of the amount of bid. As such the respondents are not entitled to refund of 10% amount of bid and the interest thereon.

That the learned District Forum erred in not considering the facts that there is no deficiency on the part of the appellant and the respondents were well aware of the situation of the plot at the time of auction. Even the complaint filed by the respondents was not maintainable as the impugned order is appeal able order.

It is, therefore respectfully prayed that the appeal may kindly be accepted and the order dated 15.6.1998 passed by the learned District Forum be set aside with costs.

A N D

It is further prayed that the operation of the impugned order passed by the learned District Forum may kindly be stayed till the decision of the appeal

(OM PARKASH SHARMA)
ADVOCATE,
COUNSEL FOR THE APPELLANT.

CHANDIGARH
DATE : 7.1998

BEFORE THE HON'BLE NATIONAL CONSUMER DISPUTES REDRESSAL COMMISSION
NEW DELHI

I.A. NO.– –337– – – – – –/1999

IN

REVISION PETITION NO. – –491– – – – –/1999

IN THE MATTER OF;

H.U.D.A ....Appellant/ Petitioner

Versus -

H.R. Bangia & Anr. "" – Respondent

APPLICATION FOR STAY

The humble petition on behalf

Of the appellant above-named

MOST RESPECTFULLY SHOWETH:

1. That the Appellant has filed the present Revision Petition under Section 21(B) of the Consumer Protection CP Act, 1986 against the order dated 24.7.1998 passed in First Appeal No. 837/98 by the Hon'ble State Consumer Disputes Redressal Commission, Haryana, Chandigarh.

2. That the sake of brevity and in order to avoid repetition of the same facts and grounds, the appellant craves indulgence of this Hon'ble Commission to refer the same as part and parcel of this Application.

3. That the Appellant has got a good prima facie case in its favour and is hopeful of succeeding before this Hon'ble Commission.

4. That the balance of convenience is also in favour of the appellant and against the respondent as per the facts and circumstances of the case.

5. That the appellant will suffer a great loss if the operation of judgment and order dated 24.7.98 passed by the Hon'ble State Commission, Chandigarh in F.A. No.837/98 is not ordered to be stayed.

P R A Y E R

It is, therefore, prayed that this Hon'ble Commission may be pleased to :

(a) stay the operation of the Order dated 24.7.98 passed in First Appeal No.837/98 by the State Consumer Disputes Redressal Commission Haryana, Chandigarh;

(b) pass such other or further order/orders that this Hon'ble National Commission may deem just and proper in the interest of justice.

Drawn & Filed by

(Ravindra Bana)
ADVOCATE FOR THE PETITIONER

FILED ON:

ANNEXURE XVIII
BEFORE THE HON'BLE NATIONAL CONSUMER DISPUTES REDRESSAL COMMISSION, NEW DELHI

REVISION PETITION NUMBER .491 OF 1999

HUDA ....Petitioner

Versus

H.R. Bangia and another .... Respondents

INDEX

S.No.	Particulars	Date	Page(s)
1.	Reply/version of respondents	22.8.2K	1-5
2.	Affidavit	22.8.2K	6
3.	Annexure R-1 Pamphlet		7 -7A
4.	Annexure R-2 Advertisement	23.11.97	8
5.	Annexure R-3 lay out plan prepared by respondents	–	9
6.	Power of attorney	–	10

GURGAON

DATED 22.8.2000

Sd/-
(G.L. MALIK)
ADVOCATE
CHAMBER No. 90,
NEW COURTS
COUNSEL FOR RESPONDENTS

POSTAL RECEIPT DT. 22.8.2K
SPEED POST REGN. NO. EE 00021887

DIARY NO. 9080 OF NCDRC NEW DELHI
DATED : 22/8/2000

BEFORE THE HON'BLE NATIONAL CONSUMER DISPUTES REDRESSAL COMMISSION, NEW DELHI

REVISION PETITION NUMBER 491 OF 1999

HUDA Versus H.R. BANGIA and another
REPLY VERSION OF THE CASE BY RESPONDENTS

Respectfully showeth:

1. That the petitioner being an organ of the State is supposed to act fairly. In the petition in hand, the petitioner by virtue of annexures R-1 and R-2 has before auction depicted the plot in question to be a prime residential plot whereas immediately after auction when the plot was seen by the respondents, it was found to be almost valueless as it was in ditches, encroached, and not two side open as demonstrated in the site plan displayed by the petitioner prior to the auction and more so the plot is not habitable and worth living.
2. That to dilute appreciation of the controversy, the petitioner has not produced copies of pamphlet and advertisement dated 23.11.97 in'the Times of India' pertaining to the auction mentioned in paragraph number 2 of the complaint and lay out plan mentioned in paragraph number 4 of the complaint. So, these are being produced herewith as annexures R-1, R-2, and R-3 respectively.

3. That regulation number 6 sub clause (2) of the Haryana Urban Development (disposal of land and buildings) Regulations 1978 is irrational, arbitrary and inconsistent with regulation 5(5) of the said regulations and so not enforceable in law.
4. That said regulation does not find any mention in annexures R-1 and R-2 and it would be deemed that petitioner had abandoned its benefit qua the transaction in question.
5. That the transaction in question was achieved by petitioner by practicing fraud and misrepresentation on respondents which is evident from the fact that averments made out in paragraphs number 4 and 7 of the complaint have not been controverted by the petitioner in its Written Statement before the Ld. District Forum.
6. That since the said avertments have not been controverted, these would be deemed to have been admitted resulting in vitiation of the whole transaction.
7. That it was not possible for the respondents to inspect all the plots offered in auction and so the respondents had given the bid on the basis of the site plan displaced by petitioner. When the respondents physically saw the plot in question after completion of the bid, the respondents found the deficiencies as mentioned in paragraphs number 4 and 7 of the complaint. The respondents, on the very same day i.e. on 27.11.97 informed in person and applied to Estate Officer, HUDA for refund of Rs.1,00,000.00 deposited by the respondents. It was therefore wrongly and for the first time pleaded before the hon'ble State Commission and now is being repeated before this hon'ble commission that the respondents were well aware of the situation of the plot at the time of the auction. That defence finds no mention in petitioner's reply before the hon'ble District Forum.

8. That it was represented by the petitioner through pamphlet annexure R-1 and advertisement in 'the Times of India' annexure R-2 that the 'auction was of prime residential plots in sector 15-II, Part 30, 56 and 17 Gurgaon'. But this is patently belied by the state of affairs on the spot which have been demonstrated by the respondents through site plan annexure R-3. Since the plot is encroached, not two side open, and in utter dal-dal, its possession can not be delivered by the petitioner to the respondents and the contract would be deemed to have been frustrated/become impossible of performance on the part of petitioner. Therefore allotment letter issued by petitioner to respondents is meaningless and non-est in the eyes of law.
9. That no fault can be found with well reasoned orders of the courts below and as such these orders deversde to be sustained.
10. That deficiency in service on the part of petitioner is thoroughly made out from the averments in paragraphs number 4 to 7 of the complaint which have not been questioned by the petitioner.

It is therefore prayed that the petition may be dismissed with costs.

GURGAON
DATED 22.8.2000

Sd/-
(G.L. MALIK)
ADVOCATE
CHAMBER No. 90,
NEW COURTS
COUNSEL FOR RESPONDENTS

ANNEXURE XIX
Urgent/Date Bound/By Hand

From : The Estate Officer,
HUDA. Gurgaon

To

i. Sh. H.R. Bangia
ii. Smt. Subhash Bangia
R/O G-50B (FF), Kalkaji,
New Delhi.

Memo No.13266 Dated: 6/9/2000

Subject: HUDA V/S H.R. Bangia - Summon/Notice to the respondents

Kindly find enclosed herewith the Dasti summon/ Notice passed by the Hon'ble State Commission, Haryana Chandigarh for appearing on 13.9.2K at 11.00 A.M. before Hon'ble State Commission Haryana, Chandigarh. The receipt of said summon may be acknowledged.

DA/As above.
Summon

Sd/-
Estate Officer,
HUDA, Gurgaon

Endst.No. Dated:

A copy is forwarded to the Chief Administrator, HUDA (Legal Cell) for information and w.r.to his endst. No.DDA-2000/8123 dated 29.8.2000.

Sd/-
Estate Officer,
HUDA, Gurgaon

Dasti No. SCDRC/A.II/2000 dated Chandigarh

STATE CONSUMER DISPUTES REDRESSAL COMMISSION, HARYANA
KOTHI NO 543 SECTOR 8-B, CHANDIGARH.

R.P. NO. 36 OF 2000

H U D A APPELLANTS

Versus

H.R. BANGIA Respondents

To

1. Sh. H.R. Bangia
2. Smt. Subhash Bangia

R/o G-50 B (FF) Kalkaji, New Delhi

The above said RP (copy enclose) has been fixed for hearing before the State Consumer Disputes Redrssal Commission Haryana, on 13-9-2000 at 11.A.M.

You are directed to appear in person or through some authorized agent on the said date and time and also bring with you all the documents/evidence upon which you intend to reply.

Take notice that in default of your appearance on that day before mentioned, the appeal will be heard and determined in your absence.

Given under my hand and the seal of this Commission On this 9th day of May 2000.

Sd/-
Superintendent.

ANNEXURE XX

BEFORE THE HARYANA STATE CONSUMER DISPUTES REDDRESSAL COMMISSION AT CHANDIGARH

FIRST REVISION NO. 36 OF 2000

HUDA APPELLANT

VERSUS

H.R. BANGIA AND ANOTHER RESPONDENT

I N D E X

S.No.	Particulars	Date	Page(s)
01.	Application u/s 151 of CPC	21.04.2000	01
02.	Grounds of Revision	21.04.2000	02 - 04
03.	Copy of order	7.03.2000	05 -07
04.	Execution application		08 - 09
05.	Copy of reply	28.12.1999	10
06.	Power of attorney		

PLACE: CHANDIGARH
DATED: APRIL 21, 2000

Sd/-
(AMANDEEP SINGH)
ADVOCATE
COUNSEL FOR THE APPLICANT

BEFORE THE HARYANA STATE CONSUMER DISPUTES REDRESSAL COMMISSION AT CHANDIGARH

CIVIL MISC. NO.—————————OF 2000

IN

REVISION NO.———OF 2000

HUDA APPELLANT

H.R. BANGIA AND ANOTHER Respondents

APPLICATION UNDER SECTION 151 OF CPC FOR STAY OF IMPUGNED ORDER DATED 07.03.2000

RESPECTFULLY SHOWETH:-

1. That the appellant is filing the accompanying first Revision which is likely to Succeed on the grounds taken therein. The contents of grounds be read as part of this application.
2. That balance of convenience is in favour of the appellant and against the respondent.
3. That the appellant would suffer an irreparable loss and injury, if the operation of the impugned order dated 07.03.2000 is not stayed.

It is, therefore, respectfully prayed that the operation of the impugned order dated 07.03.2000 may kindly be stayed.

PLACE; CHANDIGRH
DATED: April 21,2000

Sd/-
(AMANDEEP SINGH)
ADVOCATE

BEFORE THE HARYANA STATE CONSUMER DISPUTES REDRESSAL COMMISSION AT CHANDIGARH

REVISION PETITION NO.– – –OF 2000

Haryana Urban Deelopment Authority
throughits Estate Offier, Gurgaon, Haryana —Appellant

VERSUS

1. H. R. Bangia 2. Smt. Subhash Bangia,
residents of G-50 B (FF) Kalkaji, New Delhi — Respondents

REVISION UNDER SECTION 15 OF THE CONSUMER PROTECTION ACT, 1986 AGAINST THE IMPUGNED ORDER DATED 07.03.2000 PASSED BY DISTRICT FORUM, GURGAON.

Claim in Appeal: For the acceptance of appeal by setting aside the impugned order dated 07.03.2000.

RESPECTFULLY SHOWETH:-

1. That the impugned order dated 07.03.2000 passed by learned District Consumer Dispute Redressal Forum, Gurgaon is against the law and facts brought on the record of the file.
2. That this revision is directed against the order of the Learned District Consumer Forum, Gurgaon dated 07.03.2000 passed in Execution Application No. 207 of 12.11.1999.
3. That according to condition No. 7 of the allotment letter it was made clear to the allottee that the possession of site shall be offered after the completion of the development work in the area as the area was fully developed hence the possession was offered to complainant on dated 18.12.1997. So possession is offered within one month from the date when the

allottee had deposited the earnest money hence there is no deficiency on the part of HUDA.

4. That as already said in the foregoing para that it was made clear to the allottee that the possession of the site shall be offered after the completion of the development work in the area. The possession of the plot was offered on 18.12.1997 but the complainant has not come forward for taking the physical possession of the plot rather he requested to refund his earnest money along with interest @ 18% p.a. As there is no such policy in the HUDA Act to refund the earnest money so the Ld. Forum committed a grave illegality by saying that earnest money be refunded to him along with interest @ 15%.
5. That the Ld. Forum by ignoring the above said aspect of the matter allowed the complaint filed by the complainant and directed the appellant to refund the earnest money along with interest @ 15% p.a. on the amount deposited by him.
6. That the Ld. Forum has granted interest @ 15% which is quite excessive. The Ld. Forum did not take into consideration the facts and circumstances of the case. The possession is offered to the complainant within one month of his depositing his earnest money but the complainant was not in the position to construct the same and he applied to refund his earnest money so there is no deficiency of service on the part of the appellant.
7. That the Ld. Forum has erred in granting interest @ 15% when Hon.'ble Supreme Court has granted interest @ 10% in such like cases.
8. That since the matter is pending in the Hon'ble National Commission the District Consumer Forum committed a grave illegality by allowing the execution application filed by the complainant.
9. That views from any angle the order passed by Learned District Forum, Gurgaon is wrong, illegal and is unsustainable in the eyes of law.

It is, therefore, respectfully prayed that the present revision may kindly be allowed and the impugned order dated 07.03.2000 passed by District Forum, Gurgaon may kindly be set aside.

Sd/-

PLACE: CHANDIGARH (AMANDEEP SINGH)
DATED: April 21, 2000 ADVOCATE
Counsel for the appellant

PRESIDENT: DISTRICT CONSUMER DISPUTES REDRESSAL FORUM GURGAON

Execution Appl. No. 207/12.11.99

Date of decision 7.3.2000

H.R. Bangia **2. Smt. Subhash Bangia**

Residents of G 50 B (FF) Kalkaji, New Delhi
... **Complainants**

VERSUS

Haryana Urban Development Authority, Sector - 14, Gurgaon
through its Estate Officer
— Respondent

Present : Complainant in person
Sh. Dharmesh Sharma, Counsel /ADA for the respondent.

ORDER:

By this order we are going to dispose of this execution application filed by the applicant under section 27 of Consumer Protection Act for due execution of our order dated 15.6.98 in CPA No. 207 of 1998.

2. Brief facts of the case are that the complainant filed a complaint before this Forum against the respondent which was decided on 15.6.98 ordering the respondent to refund Rs. One lac with interest @ 15% to the complainant but the respondent has not made the compliance of the order. So the complainant filed execution application which was decided on 12.10.99 and the following order was passed.

"In this view of the matter the respondent-HUDA is afforded another opportunity to refund the amount of Rs. One Lac with interest @ 15% per annum from the date of deposit till the payment within 25 days of the order of this case ; failing which the HUDA and its concerned functionaries will be proceeded against as per provisions of Section 25/ 27 of CP Act".

But when the compliance was not made, the applicant filed this 2nd execution application.

3. Notice of the application was given to the respondent and the respondent appeared through their ADA and filed reply taking the plea that that the complainant gave highest bid for plot No. 1578/15 II, Gurgaon and also deposited Rs. 1 lac being 10% of the total cost at the time of auction. The complainant had given bid in open auction so he is not a consumer as per settled law. The orders passed by Hon'ble DCF, Gurgaon have been **challenged in the Hon'ble National Commission, New Delhi** through Sh. Ravindra Bana, Advocate. It is submitted that the orders of the DCF Gurgaon shall be complied with the prior approval of the competent authority.

4. We have heard the complainant in person and the counsel for the respondent and have gone through the evidence and record on the file. The complainant had purchased plot Number 1578 Sector 15-II in a public auction held on 27.11.97. He had deposited Rs. One lac but the said plot was not fit for construction. So the complainant approached the respondent for the refund of Rs. One lac but the respondent failed to do so so far. So the complainant filed C.P.A. No.287/3.3.98 decided on 15.6.98 but all in vain. The complainant again filed execution application under

Section 25 & 27 C.P.Act in which it was ordered that the respondent shall refund the amount of Rs. One lac with interest @ 15% from date of deposit till the date of payment within 25 days of the order dated 12.10.99. HUDA again failed to comply with the order passed by this Forum.

So the applicant again filed an execution application against the order dated 12.10.99. Several show cause notices were given to the respondent for comply with the order but the respondent stated that the **order passed by this Forum have been challenged in the Hon'ble National Commission but no copy of stay order has been placed on the file. No copy of complaint has been placed on the file. No any proceedings of Hon'ble National Commission in respect of the complaint has been filed by the respondent-HUDA. No affidavit in this regard has been filed by the HUDA.**

So in these circumstances, the respondent is directed to refund the amount of Rs. One lac to the complainant with interest @ 15% per annum from the date of deposit till the date of payment within 25 days from today; failing which HUDA shall pay Rs. 100/- per day to the complainant and strict action will be taken.

No order as to costs

Announced:	Sd/-
7.3.2000	**B.S. Indora**
Sd/-	President.
Mrs. Asha Barak, Member	Distt. Consumer Disputes Redressal Forum, Gurgaon

BEFORE THE DISTRICT CONSUMER DISPUTES REDRESSAL FORUM: GURGAON

H.R. Bangia Vs. HUDA

Reply to application for under section 25&27 of the C.P.Act.

Sir,

It is humbly submitted as under:-

1 & 2 That paras No. 1 & 2 of the application are informative and matter of court records.

3. It is submitted that the complainant gave highest bid for plot No.1578/15-II Gurgaon and also deposited Rs. 1 lac being 10% of the total cost at the time of auction. **The complainant had given bid in open auction so he is not a consumer as per settled law.** The orders passed by Hon'ble DCF, Gurgaon have been challenged in the Hon'ble National Commission, New Delhi through Sh. Ravindera Bana, Advocate. It is submitted thatthe orders of the DCF, Gurgaon shall be complied with with the prior approval of the competent authority.

It is, therefore, prayed that the application under reply may kindly be dismissed.

Respondent
Sd/-
Haryana Urban Dev. Authority
Through Estate Officer, Gurgaon.

Dated. 28.12.1999

Revision Petition No 36 of 2000

H U D A Vs H.R. Bangia

Present : Mr. Amandeep Singh, Advocate for the petitioner.

Notice for 1st August 2000. Operation of the impugned order stayed till further orders. Dasti as prayed for.

Sd/-
(Amarjeet Chaudhary)
President

Sd/-
(A. D. Malik)
Member

Seal : District Consumer Disputes Redressal Commission, Haryana, Chandigarh.

May 9, 2000

ANNEXURE XXI
STATE COMMISSION DISPUTES REDRESSAL COMMISSION
HARYANA, CHANDIGARH

Revision Petition ; No. 36 of 2000

Date of Decision: 15-2-2001

Haryana Urban Development Authority through its Estate Officer, Gurgaon, Haryana

APPELLANT(S)

VS

1. H.R. Bangia 2. Smt. Subhash Bangia, residents of G 50B (FF), Kalkaji, New Delhi

Respondent(s)

Present: Mr. Amandeep Singh, Advocate for the appellant
Mr. H.R. Bangia, respondent. In person

BEFORE:
Hon'ble Mr. Justice Amarjeet Chaudhary, President
Mr. A.D. Malik, Member

O R D E R

Amarjeet Chaudhary J.(Oral)

Haryana Urban Development Authority has come up in revision against the order of the District Forum, Gurgaon dated 7.3.2000 vide which the District Forum on an execution application filed by H.R. Bangia & another had issued direction to the petitioner to refund Rs.one lac to the complainants with interest @ 15% per annum from the date of deposit till the date of payment within 25 days from today; failing which HUDA shall pay Rs.100/- per day to the complainants.

2. Notice of the revision petition was issued and in pursuance of which the respondent has put in appearance in person.

3. We have heard the counsel for the petitioner as well as respondent in person and have also perused the impugned order. After taking into consideration their respective submissions, we are convinced that there was no justification for imposing penalty of Rs. 100/- per day upon the petitioner - HUDA and the same is waived off. The rest of the order is maintained. The impugned order is modified in the manner indicated above and the revision petition stands disposed of accordingly. However, it is made clear that order of the District Forum is to be implemented within one month from the receipt of the copy of the order; failing which penal action will be initiated under Section 27 of the Consumer Protection Act against the petitioner - HUDA.

Sd/-
(Justice Amarjeet Chaudhary)
President

Sd/-
(A.D. Malik)
Member
February 15, 2001

Supdt. Sd/- 23.3.2001
State Consumer Redressal
Commission, Haryana, Chandigarh

ANNEXURE XXII

H.R. BANGIA

Phone: 6838559
II-E/99, (Top Floor)
Lajpat Nagar,
Central Market,
New Delhi - 110 024

27th March, 2001

The Chief Administrator,
Haryana Urban Development Authority,
Panchkula, Sector - 6,
Panchkula

Subject:

Revision Petition No. 36 of 2000
HUDA Vs H.R. Bangia And
Smt. Subhash Bangia,
both residents of II-E/99 Top Floor,
Central Market, Lajpat Nagar,
New Delhi-110024

Sir,

The above case was decided on February 15, 2001 by the State Consumer Disputes Redressal Commission, Haryana, Chandigarh. The case was attended by Shri Amandeep Singh, Advocate who represented from HUDA. The undersigned was also present in the Hon'ble Court when the case was announced by Hon'ble Court. It was decided to comply with the orders with immediate effect.

It is informed that the said orders have not yet been complied with as per the directions given on 15th February, 2001.

Yours faithfully,

Sd/-
(H.R. Bangia)
II-E/99 Top Floor,
Central Market,
Lajpat Nagar,
New Delhi-110 024

Copy for information and similar action to

Estate Officer,
Haryana Urban Development Authority,
Sector 14, Gurgaon

ANNEXURE XXIII

Registered Post

H.R. Bangia
Master of Public Administration
PGD Labour Law
(Indian Law Institute)

E-99 (Top Floor)
Lajpat Nagar II
Central Market,
New Delhi- 110 024
Phone: 683-8559

Estate Officer,
Haryana Urban Development Authority,
Sector 14, HUDA OFFICE COMPLEX,
Gurgaon (Haryana)

Subject: Compliance of decision dated 15.2.2001 in Revision Petition No. 36 of 2000 of HUDA Vs. H.R. Bangia & Smt. Subhash Bangia, both resident of E-99 (Top Floor) Lajpat Nagar II, Central Market, New Delhi-110 024

Sir,

I enclose copy of order dated 23rd March, 2001 of State Consumer Disputes Redressal Commission, Haryana, Chandigarh in respect of the Revision Petition No. 36 of 2000 (decided on 15.2.2001) of HUDA Vs. H.R. Bangia & Subhash Bangia both resident of E-99 (Top Floor), Lajpat Nagar II, Central Market, New Delhi-110 024 for favour of your kind perusal with the request to kindly comply with the orders accordingly.

It also refers to my registered letter dated March 27, 2001.

Thanking you,

Yours faithfully,

Sd/-
(H. R. Bangia)
10.4.2001

P.S. Please note the address changed
Encls: Copy of Order dt. 23.3.2001

Registered Letter No. 1113 dated 10.4.2001

Sd/-
Haryana Urban Dev. Authority–
Thru' Estate Officer, Gurgaon.

ANNEXURE XXIV

BEFORE THE DISTRICT CONSUMER DISPUTES REDRESSAL FORUM, GURGAON

I, H,R.. Bangia 2. Smt. Subhash Bangia, both residents of E-99 (Top Floor) Lajpat Nagar II, Central Market, New Delhi-110024

..... Complainants

Versus

Haryana Urban Development Authoriy,
Sector 14, Gurgaon through its Estate Officer,

.....Respondent

Complaint under Section 25/27 of Consumer Protection Act, 1986.

1. That the Complainant No. 1 retired on 30.6.1998 as Administrative Officer from National Institute of Public Cooperation and Child Development which is working as an autonomous organization under the Ministry of Human Resource Development (Department of Women and Child Development) Government of India, New Delhi. The complainants were not having any house/land/plot either in Delhi or in Gurgaon so they wanted to have a plot to construct their house on urgent basis as the Complainant No. 1 was to retire on June 30, 1998.
2. That the respondent advertised for the auction of Prime residential plot in Sector 15, Gurgaon through advertisement in Times of India News paper as well as through hand pamphlet containing terms and

conditions. One of such pamphlet and Photostat copy of Times of India advertisement dated 23.11.1997 are attached herewith as **Annexure 1 & Annexure II** respectively.

3. That the venue of auction on 27.11.1997 at 11.00 a.m. was Estate Office, HUDA, Sector 14, Delhi Road, Gurgaon. The Complainants were tempted to come all the way to Gurgaon and they participated in the auction for Prime Residential Plots being the highest bidder at the rate of Rs. 7300/-(Rupees Seven thousand three hundred only) per Sq. Mtr. for Plot of six *marle* in Sector 15 Part II bearing Plot No. 1578, a sum of Rs. 1,00,000/- (Rupees one lakh only) was deposited vide Cash Receipt No. 413 (Book No. nil) dated 27.11.1997 (Photocopy of **Annexure III** enclosed).
4. That immediately after the completion of the bid the Complainants went to the spot and found that the said plot was lying undeveloped and was situated at a live high tension wire passing near the plot and there was *dal-dal* on the site and was not at all fit for raising construction over it for residential purposes and there was encroachment over this plot by the house of an already existing unauthorized colony inhabitants and as such the said plot was not qualifying for adjective 'Prime' Plot as advertised in the pamphlets widely distributed at the time of auction and also in the Times of India dt. 23.11.1997 newspaper (as mentioned at para 2 above). There was no construction on the left and right side of the said plot. Since the live high tension wire was passing by the side of this plot, all the plots opposite this plot though allotted for more than five years were not given possession to the allottees. The length of the plot was also not 18.2 mtrs as specified in the auction and the pamphlets distributed to the public. It was also not two side open as was declared at the time of auction. The said facts were reported

in my petition dt. 3.3.1998 (Photocopy of Petition dt. 3.3.1998 is at **Annexure IV.**). It caused a great mental agony and tension to the complainants and he suffered a heart-attach on 4.3.1998 (On the night of 3.3.1998) and he was admitted to the St. Stephen's Hospital, Tis Hazari, Delhi. He was advised bed rest for two months by the Attending Medical Expert, Dr. Madhukar Shahi, MD DM DNB, Consultant, and Cardiologist. He had been advised not to undergo any mental or physical stress for another period of six months vide his certificate dt. 22.10.98 (Already furnished to the Forum with application dt. 9.11.1998). Thus a letter for cancellation of the auction for the refund of earnest money of Rs. 1,00,000/- was given to the Estate Officer, Gurgaon by the complainants on the same day i.e. 27.11.1997(**Annexure V**).

5. That the complainant No. 1 thereafter sent a letter dt. 30.11.1997 to Shri R.S. Verma, Chief Secretary, Government of Haryana Chandigarh for the refund of earnest money of the plot in question stating therein all the facts about which mention had been made in the above paras, stating therein the full facts about the highhandedness and deficiency in service on the part of the respondent (Photo copy furnished with petition dt. 3.3.1998)
6. That a letter dt. 19.12.1997 was written by the office of the Chief Administrator, HUDA, Panchkula to the Estate Officer, HUDA, Gurgaon for the early disposal of the case of the Complainant No. 1 (Photocopy already furnished with petition dt. 3.3.1998). Thereafter the complainant No. 1 wrote a letter on 22.12.1997 to Estate Officer, Gurgaon, HUDA and requested him to refund the amount of Rs. 1,00,000/- but no action was taken by him in spite of telegram dt. 31.12.1997 (Photocopies furnished with Petition dt. 3.3.1998). Another letter dt. 21.1.1998 was written by the complainant No.

1 to the Administrator, HUDA, Gurgaon stating therein again full facts for the refund of the earnest money of Rs. 1,00,000/- in respect of the plot No. 1578 Sector 15, Part II, Gurgaon but nothing had been done by the respondent..(Photocopy furnished with petition dt. 3.3.1998).

7. That the plot in question was not free from encumbrance and did not meet the specification as set in auction as per pamphlet distributed widely to the public and was not a prime residential plot as advertised in Times of India dt. 23.11.1997 and the complainants had been duped by the respondent and was forced to part with his hard earned money in order to dump it in the mud which is altogether a great deficiency in service on the part of the respondent and hence the complainants became entitled to file the suit on 3.3.1998 for refund of the earnest money of Rs. 1 lac along with interest @ 18% and also for damages for mental agony and harassment.
8. That the complainant No. 1 and complainant No. 2 prayed vide their petition dt. 3.3.1998 that the Respondent-HUDA be directed to refund the amount of Rs.1,00,000/- deposited by the complainants on 27.11.1997 as an earnest money to the Plot No. 1578 Sector 15 Part II, Gurgaon along with interest @ 18% p.a. from the date of deposit till final payment. It was also prayed to award damages for mental agony and harassment to the tune of Rs. 10,000/- besides costs of proceedings.
9. That the Petition dated 3.3.1998 before the District Consumer Dispute Redressal Forum, Gurgaon was heard vide CPA No.297/3.3.1998 but the respondent -HUDA did not even furnish the reply to Petition dated 3.3.1998 to the learned President Shri D.D. Yadav and the Members present in the Forum. The Forum vide their decision dt. 15.6.1998 ordered that the amount of Rs. 1,00,000/- be refunded to the

complainant with interest at the rate of 15% per annum from the date of deposit till the date of repayment.

10. That the Complainants vide their letter dated July 20, 1998 handed over the orders dt. 15.6.1998 personally at the office of the Estate Officer, HUDA, Gurgaon on 20.7.1998 itself and obtained the receipt from his office. Another request dt. 9.9.1998 as a reminder was also sent by Regd. Post for refund as per decision dt. 15.6.1998 and to comply with the orders of the Forum. But the same was not complied with.
11. That the Complainants vide their Petition dt. 9.11.1998 CPA No. 1899 moved the District Forum for taking action under Section 25 and Section 27 of the CPA.(**Annexure VI**).
12. That the Hon'ble District Forum decided on 12.10.99 (Order dt. 12.10.1999 enclosed as Annexure VI) to refund the amount of Rs. One lac with interest @ 15% p.a. from the date of deposit till payment within 25 days of the order of the same; failing which the HUDA and its concerned functionaries will be proceeded again as per provisions of Section 25/ 27 of C.P. Act.
13. That HUDA again failed to comply with the order passed by the District Forum. The forum served several show causes notices to the Respondent for comply with the order but the respondent-HUDA stated that the order passed by the Forum have been challenged in the Hon'ble National Commission but no copy stay order had been placed on the file. No copy of complaint had been placed on the file. No any proceedings of Hon'ble National Commission in respect of complaint had been filed by the respondent-HUDA. No affidavit in this regard had been filed by the HUDA.
14. That in those circumstances, the respondent – HUDA was directed to refund the amount of Rs. One lac

to the complainant with interest @15 per cent annum from the date of deposit till the date of payment within 25 days from the date of order i.e. 7.3.2000; failing which HUDA shall pay Rs. 100/- per day to the complainant and strict action will be taken. (Order dt. 7.3.2000 is at **Annexure VIII**).

15. That complainants received Memo No. 13266 dt. 6.9.2000 on 11.9.2000 from the Estate Officer, HUDA, Gurgaon as Dasti Summon/Notice passed by the Hon'ble State Commission, Haryana Chandigarh for appearing on 13.9.2k at 11.00 a.m. before the Hon'ble State Commission, Haryana, Chandigarh.
16. That the complainant No. 1 appeared before the Hon'ble State Commission Haryana, Chandigarh on 13.9.2000 in connection with Revision Petition No. 36 of 2000 of HUDA VS H.R. Bangia
17. That the Hon'ble State Commission Haryana, Chandigarh decided the case vide Order dated 15.2.2001 (**Annexure IX**).

    Para 3 of the order dated 15.2.2001 is reproduced below for brevity:

    We have heard the counsel for the petitioner as well as respondent in person and have also perused the impugned order. After taking into consideration their respective submission, we are convinced that there was no justification for imposing penalty of Rs. 100/- per day upon the petitioner - HUDA and the same is waived off. The rest of the order is maintained. The impugned order is modified in the manner indicated above and the revision petition stands disposed of accordingly. However, it is made clear that order of the District Forum is to be implemented within one month from the receipt of the copy of the order; failing which penal action will be initiated under section 27 of the Consumer Protection Act against the petitioner - HUDA.

18. That the complainant No. 1 vide his Regd. Post No. 1113 latter dated 10.4.2001 informed the Estate Officer with photo copy of the order dated 15.2.2001 to comply with the said orders accordingly **(Annexure X)**
19. That since then neither the said amount with interest nor any reply has been furnished to the complainants. Section 25 of CPA are clear about the enforcement of orders by the Forum, the State Commission or the National Commission, which indicates that every order made by the District Forum, the State Commission or the National Commission may be enforced by the District Forum, the State Commission or the National Commission, as the case may be, in the same manner as if it were decree or order made by a court in a suit pending therein and it shall be lawful for the District forum, the State Commission or the National Commission to send in the event of its inability to execute it, such order to the court within the local limits of whose jurisdiction -

    a. In the case of an order against a company, the registered office of the company is situated, or
    b. In the case of an order against any other person, the place where the person concerned voluntarily resides or carries on business or personally works for gain, is situated, and thereupon, the court to which the order is so sent, shall execute the order as if it were a decree or order sent to it for execution.
20. That it is prayed that the respondent - HUDA be directed to refund the amount of Rs. 1,00,000/- (Rupees one lac only) to the complainants with interest at the rate of 15% per annum from the date of deposit i.e. 27.11.1997 till the date of repayment and further order to the Respondent - HUDA be given as per Section 25/27 of the

Consumer Protection Act, 1986 for non-compliance of the order of the Hon'ble State Consumer Disputes Forum, Gurgaon dated 7.3.2000 regarding HR Bangia vs. HUDA till the date of the present petition besides costs of the present proceedings which may be deemed fit by the Hon'ble Forum, Gurgaon.

VERIFICATION

Verified that the contents of the above complaint are true and correct to the best of our knowledge and belief.

Verified at Gurgaon on 20.06.2001

Sd/-
H.R. Bangia
Complainant No. 1

Sd/-
Smt. Subhash Bangia
Complainant No. 2

Both residents of E-99, Lajpat Nagar II, Central Market, New Delhi-110024

Encls : As above.

ANNEXURE XXV

Before the District Consumer Disputes Redressal Forum, Gurgaon

H.R. Bangia Versus H.U.D.A.

Reply to application dated 23.8.2001

Sir,

The respondent humbly submits as under:-

That the application filed by the complainant is not maintainable in law, as there is no provision to replace the page of petition in lieu of the original page of the petition, as alleged.

It is, therefore, most humbly prayed that the application under reply, may kindly be dismissed with costs.

Respondent
Sd/-
Haryana Urban Development Authority
Through its Estate Officer,
Gurgaon.

Dated 5.9.2001

Through Sh. Satbir Singh Tanwar,
Advocate, Gurgaon.

H.R. Bangia Vs. HUDA

Present: Complainants in person.
Counsel for the respondent.

The complainant Sh. H.R. Bangia has moved an application stating that the page no. 7 of the above mentioned case may please be replaced by the copy annexed due to typographical error as the HUDA had also not complied with the order dated 15.2.2001 passed by Hon'ble State Commission, Haryana, Chandigarh in case No. R.P. 36 of 2000. Notice was issued to the respondent and the respondent appeared through counsel and filed reply taking the plea that the application filed by the complainant is not maintainable in law as there is no provision to replace the page of petition in lieu of the original page of the petition, as alleged and the application of the complainant may kindly be dismissed.

Heard.

After taking into consideration all the facts mentioned in the application and in the interest of justice, the application filed by the complainant is hereby allowed. Now the case is adjourned to 8.10.2001 for the personal appearance of the E.O.HUDA. In this respect the Ahlmad is directed to issue the notice to the E.O.Huda with the direction to appear in person before this Forum on 8.10.2001 with the compliance report.

1. Sd/ Member
2. Sd/- Member

Sd/-
President
DCDRF, GGN.
6.9.2001

Annexure XXVI

Dasti 8.11.2001
10 AM

H.R. Bangia Vs HUDA

To

The Estate Officer,
HUDA Deptt. Gurgaon.

Memo in the above note

Sir,

You are hereby directed to appear in person before this Forum on 8.11.2001 with the relevant record of this case (For compliance)

Sd/-

President, Distt. Consumer Disputes Redressal Forum,
Gurgaon
23/X/2001

ANNEXURE XXVII

HR Bangia Vs HUDA Present: Complainant in person
Shri Satbir Singh Tanwar, Counsel for the complainant

Vide Order dated 23.10.2001 the Estate Officer, HUDA Gurgaon was directed to appear in person before this Forum for compliance of the order passed by this Forum on dated 15.6.1998 by which the respondent-HUDA was directed to refund the amount of Rs. 1,00,000/- to the complainant with interest at the rate of 15% per annum from the date of deposit till the date of payment and failing which strict action will be taken. Thereafter, the opposite -party-HUDA went in appeal against that order and the following order was passed by the Hon'ble State Commission on dated 15.2.2001

"We are convinced that there was no justification for imposing penalty of Rs.100/- per day upon the petitioner-HUDA and the same is waived off. The rest of the order is maintained."

In compliance to the order of this Forum, Sh. Pardeep Kumar, Estate Officer, HUDA has appeared before this Forum on dated 9.11.2001 and made a statement that he will comply with the order of the Forum after receiving the approval of Chief Administrator, HUDA, Chandigarh within a month. But no action has been taken by the opposite party till date. So notice be issued to the Chief Administrator, HUDA, Chandigarh with the direction to approve the case and approval of the same be sent before this Forum on or before 15.1.2002 so that compliance of the order is made accordingly.

Sd/-
President,
DCDRF, GGN
14.12.2001

ANNEXURE XXVIII

NATIONAL CONSUMER DISPUTES REDRESSAL COMMISSION, NEW DELHI

Revision Petition No. 491 of 1999 (From the Order dated 24.7.98 in f.a.No.837/98 of the State Commission, Haryana) H.U.D.A. Vs. H.R. Bangia came up for hearing on 21.12.2001..

The case came before: Hon'ble Mr. Justice D.P. Wadhwa, President,
Hon'ble Mr. Justice J.K. Mehra, Member
Mrs. Rajyalakshmi Rao, Member
Mr. B.K. Taimni, Member

For the Appellant Mr. Ravindra Bana, Advocate

For the Respondent Mr. G.L. Malik, Advocate

21.12.2001

O R D E R

J.K. MEHRA J MEMBER

In this case the Respondent/Complainant had purchased a plot at an open auction and as per the terms deposited 10% of the price. Thereafter, he went to seek an inspection of the plot and was shown the plot and discovered to his dismay that the plot had a high-tension wire passing over it, apart from that it had a depression where water had collected which need to be reclaimed. He approached the Petitioner for cancellation of his plot in view of the above serious deficiencies on the plea that he had made his bid for a developed plot free from any such problems

The Petitioner took up the stand that as per the terms of the auction if the bidder does not pay the 15% further amount within 30 days, the HUDA administration was within its rights to forfeit the 10% amount deposited. The Complainant filed a complaint alleging that HUDA could do so only if it had offered an inspection of the site before the auction. Since no inspection was offered at the time or before the auction before the bids, no such plea would come to its avail and it was liable to refund the amount which had been deposited on his successful bidding. The District Forum upheld the contention of the Respondent and decided in his favour, directing the Petitioner to refund the amount with interest at the rate of 15% p..a. The State Commission also agreed with the District and sustained that order. We see no jurisdictional error or infirmity in the concurrent findings of the two for a below which would merit our interference under Sec. 21(b) of the Consumer Protection Act, 1986.

The Revision Petition is dismissed

Sd/-
(D.P. WADHWA)
PRESIDENT

Sd/-
(J.K. MEHRA)
MEMBER

Sd/-
(RAJYALAKSHMI RAO)
MEMBER
Sd/-
(B.K. TAIMNI)
MEMBER

ANNEXURE XXIX
ADVERTISEMENT IN TIMES OF INDIA DATED 23.11.1997 & PAMPHLET DISTRIBUTED & DISPLAYED AT SITE

HUDA OFFERS A GREAT INVESTMENT OPPORTUNITY YOU SIMPLY CANT AFFORD TO MISS !

BUY A PIECE OF FUTURE

I AUCT[illegible] OF PRIME COMMERCIAL SITES IN SECTOR 4, 5, 15-II, 18, 21, 22, 23-23A (DISTT. SHOPPING CENTRE), 31,31-32A, 32 INSTITUTIONAL & 55 GURGAON

II AUCTION OF PRIME RESIDENTIAL PLOTS IN SECTOR 15-II, PART-30, 56 AND 17 GURGAON

AUCTION DATE 27.11.97 TIME 11.00 A.M.
VENUE: ESTATE OFFICE HUDA, SECTOR 14, DELHI ROAD GURGAON.

Sr. No.	Sector No.	Particulars	Sr. No. of Sites	Dimension In Mtrs	Area in Sq. Mts.
1.	4	SCF Site	18,31	5.5x24.4	134.2
2.	4	Booth Site	81 to 83	2.75x8.25	22.68
3.	5	D/S Shop Site	46,57	5.5x13.75	75.62
4.	5	D/S Shop Site	43 Cor, 58 Cor.	5.73x13.75	78.78
5.	5	Booth Site	39 to 41	2.75x8.25	22.68
6.	15-II	Booth Site	132 to 134	2.75x8.25	22.68
7.	18	Booth Site	111 to 115	2.75x8.25	22.68
8.	21	Booth Site	34 to 36	2.75x8.25	22.68
9.	22	Booth Site	135 Cor, 146 Cor,	2.865x8.25	23.636
10.	22	Booth Site	64 to 66, 136, 145,	2.75x8.25	22.68
11.	23-23A (Distt. Shopping Centre)	SCO Site three Storey with basement	13,14,35,36	5.5x25	137.5
12.	23-23A (Distt. Shopping Centre)	SCO Site three Storey with basement	8 Cor., 20 Cor, 30 Cor, 33 Cor,	5.73x25	143.25
1.	23-23A (Distt. Shopping Centre)	Booth Site	98 to 103	2.75x8.25	22.68
14.	31	Double Storey Shop Site with basement.	100 Cor, 101 Cor	5.73x13.75	78.78
15	31	Double Storey Shop Site with basement.	102, 103	5.5x13.75	75.62
16.	31	Booth Site	6 to 8	2.75x8.25	22.68
17.	31-32 A	SCO/F Site three storey with basement	46 Cor.	5.73x22	126.06
18.	31-32A	—do—	45	5.5x22	121
19.	32 Inst.	SCO Site three Storey with basement	13 to 16	5.5x22	121
20.	32 Inst.	Booth Site	25 to 27	2.75x8.25	22.68
21.	55	SCO Site 3 storey with basement	101 to 103	5.5x22	121
22.	55	Booth Site	75 to 78	2.75x8.25	22.68

II Detail of residential plots for auction on 27.11.97

Sr. No.	Sector	Size	Plot No.
1.	15-II	6M	1578, 1579P
2.	15-II	10M	1495A, 1495B, 1495C-P 1495F-P, 1496C, 1496D
3.	15-II	14M	788B
4.	Part-30	4M	29 to 35
5.	56	1K	582 to 586
6	17	1K	28

TERMS AND CONDITION

1. 10% of the bid amount has to be tendered on the spot at the fall of hammer either in cash or by bank draft in favour of the Estate Officer, HUDA, Gurgaon
2. Another 15% of the bid money is to be deposited with in 30 days from the date of issue of allotment letter by bank draft.
3. Balance 75% amount is to be paid with in 60 days from the date of issuance of allotment letter either as one time interest free payment or in the following manner:-
   a) In the case of Booth site, the balance 75% amount would be payable in 10 half yearly equal instalments with 15% interest.
   b) In the case of other commercial sites the balance 75% amount would be payable in 8 half yearly instalments with 15% rate of interest.
   c) In the case of residential plots the balance 75% amount would be payable in 6 half yearly instalments with 15% interest.

The Presiding Officer reserves the right to withdraw any property from the auction or reject any bid without assigning any reason.

The detailed terms and conditions will be announced at the venue, at the time of auction.

The Estate Officer, HUDA Gurgaon may be contacted on any working day for further clarifications/site plan/details etc.

A security of Rs. 2000/- will be deposited before the start of auction which is refundable after the auction

Sanjay Joon, HCS
Estate Officer
HUDA, Gurgaon
Phone:-321253

TIMES OF INDIA
23-11.97

K. S. Yadav, IAS
Administrator,
HUDA, Gurgaon.
Phone: - 321650

HUDA : BUILDING A BETTER FUTURE

HUDA Offers A Great Investment Opportunity
You Simply Cant Afford to Miss !

BUY A PIECE OF FUTURE

I Auction of Prime Commercial Sites in Sector 4, 5, 15-II, 18, 21, 22, 23-2 (Distt. Shopping Centre), 31, 31-32A, 32 Institutional & 55 Gurgaon

II Auction of Prime Residential Plots in Sector 15-II, Part-30, 56 & 17 Gurga

Auction Date 27–11–97 Time 11-00 A.M.

Venue : ESTATE OFFICE HUDA, SECTOR-14, DELHI ROAD, GURGAO

Sr. No.	Sector No.	Particulars	Sr. No. of Sites	Dimension In Mtrs.	Area i sq. Mt
1.	4	SCF Site	18, 31	5.5x24.4	134 2
2.	4	Booth Site	81 to 83	2.75x8.25	22.68
3.	5	D/S Shop Site	46, 57	5.5x13.75	75 62
4.	5	D/S Shop Site	43 Cor, 58 Cor.	5.73x13.75	78.78
5.	5	Booth Site	39 to 41	2.75x8.25	22.68
6.	15-II	Booth Site	132 to 134	2.75x8.25	22.68
7.	18	Booth Site	111 to 115	2.75x8.25	22.68
8.	21	Booth Site	34 to 36	2.75x8.25	22.68
9.	22	Booth Site	135 Cor, 146 Cor.	2.865x8.25	23.63
0.	22	Booth Site	64 to 66, 136, 145	2.75x8.25	22.68
1.	23-23A (Distt. Shopping Centre)	SCO Site three Storey with basement	13, 14, 35, 36	5.5x25	137.5
2.	23-23A (Distt. Shopping Centre)	SCO Site three Storey with basement	8 Cor, 20 Cor, 30 Cor, 33 Cor.	5.73x8.25	143.25
3.	23-23A (Disit. Shopping Centre)	Booth Site	98 to 103	2.75x8.25	22.68
4.	31	Double Storey Shop Site with basement	100 Cor, 101 Cor.	5.73x13.75	78.78
5.	31	Double Storey Shop Site with basement	102, 103	5.5x13175	75.62
6.	31	Booth Site	6 to 8	2.75x8.25	22.68
7.	31-32A	SCO/F Site three Storey with basement	46 Cor.	5.73x22	126.06
8.	31-32A	—do—	45	5.5x22	121
9.	32 Inst.	SCO Site three Storey with basement	13 to 16	5.5x22	121
0.	32 Inst.	Booth Side	25 to 27	2.75x8.25	22.68
1.	55	SCO Site 3 Storey with basement	101 to 103	5.5x22	121
2.	55	Booth Site	75 to 78	2.75x8.25	22.68

Details of residential plots for auction on 27-11-97

r. No.	Sector	Size	Plot No.
1.	15-II	6 M	1578, 1579;P
2.	15-II	10 M	1495 A, 1495 B, 1495 C-P, 1495F-P, 1496C, 1496D
3.	15-II	14 M	788 B
4.	Part-30	4 M	29 to 35
5.	56	1 K	582 to 586

Terms and conditions

1. 10% of the bid amount has to be tendered on the spot at the fall of hammer either in cash or by bank draft in favour of the Estate Officer, HUDA, Gurgaon.
2. Another 15% of the bid money is to be deposited within 30 days from the date of issue of allotment letter by bank draft.
3. Balance 75% amount is to be paid within 60 days from the date of issuance of allotment letter either as one time interest free payment or in the following manner.
   a) In the case of Booth Site, the balance 75% amount would be payable in 10 half yearly equal instalments with 15% interest.
   b) In the case of other commercial sites the balance 75% amount would be payable in 8 half year instalments with 15% rate of interest.
   c) In the case of residential plots the balance 75% amount would be payable in 6 half yearly instalments with 15% interest.
4. The Presiding Officer reserves the right to withdraw any property from the auction or reject any bid without assigning any reason.
5. The detailed terms & conditions will be announced at the venue, at the time of auction.
6. The Estate Officer, HUDA Gurgaon may be contacted on any working day for further clarifications/site plan/details etc.

   A Security for Rs. 2000/- will be deposited before the start of auction which is refundable after the auction.

SANJAY JOON, HCS
Estate Officer,
HUDA, Gurgaon
Phone: 321253

K. S. YADAV, IAS
Administrator,
HUDA, Gurgaon
Phone: 321650

HUDA: BUILDING A BETTER FUTURE

ANNEXURE XXX

LAYOUT PLAN OF HOUSE NO. 1578 SECTOR 15 PART II, GURGAON

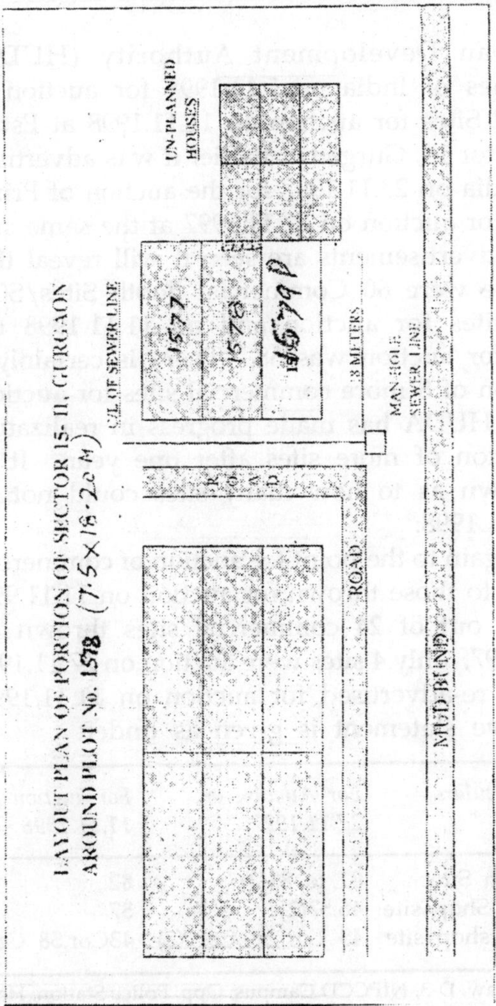

ANNEXURE XXXI
HUDA AND THE ROLE OF M.R.T.P.C.

*H.R. BANGIA

Haryana Urban Development Authority (HUDA) advertised in Times of India on 5.11.1998 for auction of Prime Commercial Sites for auction on 11.11.1998 at Estate Office, HUDA, Sector 14, Gurgaon. Earlier it was advertised in the Times of India on 23.11.1997 for the auction of Prime Commercial Sites for auction on 27.11.1997 at the same site.

If both these advertisements are seen it will reveal that on 27.11.1997 there were 60 Commercial Booth Sites/SCO and D/S shops sites for auction and on 11.11.1998 the numbers of sites for auction was 68. There is certainly a progress for auction of 8 more commercial sites for auction, which shows that HUDA has made progress in realization of money by auction of more sites after one year. It is, however, not known as to how many sites could not be auctioned on 11.11.1998.

If we go back again to the point for auction of commercial sites on 27.11.1997 to those thrown for auction on 11.11.998, it will reveal that out of 24 commercial sites thrown on auction on 27.11.1997, only 4 sites were auction on 27.11.1997 and 20 sites were re-advertised for auction on 11.11.1998.

The comparative statement is given as under:

S.No.	*Sector No.*	*Particulars*	*For Auction on 27.11.1997*	*For auction on 11.11.1998*
1.	4	Booth Site	81 to 83(3)	82
2.	5	D/S Shop site	46,57(2)	57
3.	5	D/S shop site	43 Cor.,58 Cor (2)	43Cor,58 Cor

* Consultant, Labour Law, D-3, NIPCCD Campus, Opp. Police Station, Hauz Khas, New Delhi1-110016

S.No.	*Sector No.*	*Particulars*	*For Auction on 27.11.1997*	*For auction on 11.11.1998*
4.	15-II	Booth Site	132 - 134(3)	132 - 134
5.	22	Booth Site	64-66, 136, 145(5)	64-66,136-145
6.	22	Booth Site	135 Cor, 146 Cor (2)	135 & 146 Cor
7.	31	Booth Site	6 to 8(3)	7 to 8
8.	31	D/S shop site with basement	102, 103(2)	102, 103
9.	31-32A	SCO/F sitet hree storey with basement	46Cor(1)	46Cor
10.	31-32A	SCO/F site three storey with Basement	45(1)	45
Total Prime Commercial sites for auction			24	20

The above figures however do not give the details of the Prime commercial sites of new Sectors included in auction on 11.11.1998. HUDA thus could auction only 16.66% of the Prime Commercial sites in November, 1997 and repeated for re-auction of 83.34% Prime Commercial sites for November 1998.

Apart from the reason of slump of sale of commercial property in Gurgaon it is observed that HUDA do not give certain vital information to the public in the advertisements in newspapers and also in the printed pamphlets distributed widely at the site and at the time of auction on the spot with the result that sale of such Prime Commercial sites does not attract the attention of the buyers.

The following vital information is found missing and misleading to the general public and the allottees:

The reserved price of the Prime commercial sites as well as that of Prime residential plots is not given in the advertisement and even in the pamphlets which are distributed widely at the time of auction on the spot. Before the auction of each plot the amount of reserved price is announced. Whereas the reserved price of sites/plots are made known to the public in the advertisements by other authorities e.g. DDA, UPHD Board etc. It is not known why HUDA conceals this information.

Secondly, an amount of 10% of the earnest money is deposited by the bidder after the fall of the hammer and subsequent amount is realized as per the terms and conditions as contained in the advertisement and the letter of allotment which is issued after a month or so from the date of auction. As per terms and condition No. 24, on payment of 25% price, the allottee can obtain the possession of the site/plot on any working Wednesday.

In view of the above it may be seen in the allotment under Form 'CC Term and Condition No. 4, it is mentioned that *"In case of failure to deposit the balance amount within 30 days from the date of issue of allotment letter, the allotment shall be cancelled and the deposit of 10% bid money deposited at the time of bid shall stand forfeited to the authority against which the allottee shall have no claim for damage"*. Nowhere in the advertisement or in the pamphlets or at the time of auction is this condition made known to the public. This condition is known to the allottee when he receives after a month or so the Letter of Allotment in Form 'CC' of HUDA.

It· is all the more interesting to note in terms and conditions No. 6, where it is mentioned that the possession of the site will be offered to the allottee on completion of the development works in the area. In case of building or undeveloped land, the possession shall be delivered within 90 days from the date of issue of the allotment letter. It is not known why the auctions of Prime sites are conducted when the development work is incomplete and possession cannot be made when the allottee pays 25% of the amount asked for?

The above Term and Condition is contrary to the Term and Condition No. 24 in which it is mentioned that on "Payment of 25% price the allotte can obtain possession of the site on any working Wednesday. It is more confusing when we look at Term and Condition No. 4 in which the allottee is supposed to deposit the balance of amount within 30 days from the date of issue of Allotment Letter and as such by doing so the allottee has deposited 10% initially and within 30 days the allottee has already deposited another 15%, which comes to 25% deposit in all and if the allottee is not given possession of the site (as per Term and Condition No. 24) he is deprived of his Fundamental Rights to acquire the site in case the site is not yet ready for giving possession by HUDA as per Term and Condition No. 6.

Moreover, it is also observed that either the site is already encroached or some high tension live wire is on or is passing by the side of the site or the site advertised as Prime site is actually not the Prime site as advertised. This gives rise to litigations and heavy loss to the individuals as HUDA does not care to response to the aggrieved at all. By concealing the above vital information to the public and especially to the allottees, HUDA invites trouble for itself and to the allottees.

Nowhere in the advertisement or in the pamphlets widely distributed or at the time of the auction the public is informed that in case of failure to deposit the balance amount within 30 days from the date of issue of allotment letter the allotment shall be cancelled and the deposit of 10% bid money deposited at the time of bid shall stand forfeited to the Authority against which the allottee shall have no claim for damages.

It is also observed that HUDA in many cases do not honour the decisions of the District Consumer Disputes Redressal For a which tantamount to contempt of the court.

For keeping in abeyance of 83.34% Commercial sites for a year for auction, it is not known how much HUDA might have suffered a loss. It is the study of only one case in point, which reveals the way HUDA, Gurgaon is functioning. What is the state of affair of HUDA in all other Districts has not come to light so far. This is the case study for a period involving one year only.

It is a right time for HUDA to set their house in order so that the welfare of the people is kept in mind by them to not put itself to financial loss and at the same time it should maintain the welfare of the people who would also cooperate with it in their developmental activities for which HUDA was primarily set up.

In conclusion, in the absence of the above vital information, the allottees are put to utter darkness at the cost of HUDA which is minting money and depriving the allottees of their hard earned money. It is thus high time that Monopoly Restrictive Trade Practice Commission should play its role to curb this tendency of HUDA and come to the rescue of the allottees.

ANNEXURE XXXII
NATIONAL CONSUMER DISPUTES REDRESSAL COMMISSION

National Consumer Disputes Redressal Commission,
5th Floor, Oil Building,
Janpath New Delhi-110001
Phone: 011-23317890

Functional Offices of the National Commission

The National Commission shall ordinarily *function at New Delhi and perform its functions at such other places as the Central Governmen may, in consultation with the National Commission, notify in the Official Gazette, from time to time. Accordingly, the Central Government has ** notified that the National Commission shall perform its functions at the following places other than New Delhi":

1. Ahmedabad
2. Allahabad
3. Bangalore
4. Bhopal
5. Chennai
6. Hyderabad
7. Jodhpur
8. Kolkata
9. Lucknow
10. Nagpur
11. Pune

---

* Section 22C subs. by Act 62 of 202

** Vide S. O. 974(E), dated 31st August, 2004, published in the Gazette of India, Extra, Pt. II Sec. 3(ii), dated 31st August, 2004.

ANNEXURE XXXIII
ADDRESSES OF THE STATE CONSUMER DISPUTES REDRESSAL COMMISSIONS

Under Section 24-B of the Consumer Protection Act, 1986, the National Consumer Disputes Redressal Commission exercises administrative control over State Commissions. There are 34 State Commissions whose names in alphabetical order with their Presidents, Members, Registrars and addresses are as under—

Sl. No.	*State Commissions & Addresses*	*Name of the President, Members and Registrar*	*Phone No. (Office)*	*Phone No. (Res.)*
1.	**Andhra Pradesh** State Consumer Disputes Redressal Commission, 'Eruvaka' Building, Kahairatabad, HYDERABAD - 500004 STD Code: 040 E-mail : ap-sforum@nic.in	Hon'ble Mr. Justice D. Appa Rao President	23391273 23318456 Cell-9949589595	040-27763050 040-27762306
		Mrs. M. Shreesha, Member	23394399	235540099 9866354555
		Vacant Member	23394399	
		Mr. M. Lakshminarayana Registrar	Fax:23394399	040-23302704 9866793339

1	2	3	4	5
2.	**Arunachal Pradesh** State Consumer Disputes Redressal Commission, Near Pawan Hans Office, (Old Secretariat Complex) Naharlagun, ITANAGAR	Hon'ble Mr. Justice Beryl Lamare President	0360-2247661	361-2483767
		Mr. Larbin Nasi, Member	-	2351673
	STD CODE: 0360	Mrs. P. L. Ete, Member	-	2214263
	E-mail : arp-sforum@nic.in	Mr. B. J. Dey Registrar	2248620 Fax :2350837	2246698
3.	**A & N Islands** State Consumer Disputes Redressal Commission, Dte of Civil Supplies, Civil Supplies Complex, PORT BLAIR-744102	Hon'ble Mr. Justice P. N. Sinha President	244585	033-24003130
	STD CODE: 03192	Mr. Bimal Behari Chakraborthy, Member	232321	9434285822
	E-mail : an-sforum@nic.in	Mrs. Vijay Lakshmi Member	232321	9434260444

1	2	3	4	5
		Mr. Ravinder Dhall, Registrar	232321 Fax :232321	
4.	**Assam** State Consumer Disputes Redressal Commission, Housefed Complex, Central Block, 5th Floor, Front Portion, Beltola Bashistha Road, Guwahati - 781 006 STD CODE: 0361 E-mail : asm-sforum@nic.in	Vacant President	0361-2229766	
		Mrs. Basanti Lahkar Member	2631057	9957187082
		Mr. M. K. Barooah Member	2631057	9435017004
		Mrs. Leena Das Registrar	Fax: 2631057	9864039868
5.	**Bihar** State Consumer Dicputes Redressal Commission, R - Block, Road No.2, South of Daroga Prasad Rai Memorial Trust, PATNA - 800 001 STD CODE: 0612 E-mail: scdrc@sancharnet.in & bih-sforum@nic.in	Hon'ble Mr. Justice Prithvi Narayan Yadav President	2207394	2350509
		Mr. Anil Kumar Verma Member	2207394	
		Vacant Member		

1	2	3	4	5
		Mr. Vieheshwarnath Mishra Registrar / Secretary	2207395 Fax: 2207395	2267496
6.	**Chandigarh** State Consumer Disputes Redressal Commission, Plot No. 5-B, Madhya Marg, Sector - 19 B, Chandigarh -160 019 STD CODE: 0172 E-mail: stcomm@chd.nic.in & cdg-sforum@nic.in	Hon'ble Mr. Justice Pritam Pal President	2700183 Fax: 2784225	2728220
		Maj. Gen. S.P. Kapoor, Member	2700183	2576504
		Mrs. Neena Sandhu Member	2700183	2601138 4635138
		Mr. Rakesh Singh Rawat, Secretary	2700183	2714637
7.	**Chhattisgarh** State Consumer Disputes Redressal Commission, Behind New Bus Stand, Pandri, RAIPUR - 492 004 STD Code : 0771 E-mail : chg-sforum@nic.in	Hon'ble Mr. Justice Subhash Chandra Vyas President	2582901 2582904	2444667
		Mrs. Veena Mishra, Member	2236215	5650525 2445603

1	2	3	4	5
		Mr. R. S. Awasthi Member	2236215	2424351
		Mr. Ashok Kumar Pathak Registrar	2582902 Fax: 2582904	2262901
8.	**Dadra & Nagar Haveli & Daman & Diu** State Consumer Disputes Redressal Commission, Department of Civil Supplies, Collectorate, DAMAN - 396220 STD CODE: 0260 Email : daman@guj.nic.in & dnh-sforum@nic.in	Hon'ble Mr. Justice D. G. Deshpande, President	0260-230689	022-28449091
		Mr. Avinash S. Korgaonkar, Member	0260-230689	022-28082717 022-28056578
		Mrs. Manjushri Chand, Member	0260-230689	0260-2261691
		Mr. J.M.Dali, Registrar	2230689 2230698 Fax 2230689	0260-2231185
9.	**Delhi** State Consumer Disputes Redressal Commission, 'A' Block, First Floor,	Hon'ble Mr. Justice B. A. Zaidi President	23370258 23378644 23378566	23093695 23092739

1	2	3	4	5
	Vikas Bhawan, I.P. Estate, NEW DELHI -110 002	Ms. Ramnita Mittal, Member	23379146	22500262
	STD CODE: 011	Vacant Member	23379146 23378565	27868767
	Email: statecommission@vsnl.net & del-sforum@nic.in	Mr. Rajender Singh Registrar	23370799 Fax: 23370258	
10.	**Goa** State Consumer Disputes Redressal Commission, Junta House, 1st Lift, 4th Floor, Vivekanand Road, PANAJI - 403 001	Hon'ble Mr. Justice D. Govindrao Deshpande President	2421792 Fax:2425365	
		Mrs. Sandra Vaze--e-Correia, Member	2222466	2531111
	STD CODE: 0832	Mrs. Caroline Collasso Member	2222466	22254947
	E-mail: gcdrc@goa.nic.in & goa-sforum@nic.in	Mrs. Maria Gonsalves, Registrar	2222466	2416304

1	2	3	4	5
11.	**Gujarat** State Consumer Disputes Redressal Commission, 4th Floor,' A' Block and Ground Floor,'C' Block, Multistoried Building, Laldarwaja, AHEMDABAD – 380009	Hon'ble Mr. Justice R. P. Dholakia President	25501623 25501624 Fax: 25501624 26442875	26850324
		Mrs. Leenaben P. Desai, Member	25501625	26461750
	STD CODE: 079	Dr. M.K. Joshi, Member	25501625	9879094226 26760540
	E-mail : guj-sforum@nic.in	Dr. Jatin P Vaidya Member	25501625	9825292608 26576277
		Mr. A. D. Bagul Registrar	25501625 Fax: 25501624	9925811311
		Mr. K. B. Bhavsar Secretary	25501625	9824361495
12.	**Haryana** State Consumer Disputes Redressal Commission, Bays No. 3 - 6, Sector – 4, Panchkula, Haryana	Hon'ble Mr. Justice Ripudaman Singh Madan President	2567601 Fax:2567502	2585744

1	2	3	4	5
	STD CODE: 0172	Dr. Rekha Sharma Member	2566322	4655156
	E-mail : har-sforum@nic.in	Vacant Member	2566322	2403388
		Mr. Ashwani Sharma, Secretary	2567364	22616914
13.	**Himachal Pradesh** State Consumer Disputes Redressal Commission, Block No.33, 2nd Floor, H.P. Nagar Vikas Pradhikaran Commercial Building, Kusumpati, SHIMLA – 171 009	Hon'ble Mr. Justice Arun Kumar Goel President	2620854 Fax: 2622491	2624315
		Shri Chander S. Sharma Member	2622491	
	STD CODE: 0177	Smt. Saroj Sharma Member	2620855	
	E-mail : hp-sforum@nic.in	Mr. R. K. Sharma Registrar	2620797 Fax: 2622491	
14.	**J & K** State Consumer Disputes Redressal Commission,			

1	2	3	4	5
	i) 3, Manda Hill, Rehari, Jammu Tavi, Jammu & Kashmir ii) Near Municipality Office, Municipality Complex, SRINAGAR	Hon'ble Mr. Justice G. D. Sharma President	2545232 0194-2477195	2459681
	STD CODE: Jammu -- 0191, Srinagar- 0194	Mr. Khalid Hussain, Member	2545232	2107326 9419183485
	E-mail : jk-sforum@nic.in	Mrs. Ritat Aijaz Member	0191-23252	9906920305
15.	**Jharkhand** State Consumer Disputes Redressal Commission, Near High Court,Dauranda, RANCHI - 834002	Hon'ble Mr. Justice D. P. Singh President	2480171	
		Vacant Member	2481589	-
	STD CODE: 0651	Smt. Kalyani Kar Roy, Member	2481589	2413109
	E-mail : jkh-sforum@nic.in	Mr. S.B. Prasad Registrar	2481589	2562510
16.	**Karnataka** State Consumer Disputes Redressal Commission,	Hon'ble Mr. Justice K. Ramanna President	22260590 22262865	26763749

1	2	3	4	5
	Basava Bhavan, High Grounds Basaveswara Circle, BANGALORE - 560001	Mrs. Rama Ananth, Member	22262865	23229683
	STD CODE: 080	Mr. T. Hariappa Gowda Member	22262865	26420569
	E-mail : karscdrc@kar.nic.in & kar-sforum@nic.in	Mr. S. A. Hidayathulla Shariff Registrar	22355065 22262865 Fax: 22260590	
17.	**Kerala** State Consumer Disputes Redressal Commission, Sisu Vihar Lane,Vazhuthacaud, THIRUVANANTHAPURAM - 695 010.	Hon'able Mr. Justice K. R. Udayabhanu President	2313158 2725158 Fax:2320578	2446040 9447090113
	STD CODE: 0471	Smt. Valsala Sarngadaran Member	2725157	2541261
	E-mail : ker-sforum@nic.in	Justice M. V. Viswanathan Member	2727299	2437288
		Shri Chandramohan Nair Member	2725157	2353084

1	2	3	4	5
		Shri S. Abdulla Sona Member	2725157	2380080
		Mrs. S. K. Rajalekshmy Secretary & Registrar	2727220	2558557
18.	**Lakshadweep** State Consumer Disputes Redressal Commission, C/o Assistant Controller of Legal Metrology, Department of Legal Metrology & Consumer Affairs, U.T. of Lakshadweep. KAVARATTI - 682555	Hon'able Mr. Justice K. R. Udayabhanu President	04896-262087 263852 Fax: 263298	0471-2437521 2726040
		Ms. A. Haraja, Member	262087	04894-242031
		Ms. Jeena Joseph, Member	262087	0484-2397132
	STD CODE: 04896			
	E-mail : lak-accal@hub.nic.in & lak-sforum@nic.in	Mr. M. K. Abdul Khader Registrar	262087 Fax: 263298	04896-262545
19.	**Madhya Pradesh** State Consumer Disputes Redressal Commission Plot No.- 76, Arera Hills BHOPAL - 462 001	Hon'ble Mr. Justice S. K. Kulshreshtha President	2554270 Fax:2554270	

1	2	3	4	5
	STD CODE: 0755	Mrs. Promila S. Kumar Member	2763024	2661363
	E-mail: scdrcbho@mp.nic.in & mp-sforum@nic.in	Mrs. Neerja Singh Member	2763024	2552856
		Mr. B. S Parmar, Registrar	2763673 Fax : 2554270	2431477
20.	**Maharashtra** State Consumer Disputes Redressal Commission, Old Administrative Staff College Bldg., Opp. C.S.T. Station, Hazarimal Somani Marg, MUMBAI – 400 001	Hon'ble Mr. Justice S. B. Mhase President	22072097 22057409 Fax: 22018539	22821220
		Mr. P. N. Kashalkar Member	22094290	24930015 9323030364
	STD CODE: 022	Mrs. Swati P. Lale Member	22072097	28820151
	E-mail : mah-sforum@nic.in	Mr. M. N. Ahmed Member (*Nagpur CB*)	0712-2562259	0712-3255918
		Smt. S. G. Nagarale Member (*Nagpur CB*)	0712-2562259	9869408873

1	2	3	4	5
		Mr. A. M. Naik Registrar	22018539 22057409 Fax : 22018539	9822544183
		Mr. D.J.Khairnar I/C Registrar (Legal)	22072097	27651713
		Mr. S. V. Shinde I/C Registrar (Legal) (*Nagpur Circuit Bench*)	0712-2562259 (Fax)	9422105108
21.	**Manipur** State Consumer Disputes Redressal Commission, Deptt of Food & Civil Supplies, Sangaiprou, IMPHAL	Vacant President	2220032	0385-2229310
		Mr. T. Gogonchandra Singh, Member	2220032	0385-2442314
	STD CODE: 0385	Dr. Ch. Jamini Devi Member	2220032	9436281099
	E-mail : man-sforum@nic.in	Mr. H. Kulachandra Singh, Registrar	2220391	9856161326
22.	**Meghalaya** State Consumer Disputes Redressal Commission,	Hon'ble Mr. Justice B. Lamare, President	2222629 Fax:2222629	2537765

1	2	3	4	5
	Horse Shoe Building, Lower Luchumiere, SHILLONG - 793 001	Mr. R.K. Bawri, Member	2222629	2224074 Fax: 2224180
	STD CODE: 0364	Mrs. A.S. Rangad, Member	2225381	2500035
	E-mail : meg-sforum@nic.in	Mr. A. Marbaniang Secretary	2222629 Fax:2222629	2548443
23.	**Mizoram** State Consumer Disputes Redressal Commission, Zodian Square, AIZWAL - 796 001 STD CODE: 0389	Vacant President	2327754	0385-2229310 9436025435
		Mr. Tlanglianruma Member	2327754	2340415
	E-mail : miz-sforum@nic.in	Mrs. V. L. Hrimi Member	2327754	2340287
		Mr. R. Thanga, Registrar	2327754 2341453	2341454 2325121
24.	**Nagaland** State Consumer Disputes Redressal Commission, Guwahati High Court,	Hon'ble Mr. Justice I. A. Ansari President	2221686 2221661	2243098

1	2	3	4	5
	Kohima Bench, KOHIMA - 797 001	Mr. N.Z. Makritsu, Member	2221661	2228259
	STD CODE: 0370	Dr. (Mrs.) Alngla, Member	2240206	2221718
	E-mail : nag-sforum@nic.in	Mr. M. Kikon, Dy. Registrar	2221505	2221885
25.	**Orissa** State Consumer Disputes Redressal Commission, Sector - 1, Near Sati Choura Chowk, C.D.A. Bidanasi, CUTTACK - 14	Hon'ble Mr. Justice A. K. Samantaray President	2365398 Fax:2363604	
		Mr. Subash Mahatab Member	2603604	2647350
	STD CODE: 0671	Smt. Basanti Devi, Member	2603604	2580321 9861148025
	E-mail : ors-sforum@nic.in	Mr. Dhirendra Kumar Pattanayak, Secretary	2363604	

1	2	3	4	5
26.	**Puducherry** State Consumer Disputes Redressal Commission, Plot No.3, D.P. Thottam, Behind Hotel Sarguru, Muthialpet, T.V. Nagar, PUDUCHERRY - 605 003	Hon'ble Mr. Justice N. V. Balasubramanian President	2213862 2210503	24642137
	STD CODE: 0413	Mrs. P.V.R. Dhanalakshmi Member	2213862	2334215
	E-mail : scdrc@pondy.pon.nic.in & pon-sforum@nic.in	Vacant Member	2213862	
		Mrs. C. P. Prasanna Registrar	2213862, 2210503	2356794
27.	**Punjab** State Consumer Disputes Redressal Commission, SCO Nos. 3009-3010, Sector - 22-D, CHANDIGARH-160 022	Hon'ble Mr. Justice S. N. Aggarwal President	2702962 Fax:2707062	2702841 9876716983
	STD CODE: 0172	Ms. Jasbir Kapoor Member	2707062	2699830
	E-mail : pun-sforum@nic.in	Lt. Col. Darshan Singh Member	2707062	2220986
		Mr. Bhag Singh Registrar	2707062	
		Ms. Veena Rani Secretary	2707062	

1	2	3	4	5
28.	**Rajasthan** State Consumer Disputes Redressal Commission, Handloom Haveli, Ashok Marg, C-Scheme 1st Floor, JAIPUR- 302 001	Hon'ble Mr. Justice Sunil Kumar Garg, President	2371837 Fax: 2372237	2553210
	STD CODE: 0141	Mr. T.P. Gupta, Member	2360316	2441234
	E-mail : raj-sforum@nic.in	Smt. Vimala Shathia Member	2360316	9413403317
		Shri G. S. Hora Member	2370248	9829012888
		Shri Sikandhar Panjabi Member	2370248	9413331139
		Mr. R. S. Kulhari, Registrar	2372237	2721485
29.	**Sikkim** State Consumer Disputes Redressal Commission, Palzor Stadium Road, Near Sikkim Nationalised Transport, GANGTOK – 737 101	Hon'ble Mr. Justice A. P. Subba President	205027 Fax:205027	205068
		Mr. D. T. Bhutia Member	225027	224806

1	2	3	4	5
	STD CODE: 03592	Mr. M.K. Pradhan, Member	225027	204387
	E-mail : sik-sforum@nic.in, Statecommission sikkim@hub.nic.in	Mr. H.K. Sharma, Registrar	225027	223377
30.	**Tamil Nadu** State Consumer Disputes Redressal Commission, Slum Clearance Board Building, II Floor, (Southern Wing), No.212, R.K. Mutt Road, Mylapore, CHENNAI - 600 004	Hon'ble Mr. Justice M. Thanikachalam President	24951718 24640687	24492737
		Mr. Pon. Gunasekaran Member	24640687	24819546
	STD CODE: 044	Vacant Member	24640687	
	E-mail : scdrc@tn.nic.in & tn-sforum@nic.in	Mr. D. R. Rajareegam Registrar	24640687 Fax:24618900	22760899
31.	**Tripura** State Consumer Disputes Redressal Commission, Ramangar Road No.1, AGARTALA - 799 002	Hon'ble Mr. Justice A. B. Pal, President	2225975 Fax: 2326308	2321857
		Mrs. Gauri Sarkar, Member	2225975	2319367

1	2	3	4	5
	STD CODE: 0381 E-mail : tri-sforum@nic.in	Mr. B. K. Sharma, Member	2225975	2351995
		Mr. Arun Kr. Debbarma Secretary	2225975	2385929
32.	**Uttar Pradesh** State Consumer Disputes Redressal Commission, C – 1, Vikrant Block – 1, Near Shaheed Path, Gomati Nagar, LUCKNOW – 226 010	Hon'ble Mr. Justice Bhanwar Singh, President	2306688 2306677 Fax:2306645	2617575
		Mrs. Rachna Pal, Member	2306642	2204288
	STD CODE: 0522	Vacant Member	2306655	
	E-mail : up-sforum@nic.in	Vacant Member	2306655	
		Vacant Member	2306655	
		Mr. Devender Kumar Mishra, Registrar	2306655	
33.	**Uttarakhand** State Consumer Disputes Redressal Commission, 2nd Floor, F.T.C. Building,	Hon'ble Mr. Justice Irshad Hussain President	2722763 2724079 Fax: 2714089	2654411

1	2	3	4	5
	District Court Compound, DEHRADUN - 248 001	Mr. C. C. Pant Member	2724079	
	STD CODE: 0135	Smt. Kusum Lata Sharma, Member	2724079	
	E-mail : utr-sforum@nic.in	Mr. Srikant Pandey Registrar	2722768	2674715
34.	**West Bengal** State Consumer Disputes Redressal Commission, Bhabani Bhavan, (Ground Floor), 31, Belvedere Road, Alipore, Kolkata - 700 027	Hon'ble Mr. Justice Alok Chakrabarti President	24790378 Fax: 24794916	2324291
	STD CODE: 033	Mr. A.K. Ray, Member	24790378	25425005
	E-mail : wb-sforum@nic.in	Mr. P.K. Chattopadhyay Member	24790378	23356165
		Ms. Shilpi Majumdar Member	24790378	23599217
		Mr. S. Coari	24790378	24177282
		Mr. Debi Prasad Jana Registrar	24790378	23373776 9433073799

ADDRESSES OF DISTRICT FORUMS (ALPHAPETICABLE ORDER)

Sl. No.	*States/District Forum*	*Address*	*Phone/ Fax No.*
	ANDHRA PRADESH		
1.	Adilabad District Forum	District Court Complex Adilabad 504002	08732-225078
2.	Anantapur District Forum	District Court Premises Anantpur 501001	08554-220893
3.	Chittoor - I District Forum	District Court Compound Chittoor 517501	08572-233577
4.	Chittoor - II District Forum	7-131 Shanthi Nagar M. R. Palli Tirupathi Chittoor Distt.	08577-2246744
5.	Cuddapah District Forum	Collectorate Compound Cuddapah 516001	08562-247201
6.	East Godavari - I District Forum	Ground Floor Civil Supplies Bhawan Collectorate Compound East Godavari District Kakinada 533001	0884-2378821
7.	East Godavari - II District Forum	D. No. 12-21-13/3, 2Nd Floor Near Court Complex Aaryapuram Rajahmundry E.G. District	0883-2467288
8.	Guntur District Forum	District Court Compound Guntur 522004	0863-2241500

Sl. No.	*States/District Forum*	*Address*	*Phone/ Fax No.*
9.	Hyderabad - I District Forum	9Th Floor Chandravihar Complex M. J. Road Nampally Hyderabad	040-24733368
10.	Hyderabad - II District Forum	9Th Floor Chandravihar Complex M. J. Road Nampally Hyderabad	040-24747733
11.	Hyderabad - III District Forum	5Th Floor Chandra Vihar Complex M. J. Road Nampally Hyderabad	040-24746001
12.	Karimnagar District Forum	Collectorate Complex Karimnagar	0878-2232577
13.	Khammam District Forum	Varadhaiah Nagar Khammam 507002	08742-0254347
14.	Kurnool District Forum	Junior Civil Judges Court Compound Kurnool	08518-245688
15.	Machilipatnam District Forum	District Consumer Forum - I Near Pinnamaneni Teachers Guild Association Edepalli, Machilipatnam Krishna District	08672-229832
16.	Mahabubnagar District Forum	Collectorate Compound Mahaboobnagar	08542-245633
17.	Medak At Sangareddy District Forum	Collectorate Premises Sangareddy Medak District	08455-275355
18.	Nalgonda District Forum	District Court Compound Nalgonda 508001	08682-232979

Sl. No.	*States/District Forum*	*Address*	*Phone/ Fax No.*
19.	Nellore District Forum	Golden Jubilee Bhawan Collectorate Compound Nellore	0861-2337063
20.	Nizamabad District Forum	Old Lic Building Yellamunagunta Chowrastha Nizamabad 503003	08462-233275
21.	Ongole District Forum	9-1-19 Court Street Ongole 523002	08592-231292
22.	Rangareddy District Forum	8-1, Vikas Nagar Dilsukhnagar Hyderabad	040-24047675
23.	Srikakulam District Forum	Near Ttd Kalaynapandapam Srikakulam	08942-224468
24.	Vijayawada District Forum	District Consumer Forum - Ii D. No. 40-5-19/9A Opp. Siddhartha Arts College Mogalrajapuram Vijaywada 10	0866-2573161
25.	Vishakapatnam - I District Forum	III Floor Criminal Court Complex District Court Complex Prakashrao Pet Visakhapatnam	0891-2746026
26.	Vishakapatnam - II District Forum	III Floor Criminal Court Complex District Court Complex Prakashrao Pet Visakhapatnam	0891-2734128
27.	Vizianagaram District Forum	Pradeep Nagar Near District Court Complex Vizianagaram 535001	08922-221640

Sl. No.	*States/District Forum*	*Address*	*Phone/ Fax No.*
28.	Warangal District Forum	H. No. 1/706-1 1St Floor, Samata Sadan Near Eakasila Park Balasamundram Hanumakonda 506001	0870-2567995
29.	West Godavari District Forum	District Court Premises W. G. District Eluru 534006	08812-239670
		A & N ISLANDS	
1.	**A & N Islands District Forum**	District Forum District Court Complex, Port Blair – 744101.	
		ARUNACHAL PRADESH	
1.	**Upper Subansiri District Forum**	P.O. Daporijo Arunachal Pradesh	03792 – 223223 Fax - 223330
2.	**Lower Subansiri District Forum**	P.O. Ziro Arunachal Pradesh	03788 – 224255 Fax - 224325
3.	**Tawang District Forum**	P.O. Tawang Arunachal Pradesh	03794 – 222221 Fax - 222250
4.	**West Kameng District Forum**	P.O. Bomdila Arunachal Pradesh	03782 – 222021 Fax- 222378
5.	**East Kameng District Forum**	P.O. Seppa Arunachal Pradesh	03787 – 222338 Fax - 222427
6.	**East Siang District Forum**	P.O. Pasighat Arunachal Pradesh	0368 - 2222340 Fax-2222302

Sl. No.	*States/District Forum*	*Address*	*Phone/ Fax No.*
7.	**West Siang District Forum**	P.O. Along Arunachal Pradesh	03783-222221 Fax - 222785
8.	**Upper Siang District Forum**	P.O. Yuhgkiong Arunachal Pradesh	03777 - 222221 Fax - 222324
9.	**Lohit District Forum**	P.O. Tezu Arunachal Pradesh	03804 - 223666 Fax - 222540
10.	**Tirap District Forum**	P.O. Khonsa Arunachal Pradesh	03786 - 222222 Fax - 222224
11.	**Changlang District Forum**	P.O. Changlang Arunachal Pradesh	03808 - 222221 Fax - 222221
12.	**Lower Dibang Valley District Forum**	P.O. Roing Arunachal Pradesh	03803 - 222223 Fax - 222380
13.	**Papum Pare** District Forum	P.O. Yupia Via-Naharlagun Arunachal Pradesh	0360 - 2284900 Fax– 2284901
14.	**Kuring Kumey District Forum**	(Newly established) P.O. Koloriang Arunachal Pradesh	03788 - 225512
15.	**Dibang Valley**	(Newly Established) P.O. Anini Arunachal Pradesh	03801 - 222222 Fax - 222222

ASSAM

1.	Barpeta DF		03665-252223
2.	Bongaigaon DF		03664-221060
3.	Cachar DF		03842-232597
4.	Darrang DF		03713-222238

Sl. No.	*States/District Forum*	*Address*	*Phone/ Fax No.*
5.	Dhemaji DF		037532-224213
6.	Dhubri DF		03662-230024
7.	Dibrugarh DF		0373-95712
8.	Goalpara DF		03663-240181
9.	Golaghat DF		03762-2480072
10.	Guwahati DF		0361-2668616
11.	Hailakandi DF		03844-222719
12.	Jorhat DF		0376-2371414
13.	Karbi-Anglong DF		03671-
14.	Karimganj DF		03843-262636
15.	Kokrajhar DF		03661-70741
16.	Lakhimpur DF		03752-222337
17.	Morigaon DF		03678-240311
18.	N. C. Hills DF		03673-
19.	Nagaon DF		03372-234002
20.	Nalbari DF		03624-220320
21.	Sibsagar DF		03762-2222146
22.	Sonitpur DF		03712-957112, 231431
23.	Tinsukia DF		0374-2331258
		BIHAR	
1	Araria District Forum	Collectorate Compound Araria	06453-224421
2	Aurangabad District Forum	Collectorate Compound Aurangabad	06186-225266

Sl. No.	*States/District Forum*	*Address*	*Phone/ Fax No.*
3	Banka District Forum	Collectorate Compound Banka	06424-233613
4	Begusarai District Forum	Collectorate Compound Begusarai	06243-210678
5	Bhagalpur District Forum	Collectorate Compound Bhagalpur	0641-2403419
6	Bhojpur District Forum	Collectorate Compound Ara	06182-242280
7	Buxar District Forum	Collectorate Compound Buxar	06183-224258
8	Darbhanga District Forum	Collectorate Compound Darbhanga	06272-240430
9	E. Ch. Motihari District Forum	Collectorate Compound Motihari	06252-2234126
10	Gaya District Forum	Collectorate Compound Gaya	0631-2429321
11	Gopalganj District Forum	Collectorate Compound Gopalganj	06156-227476
12	Jehanabad District Forum	West Gandhi Maidan Jehanabad	06114-226420
13	Jamui District Forum	Collectorate Compound Jamui	06345-223946
14	Kaimur District Forum	S.D.O. Court Compound Bhabhua	06189-224439
15	Katihar District Forum	Collectorate Compound Katihar	06452-249234
16	Khagaria District Forum	Collectorate Compound Khagaria	06244-226452
17	Kishanganj District Forum	Collectorate Compound Kishanganj	06456-226140
18	Lakhisarai District Forum	Collectorate Compound Lakhisarai	06346-233033

Sl. No.	*States/District Forum*	*Address*	*Phone/ Fax No.*
19	Madhepura District Forum	Collectorate Compound Madhepura	06476-224967
20	Madhubani District Forum	Collectorate Compound Madhubani	06276-226845
21	Mungher District Forum	Collectorate Compound Mungher	06344-226390
22	Muzaffarpur District Forum	Collectorate Compound Muzaffarpur	0621-2210609
23	Nalanda District Forum	Collectorate Compound Bihar Sharif	06112-227629
24	Nawadah District Forum	Collectorate Compound Nawadah	06324-210355
25	Patna District Forum	Biscomaun Tower 3Rd Floor Patna	0612-2221896
26	Purnia District Forum	Collectorate Compound Purnia	06454-241699
27	Rohtas District Forum	Collectorate Compound Sasaran	06184-227591
28	Saharsa District Forum	Collectorate Compound Saharsa	06478-222500
29	Samstipur District Forum	Collectorate Compound Samstipur	06274-221431
30	Saran District Chapra	Collectorate Compound 06152-244156	
31	Shaikhpura District Forum	Collectorate Compound Shaikhpura	06341-223410
32	Sheohar District Forum	Collectorate Compound Sheohar	06222-257195
33	Sitamarhi District Forum	Collectorate Compound Sitamarhi	06226-255055
34	Siwan District Forum	Collectorate Compound Siwan	06154-227740

Sl. No.	*States/District Forum*	*Address*	*Phone/ Fax No.*
35	Supaul District Forum	Collectorate Compound Supaul	06473-225426
36	Vaishali District Forum	Block Campus Hajipur	06224-276014
37	W. Ch. Bettiah District Forum	Collectorate Compound Bettiah	06254-237184
		CHANDIGARH	
1.	**District Forum-I Union Territory, Chandigarh**	District Consumer Forum-I,Plot No.5-B, Sector 19-B, Madhya Marg, CHANDIGARH	0172-2549196
2.	**District Forum-II Union Territory, Chandigarh.**	District Consumer Forum-II,Plot No.5-B, Sector 19-B, Madhya Marg, CHANDIGARH	0172-2549196
		CHATTISGARH	
1.	**RAIPUR** District Forum	RDA Building, Phool Chowk, Raipur	0771-2435190 0771-2535190 0771-2443015 (Resi)
2.	**BILASPUR District Forum**	Near Composite Office Complex, Bilaspur	0775-226113 0775-226113 07752-227542 (Resi)
3.	**DURG District Forum**	Shopping Complex, Near New Bus Stand, Durg.	0788-2328507 0788-2328507 0788-2328278 (Resi)
4.	**RAJNAND-GAON** District Forum	Behind Collectorate Rajnandgaon.	07744-227344 07744-223634 (Resi)

Sl. No.	*States/District Forum*	*Address*	*Phone/ Fax No.*
5.	**SARGUJA** District Forum	Near Collectorate, Sarguja	07774-235094 07774-235094 07774-225091 (Resi)
6.	**BASTAR** District Forum	District Court Premises, Jagdalpur.	07782-231082 07782-231084 (Fax)
7.	**RAIGARH** District Forum	Collectorate Premises, Raigarh.	07762-223733 07762-223644 (Fax)
8.	**KORIA** District Forum.	Collectorate, Koria.	Attached with Sarguja DCDRF.
9.	**JASHPUR NAGAR** District Forum	Collectorate, Jashpurnagar.	Attached with Sarguja DCDRF.
10.	**KANKER** District Forum	Jilla Panchayat Office Campus, Kanker.	Attached with Bastar DCDRF.
11.	**DHAMTARI** District Forum	New Collectorate Compus, Dhamtari.	Attached with Raipur DCDRF.
12.	**KORBA** District Forum	Near Additional District & Judge Court, Korba.	Attached with Bilaspur DCDRF.
13.	**JANJGIR-CHAMPA** District Forum	Additional District & Session court, Janjgirchampa.	Attached with Bilaspur DCDRF.
14.	**MAHASAMUND** District Forum	Old Collectorate Compus, Mahasamund.	Attached with Raipur DCDRF.
15.	**KAWARDHA** District Forum	Tehsil Office, Kabirdham, Kawardha.	Attached with Rajnandgaon DCDRF.
16.	**DANTEWADA** District Forum Dhantewada.	Collectorate Compus (Food Section)	Attached with Bastar DCDRF.

Sl. No.	States/District Forum	Address	Phone/ Fax No.
		DAMAN	
1.	Daman District Forum	**Office of the Collector, Civil supplies Department, Collectorate, Fort Area, Moti Daman- 396 220.**	0260 2230698 0260 2230689 0260 2230698 (Resi)
		DIU	
1.	**Diu District Forum**	Office of the Collector, Civil Supplies Department, Collectorate, Diu- 362 520.	02875-252444 02875-252333 (Fax)
		DELHI	
1.	District Forum - North De lhi.	Room Nos. - 2 & 3, Old Civil Supplies Bldg, Tis Hazari, Delhi–110 054.	23969372 23912675
2.	**District Forum - South**	C-22 & 23, Udyog Sadan, Qutub Institutional Area, Behind Qutub Hotel, Mehrauli, Delhi.	26565666 26961433
3.	**District Forum - West Delhi.**	150 - 151, Community Centre, C-Block, Pankha Road, Janakpuri, New Delhi.	25541281 25505036
4.	**District Forum-. North-East Delhi**	Bunkar Vihar Complex (Weavers Complex), Nand Nagri, Delhi.	22121591 22124114
5.	**District Forum- North-West Delhi.**	Ce ntre, Convenient Shopping Block-C, Pkt-C, Shalimar Bagh, Delhi.	27494833 27492650

Sl. No.	*States/District Forum*	*Address*	*Phone/ Fax No.*
6.	**District Forum- New Delhi**	Barracks, Kasturba Gandhi Marg, New Delhi.	23389323
7.	**District Forum- South-West Delhi.**	Sheikh Sarai, Phase –II, Local Shopping Centre, Delhi.	29259612 29259613
8.	District Forum- Central Delhi.	Mezannine Floor, I.S.B.T., Kashmeri Gate, Delhi.	23866728 23866727
9.	**District Forum- East Delhi.**	Convenient Shopping Centre, Saini Enclave, Delhi.	22373093 22379588
10.	**District Forum -**	C-22 & 23, Udyog Sadan, Qutub Institutional Area, Behind Qutub Hotel, Mehrauli, Delhi.	26533073 26533014
		GOA	
1.	**District Consumer Disputes Redressal Forum, North Goa**	Flat no.F-F-1, Goa Housing Board, Commercial-Cum-Residential Complex, Block No. A, Alto Betim, Porvorim, Bardez-Goa – 403521.	0832-2411148 dcfs@goa.nic.in
2.	**District Consumer Disputes Redressal Forum, South Goa.**	Ist Floor, Blessings Pioneer Commercial Complex, Opposite District Court, Old Market, Margo-Goa. 403601.	0832-2713073 dcfs@goa.nic.in
		GUJARAT	
1.	**Ahmedabad (City) District Forum**	New Bhagwati Complex, B/s. Badsha Dairy, Near Jainmarchant Society, Paldi, Ahmedabad (City)	079-26608959 079-26608969

Sl. No.	States/District Forum	Address	Phone/ Fax No.
2.	**Ahemdabad (Rural) District Forum**	11th Floor, 'C' Wing, Apna Bazar, Ahemdabad (Rural)	079-25511278
3.	**Ahmedabad (City Additional) District Forum**	M. S. Building, 'C' Block, 11th Floor, Laldarwaja, Ahmedabad	079-25501774
4.	**Gandhinagar District Forum**	Block No. 26/2, 'GH' Type Nr. C.N.I. Church, Sector-20, Gandhinagar.	079-23262262
5.	Sabarkantha District Forum	Himatnagar District Court Compound, Ground Floor Himatnagar Sabarkantha.	02772-247678
6.	**Mehsana District Forum**	Juna Raj Mahal Building, Electrision Branch, Mehsana Distt., Mehsana.	02762-221322
7.	**Palanpur District Forum**	No. 1/2, R.R.P. Building, Palanpur (B.K.), Disttt. Banaskantha	02742-254138
8.	**Kutch-Bhuj District Forum**	Near Circuit House Kutch- Bhuj.	02832-250723
9.	**Rajkot District Forum**	District Collector Office, Block No. 1, 7th Floor M.S. Bldg. Rajkot.	0281-2474565
10.	**Rajkot (Additional) District Forum**	District Collector Office, Block No. 1, 7th Floor M.S. Bldg. Rajkot.	0281-2478723
11.	**Jamnagar District Forum**	Opp. Juna Railway Station, Jamnagar.	0288-2552977
12.	**Amreli District Forum**	Room No. 106, C-Block, 1st Floor, Rajmahal Compd, Amreli.	02792-230625
13.	**Bhavnagar District Forum**	Block No. G-1, Anax Ground Floor, M.S. Building, Bhavnagar.	0278-2422726

Sl. No.	*States/District Forum*	*Address*	*Phone/ Fax No.*
14.	**Surendranagar District Forum**	M. S. Building, Block – A, Ground Floor, Room No. 3-4, Kherali Road, Ratanpur, Surendranagar.	02752-282142
15.	**Junagadh District Forum**	Smruti Bhavan. 2nd Floor, Opp. Narsingh Vidhya Mandir, M.K. Road, Nr. Court Junagadh.	0285-2625593
16.	**Vadodra District Forum**	Room No. 70, 2nd Floor, Old Kothi Building, Raopura, Vadodra.	0265-2422098
17.	**Vadodra (Additional) District Forum**	Room No. 70, 2nd Floor, Old Kothi Building, Raopura, Vadodra.	0265-2421717
18.	**Panchmahal District Forum**	Room No. 33/4, 2nd Floor, M.S. Buldg. Collector Office Compd., Godhra, Panchmahal.	02672-246016
19.	**Nadiad District Forum**	Room No. 15/16, 2nd Floor, Sardar Patel Bhawan, Nadiad.	0268-2569301
20.	**Bharuch District Forum**	Panchbatt, Panam Plaza Building, No. 132 to 135, Ist floor, Opp. Relief Cinema Station Road, Bharuch.	02642-251604
21.	**Surat District Forum**	"A" Block, 1st Floor, M.S. Building, Nanpura, Surat.	0261-2472683
22.	**Surat (Additional) District Forum**	"A" Block, 1st Floor, M.S. Building, Nanpura, Surat.	0261-2460182
23.	**Valsad District Forum**	Damanganga Bhavan 3rd Floor, B/H. Collector Office,Valsad.	02632-242824

Sl. No.	States/District Forum	Address	Phone/ Fax No.
24.	**Anand District Forum**	1, Ajanta Society, Mahavir Marg, District Anand	02692-266022
25.	**Navsari District Forum**	Collector's Office Compound, 'C' Block, 2nd Floor, Junathana, Navsari	02637-240251
26.	**Patan District Forum**	Sardar Complex, 1st Floor, Above Hotel Kapil, Near Sipur Char Rasta, Patan	02766-233339
		HARYANA	
1.	**Ambala District Consumer Disputes Redressal Forum.**	Old SDM Office Building, Near DC Office, Ambala City - 134003.	0171-2534370
2.	**Bhiwani District Consumer Disputes Redressal Forum,**	Mini Secretariat (Judicial Complex), Bhiwani - 127021.	01664-246544
3.	**Faridabad District Consumer Disputes Redressal Forum,**	Room No. 202, Mini Secretariat, Sector 12, Faridabad - 121007.	0129-2262290
4.	**Gurgaon District Consumer Disputes Redressal Forum,**	Vikas Sadan Gurgaon - 122002.	0124-2330220
5.	**Hissar District Consumer Disputes Redressal Forum**	Mini Secretariat 4th Floor, Hissar - 124001.	01662-233104

Sl. No.	*States/District Forum*	*Address*	*Phone/ Fax No.*
6.	**Jind District Consumer Disputes Redressal Forum,**	District Improvement Trust Building, Near Bus Stand, Gohana Road, Jind-126102	01681-258100
7.	**Kaithal District Consumer Disputes Redressal Forum,**	IInd Floor, New Judicial Complex,] Kaithal - 132027	01746-235199
8.	**Karnal District Consumer Disputes Redressal Forum**	Ist Floor, (Room 1 to 5), Old Mini Secretariat, Near Civil Court, Karnal - 132001.	0184-2267887
9.	**Kurukshetra District Consumer Disputes Redressal Fourm,**	Judicial Complex, Phase - II, Kurukshetra - 132118	01744-223220
10.	**Narnaul District Consumer Disputes Redressal Forum,**	Mini Secretariat (Judicial Complex) (Monhindergarh District) Narnaul - 123001.	01282-258318
11.	**Panchkula District Consumer Disputes Redressal Forum,**	Nahan Kothi, Sector 12, Panchkula - 134109.	0171-2580300
12.	**Panipat District Consumer Disputes Redressal Forum,**	Panchayat Samiti Building, Panipat - 132103.	0180-2659701
13.	**Rewari District Consumer Disputes Redressal Forum,**	Court No.11 IInd Floor, Judicial Complex, Rewari - 123 401	01274-222731
14.	**Rohtak District Consumer Disputes Redressal Forum,**	3rd Floor, Court No. 14, New Judicial Complex, Mini Secretariat, Rohtak - 124001.	01262-245550

Sl. No.	States/District Forum	Address	Phone/ Fax No.
15.	**Sirsa District Consumer Disputes Redressal Forum,**	Mini Secretariat, Block No. 3, Near Judicial Complex, Sirsa - 125055.	01666-247800
16.	**Sonepat District Consumer Disputes Redressal Fourm**	Malik Colony, Near Judicial Complex, Sonepat - 131001.	0130-2222196
17.	**Jagadhri District Consumer Disputes Redressal Forum,**	Court Room No. 15, Judicial Complex, Jagadhri (Yamuna Nagar)–135003.	01732-227400
18.	**Jhajjar District Consumer Disputes Redressal Forum,**	Infront of District Court Complex, Jhajjar –124103.	01251-256767
19.	**Fatehabad District Consumer Disputes Redressal Forum,**	Court Room No.8, Judicial Complex, Fatehabad - 125050	01667-230100
	HIMACHAL PRADESH		
1.	**UNA District Forum**	Mini Secretariat, UNA.	01975-225801(Off) 225802(Res)
2.	**Hamirpur District Forum**		01975-225801(Off) 223802(Res)
3.	**Bilaspur District Forum**		01975-225801 223802(Res)
4.	**Mandi District Forum**	Mandi, D.C. Office complex, Phase II Ist Floor, Mandi.	01905-223770(Off) 223770(Fax)

Sl. No.	*States/District Forum*	*Address*	*Phone/ Fax No.*
			236999(Res) 01905- 222156(Res) 01905- 222656(Res)
5.	**Kullu District Forum**		01905- 223770, 236999 (Resi)
6.	**Lahaul & Spiti District Forum**		01905- 223770, 236999 (Resi)
7.	**Kangra District Forum at Dharmashala.**	Shamnagar Road, Dharamsala.	01892- 224381(Off) 01892- 224381(Fax) 226380(Res) 01892- 265665(Res) 01892- 247257(Res)
8.	**Chamba District Forum**		01892- 224381, 226380(Res)
9.	**Shimla District Forum**		0177- 2620491(Off) 0177- 2650019 (Res)
10.	**Solan District Forum**		0177- 2620491(Off) 0177- 2650019(Res)
11.	**Sirmaur at Nahan District Forum**		0177- 2620491(Off) 0177- 2650019(Res)

Sl. No.	*States/District Forum*	*Address*	*Phone/ Fax No.*
12.	**Kinnaur District Forum**		0177-2620491(Off) 0177-2650019(Res)
	JAMMU & KASHMIR		
1.	**Jammu District Forum**	District Court Premises,Jani Pore, Jammu (J&K)	Telefax : 0191-2533137
2.	**Srinagar District Forum**	Stone Building, Old Secretariate, Srinagar (J&K)	Telefax : 0194-2452912
	JHARKHAND		
1.	**Gumla District Forum**	Besides Civil SDO Office, Gumla-835207	06524-222098
2.	**Ranchi District Forum**	Collectorate Campus, Ranchi-834001	0651-2208817
3.	**Lohardagga District Forum**	Near Sub-Divisional Office, Lohardagga-835302	06526-222898
4.	**W. Singhbhum (Chaibasa) District Forum**	— —	— —
5.	**E. Singhbhum (Jamshedpur) District Forum**	Sakchi Court Campus, Sakchi-831001	0657-2435597
6.	**Dumka District Forum**	Collectorate Campus, Dumka-814101	06434-226122
7.	**Sahebganj District Forum**	In front of District Treasury, Sahebganj-816109	06436-224587
8.	**Pakur District Forum**	Besides Civil Court, Pakur-816107	06435-220746

Sl. No.	*States/District Forum*	*Address*	*Phone/ Fax No.*
9.	**Palamau District Forum**	Collectorate Campus, Palamau-822101	06562-227893
10.	**Hazaribagh District Forum**	Collectorate Campus, Hazaribagh-825301	06546-261465
11.	**Chatra District Forum**	Besides Collectorate Campus, Chatra-825401	06541-223392
12.	**Kodarma District Forum**	Collectorate Campus, Kodarma-825410	06534-252599
13.	**Giridih District Forum**	Near Collectorate Campus, Giridih-815301	06532-224633
14.	**Dhanbad District Forum**	Collectorate Campus, Dhanbad-826001	0326-2312209
15.	**Bokaro District Forum**	Collectorate Campus, Bokaro-827001	06542-223363
16.	**Deoghar District Forum**	Collectorate Campus, Deoghar-814112	06432-231718/ 06432-2237248
17.	**Garhwa District Forum**	Collectorate Campus, Garhwa-822114	06561-223733
18.	**Godda District Forum**	Near SDO Residence, Godda	06422-220614
19	**Jamtara Di strict Forum**	Officers Club, Near Dak Bungalow, Jamtara - 815351	06433-223397
20	**Saraikela District Forum**	Collectorate Campus, Saraikela - 833210	06597-234843
21	**Simdega Di strict Forum**	Near Civil Court, Simdega - 835223	06525-225992
22	**Latehar District Forum**	Near SDM Office, Latehar - 829206	06565-248158

Sl. No.	States/District Forum	Address	Phone/ Fax No.
		KARNATAKA	
1.	**Bangalore Urban District Consumer Disputes Redressal.**	Basava Bhavan, Sri Basaveshwara Circle, High Grounds, Bangalore-560001	080-2262865 2260590 080-2260590: Fax
2.	**Banglore Urban District Forum,**	Cauvery Bhavan, 8th Floor, BWSSB Wing, Kempe Gawda Road, Bangalore-560009	Telefax 080-22211137
3.	**Banglore Rural & Urban I Addl. District Forum,**	1/7, Swathi Complex, Seshadripuram, Bangalore-560020.	080-23442670 Fax : 080-23140797
4.	**Bangalore II Additional District Forum,**	1/7, Swathi Complex, Seshadripuram, Bangalore-560020.	080-23468596 Fax : 080-26673982
5	**Banglore Urban III Addl. District Forum**	No.8, VI floor, Cunningham Road, Banglore-560052	080-22352623
6	**Banglore Urban IV Addl. District Forum**	No.8, VI floor, Cunningham Road, Banglore-560052	080-22352624
7.	**Bellary District Forum,**	D.C. Office Compound, Bellary –583101	Telefax - 08392-276589 08392-254455
8.	**Belgaum District Forum,**	District & Sessions Judge Court Premises, Belagaum-590001.	Telefax- 0831-2426140
9.	**Bidar District Forum**	No. 8-11-16, Chatrapati Shivaji Road, Bidar-585401	08482-225463 Fax : 08482-224661
10.	**Bijapur District Forum,**	Sri Ganesha Nagar, Near Ibrahimpur, Managoli Road, Bijapur-586102.	08352-276257 Fax : 08352-255390

Sl. No.	States/District Forum	Address	Phone/ Fax No.
11.	**Chickmagalur District Forum,**	Nagarathna Building, Vijayapura Main Road, Chickmagalur-577101.	08262-234864
12.	**Chitradurga District Forum,**	3rd Cross, J.C.R. Layout Upstairs of the Merchants Co-op. Bank Building Chitradurga-577501.	08194-431451
13.	**Dakshina Kannada District Forum,**	Mangalore City Corporation Building, Lalbagh, Mangalore-575008.	0824-2457498
14.	**Dharwad District Forum**	Shinge Building, Opp. Vidyagiri Post Office, Vidyagiri Dharwad-580004.	0836-2460842
15.	**Gulbarga District Forum,**	Compound of Vikas Bhavan, Ist floor, Above Labout Court, Heroorkar Building, Station Road, Gulbarga-585102.	08472-256033
16.	**Hassan District Forum,**	1097, 11th Cross, K.R. Puram, Hassan- 573201.	08172-266892
17.	**Kolar District Forum,**	H.N. Gowda Building, K.No.419, I Floor, M.B. Road, Kolar-563101.	08152-241121
18.	**Kodagu District Forum,**	Shekar Complex, Mahadeva Pete, Madikeri - 571201.	08272-229852
19.	**Mandya District Forum,**	No. 2062, II Cross, Subash Nagar, Mandya - 571401.	0823-222100

Sl. No.	*States/District Forum*	*Address*	*Phone/ Fax No.*
20.	**Mysore District Forum,**	No. 845, New Kantharaj Urs Road, G.C.S.T. Layout, Kuvempu Nagar, Mysore - 570023	0821-2344902
21.	**Raichur District Forum,**	D.C. Office Compound, Raichur - 584101.	08532-233006
22.	**Shimoga District Forum,**	Shantha Mansion, Ist Floor, Gandhinagar Main Road, Shimoga - 577201.	08182-220058
23.	**Tumkur District Forum,**	Old D.C. Office Compound, Tumkur - 572101.	0816-2273037
24.	**Uttara Kannada District Consumer Forum,**	M.G. Road, Karwar - 581301.	08382-227404
25.	**Haveri District Forum**	C.D. Haveri Bldg., Parameshwara Complex, P.B. Road Haveri - 581 110	08375-832509
26.	**Chamaraja-nagar District Forum**	B.C. Manjunath Shastri Bldg., Shops Street, Chamarajanagar	08226-226502
27.	**Davanagere District Forum**	No.842, Opp. Shankar Mill, P.B. Road, Davanagere-577006	08192-256618
28.	**Koppal District Forum**	Old Civil Court Bldg., Koppal-583231	08539-220770
29	**Gadag District Forum**	Sri Siddalingeswara Nilaya Near Marata Mandhir Vakeela Chala, Gadag - 528 101	08372-532515
30	**Bagalkot District Forum**	No. 1, Sector No. 33, Navanagar Bagalkot-587102	08354-235778

Sl. No.	*States/District Forum*	*Address*	*Phone/ Fax No.*
31	**Udupi District Forum**	Vadiraja Commercial Complex Old Post Office Road, Udupi-576101	0820-2523170
		KERALA	
1.	**Consumer Disputes Redressal Commission.**	TC-14/407, Extra Police Road Palayam, Museum, PO Thiruvananthapuram-695033.	0471-2721069
2.	**Kollam District Forum**	Civil Station, Kollam- 691013.	0474-2795063
3.	**Pathanamthitta District Forum**	12/2952(2) doctors Lane Pathanamthitta-6899645.	
4.	**Alapuzha District Forum**	Beach Road, Bazar P.O., Alappuzha-688012.	
5.	**Kottayam District Forum, 686002.**	Civil Station, Collectorate Kottayam-686002.	
6.	**Painayu District Forum.**	PO, Idukki 685603, Painayu.	
7.	**Ernakulam District Forum, 682017.**	Near Govt. Homeo Hospital, Pulleppadi, Kathrikkadavu Ernakulam-682 017.	
8.	**Thrissur District Forum**	TC-50/931, Ayyanthole Thrissur-680003.	
9.	**Palakkad District Forum**	Civil Station Palakkad-679 001.	
10.	**Malappuram District Forum, 676505.**	Civil Station, Malappuram-676 505.	
11.	**Koshikode District Forum, 673020.**	Civil Station, B-Block, Kozhikode-673020.	

Sl. No.	States/District Forum	Address	Phone/ Fax No.
12.	**Wayanad District Forum, 673122.**	Civil Station, Wayanad-673122.	
13.	**Kannur District Forum**	S.N. Park Kannur-670001.	
14.	**Kasaragod District Forum**	Consumer Disputes Redressal Forum, Building No. 12/278, Near SDO Phones Office Fort Road, Kasargod-695 033.	0499-430845
		LAKSHADWEEP	
1.	**Kavaratti.**	District Consumer Disputes Redressal Forum, UT of Lakshadweep, Kavaratti-682555	04896-262087/ 04896-263852 04896-263298 (Fax) lak-accal@laksha.nic.in
		MADHYA PRADESH	
1.	Bhopal District Forum	Bhopal Plot No. 76 Area Hills, Bhopal, M.P.	0755-2551613 0755-2430527 (Resi) 0755-2551613 (Fax)
2.	Indore District Forum	Opp. Residency Club, Near Azad Nagar Police Chowki, Indore.	0731-2711030 0731-2402391 (Resi) 0731-2711030 (Fax)
3.	Gwalior District Forum	Behind S. P. Office, Civic Centre, Gwalior.	0751-2231510 0751-2344801 (Resi) 0751-2231510 (Fax)

Sl. No.	States/District Forum	Address	Phone/ Fax No.
4.	Jabalpur District Forum	Block No.15-K, Scheme No. 18 Civic Centre, Jabalpur-482001.	0761-2310636 0761-2324891 (Resi)0761-2310636(Fax)
5.	Rewa District Forum	Near Venkat Bhawan, Rewa- 486001.	07662-242451 07662-243450 (Resi)07662-242451 (Fax)
6.	Ujjain District Forum	Vishala Vikas Bhavan, Block-A, Bharatpuri, Ujjain-456001.	0734-2511435 0734-2510801 (Resi)0734-2511435 (Fax)
7.	Hoshangabad District Forum	Near District Civil Court, Hoshangabad-461001.	07574-252976 07574-252975 (Resi) 07574-252976 (Fax)
8.	Morena District Forum	H-957, Housing Board Colony, Near Civil Court, Morena-476001.	07532-232221 07532-234306 (Resi)07532-232221 (Fax)
9.	Mandsaur District Forum	Collectorate Campus, Old Election Office, Building Mandsaur-458001.	07422-245502 07422-252738 (Resi) 07422-245502 (Fax)
10.	Dhar District Forum	Near Income Tax Building, Behind District Court, Dhar-454001.	07292-237085 07292-222658 (Resi)07292-237085 (Fax)
11.	Guna District Forum	Near Collectorate, Guna-473001.	07542-250041 07542-254307 (Resi) 07542-250041 (Fax)
12.	Sagar District Forum	Opp. Commissioner Office, Near Old District Court, Sagar-470001.	07582-228442 07582-228412 (Resi) 07582-228442 (Fax)

Sl. No.	*States/District Forum*	*Address*	*Phone/ Fax No.*
13.	Satna District Forum	Near Collectorate, Civil Line Satna-485661.	07672-226775 07672-226094 (Resi) 07672-226775 (Fax)
14.	Seoni District Forum	Near Collectorate Jabalpur Road, Seoni-480661	07692-221891 07692-221951 (Resi) 07692-221891 (Fax)
15.	Khandwa District Forum	Near District Court, Khandwa-450001.	0733-2230828 0733-2230826 (Resi) 0733-2230828 (Fax)
16	Shivpuri District Forum	District Court Campus, Shivpuri-473551.	07492-233452 07492-223320 (Resi) 07492-233452 (Fax)
17.	Bhind District Forum	District Court Building, Bhind-470661.	07534-231004 07534-230803 (Resi) 07534-231004 (Fax)
18.	Vidisha District Forum	55, Club Road, Vidisha-464001.	07592-251207 07592-237206 (Resi) 07592-251207 (Fax)
19.	Damoh District Forum	Near Collectorate, Damoh-470661.	07812-223450 07812-223451 (Resi)07812-223450 (Fax)
20.	Chhindwara District Forum	District Court Campus, Chhindwara-480001.	07162-222444 07162-230396 (Resi) 07162-222444 (Fax)
21.	Khargone District Forum (clubbed with Khandwa)	Near District Court, Khandwa-450001.	0733-2230828 0733-2230826 (Resi) 0733-2230828 (Fax)

Sl. No.	*States/District Forum*	*Address*	*Phone/ Fax No.*
22.	Jhabua (Clubbed with District Forum Dhar)	District Court Building, Jhabua-457661	07392-244252
23	Dewas (Clubbed with District Forum Ujjain)	District Court Building, Dewas-455001	07272-
24	Ratlam (Clubbed with District Forum Mandsour)	Near Collectorate Rambag, Ratlam-457001.	07412-221790 07412-263337 (Resi) 07412-221790 (Fax)
25	Shajapur (Clubbed with District Forum Ujjain)	District Court Building Shajapur-465001.	07364-
26	Datia (Clubbed with District Forum Shivpuri)	District Court Building Datia-475661.	07522-
27	Shahdol	IIIrd Floor, Collectorate Compound, Shahdol.	07652-
28	Sidhi (Clubbed with District Forum Satna)	District Court Building Sidhi.	07822-
29	Panna (Clubbed with District Forum Satna)	District Court Building Panna.	07732-
30	Chhatarpur District Forum (clubbed with Damoh)	Front of Maharaja Chhatrashal College, Chhatarpur.	07682-240700 07682-240701 (Resi) 07682-240700 (Fax)
31	Tikamgarh (Clubbed with District Forum Sagar)	District Court Building Tikamgarh.	07683-247045 07683-247046 (Resi) 07683-247045(Fax)
32	Sehore(Clubbed with District Forum Bhopal)	District Court Building Sehore.	07562-

Sl. No.	States/District Forum	Address	Phone/ Fax No.
33	Raisen(Clubbed with District Forum Vidisha)	District Court Building, Raisen-464551.	07482-
34	Rajgarh(Clubbed with District Forum Guna)	District Court Building Rajgarh-465661.	07372-
35	Betul (Clubbed with District Forum Hoshangabad)	District Court Building, Betul-460001.	07141-
36	Narsinghpur (Clubbed with District Forum Chhindwara)	District Court Building Narsinghpur-487001.	07792-
37	Mandla (Clubbed with District Forum Jabalpur)	Opp. Forest Rest House, Mandla-481661.	07642-251841 07642-252677 (Resi)07642-251841 (Fax)
38	Balaghat (Clubbed with District Forum Seoni)	District Court Building Balaghat-481001.	07632-
39	Barwani (Clubbed with District Forum Khandwa)	Collectorate Building Barwani-451551.	07290-
40	Neemuch (Clubbed with District Forum Mandsour)	District Court Building Neemuch-458441.	07732-
41	Harda(Clubbed with District Forum Hoshangabad)	District Court Building Harda-461331	07577-
42	Sheopurkalan (Clubbed with District Forum Shivpuri)	District Court Building Sheopurkalan-476337	07530 -

Sl. No.	*States/District Forum*	*Address*	*Phone/ Fax No.*
43	Katni (Clubbed with District Forum Jabalpur)	District Court Campus, Katni-483501	07622-231000 07622-231637 (Resi)07622-231000
44	Dindori (Clubbed with District Forum Jabalpur)	District Court Building Dindori-481880	07644-
45	Umaria	Government Hospital Compound, Umaria-484661	07653-
		MAHARASHTRA	
1.	South Mumbai Dist. Consumer Dispute Forum	Arun Chember, 6th Floor, Tardeo, Mumbai Central (W), Mumbai.	022-23511737
2.	Central Mumbai Dist. Forum	Arum Chember, 6th Floor, Tardeo, Mumbai Central(W), Mumbai.	022-23521770
3.	Mumbai Suburban Dist. Forum	Administrative Bldg. 3rd Floor Bandra Govt. Colony, Near C.B.D. Bandra (E), Mumbai-400 034.	022-26551625
4.	Thane Dist. Forum	Room No. 214, 2nd Floor, Collector's Office Thane-400 601.	022-25344069
5.	Addl. Thane Distt. Forum	Konkan Bhawan Annexe Bldg. 4th Floor, Room Nos. 428 & 429, Opp. C.B.D. Belapur Rly. Station, Navi Mumbai - 400 614	022-27574074
6.	Raigad Dist. Forum	Patil Sadan, Block No. 6 & 8, Ist Floor, New By-Pass Road, Chandhare, Alibag, Distt Raigad- 402 201.	02141-224225

Sl. No.	States/District Forum	Address	Phone/ Fax No.
7.	Ratnagiri Dist. Forum	Collector Office Compound, Ratnagiri Distt. Ratnagiri-415 601.	02352-223745
8.	Sindhudurga Dist. Forum	Main Admn. Bldg, "C" Block, Gr. Floor, At. Post Sindhudurga Nagari, Tal-Kudal, Dist. Sindhudurga.	02362-228825
9.	Pune Dist. Forum	Pushpa Hights, Duggada Family Trust, Pune Satara Road, Bibewadi, Pune.	020-24217489
10.	Addl. Pune Dist. Forum	Pushpa Hights, Duggada Family Trust, Pune Satara Road, Bibewadi, Pune- 411037.	020-24210364
11.	Satara Dist. Forum	524/1-A, Sadar Bazar, Near Co-Operative Court, Koregaon Road, Satara-415001.	02162-237469
12.	Sangli Dist. Forum	Behind Circuit House, (Madhav Nagar Road), Near New Pride Multiplex Theatre, Sangli.	0233-2311313
13.	Kolhapur Dist. Forum	Shri Pant Balekundri Market, 1st Floor Shahupuri, 6th Lane Gavat Mandi, Kolhapur-416001.	0231-2651327
14.	Solapur Dist. Forum	Collectoral Office Compound Solapur-3.	027-2622003
15.	Nasik Dist. Forum	Collector Office Compound, Nasik-2.	0253-2580142
16.	Dhule Dist. Forum	New Admn. Bldg. Compound, Dhule.	02562-237110
17.	Nandurbar Distt. Forum	Room No. 205-206, Collector Office Compound, Nandurbar	02564-261119

Sl. No.	States/District Forum	Address	Phone/ Fax No.
18.	Jalgaon Dist. Forum	New Admn. Bldg., Besides All India Radio Station, Jalgaon.	0257-2221868
19.	Ahmednagar Dist. Forum	Parag Bldg., Near Collector Office, Ahmednagar-414001.	0241-2347917
20.	Aurangabad Dist. Forum	Collectorate Bldg. 2nd Floor, Aurangabad-431001.	0240-2321202
21.	Beed Dist. Forum	House No. 1/6/266, near Chhatrapati Shahu Bank, Pangeri Road, Shahu Nagar, Beed-431122.	02442-230501
22.	Parbhani Dist. Forum	Admn. Bldg., Compound, Parbhani-431401.	02452-222640
23.	Hingoli Distt. Forum	Admn. Bldg. G – 8, Collector Office Compound, Hangoli	02456-223888
24.	Nanded Dist. Forum	V.I.P. Road, Opp. Telephone Exchange, Nanded- 431 602.	02462-254729
25.	Latur Dist. Forum Latur.	Admn. Bldg., 2nd Floor, Collector Office Compound, Latur.	02382-242319
26.	Osmanabad Dist. Forum	Collector Office Compound, Osmanabad- 431 501.	02472-223478
27.	Jalna Dist. Forum	Survey No. 488 (62), By-Pass Road, Opp. Sports Complex, Jalna- 431 203.	02482-225473
28.	Amravati Dist. Forum	Ramyana Bldg., Biyani Chowk, Camp, By-pass Road, Amravati-444602.	0721-2662158

Sl. No.	*States/District Forum*	*Address*	*Phone/ Fax No.*
29.	Akola Dist. Forum	Collector Office Compound, Akola- 444 002.	0724-2438281
30.	Washim Distt. Forum	Patni Chowk, Balaji Complex, Near "Deshonnati" Office, Washim.	07252-235545
31.	Buldhana Dist. Forum	Govt. Admn. Bldg Compound, Opp. S.T. Bus Stand, Buldhana- 443001.	07262-243045
32.	Yavatmal Dist. Forum	Grahak Nyay Bhavan, Near Admn. Bldg., Yavatmal.	07232-243015
33.	Nagpur Dist. Forum Lines, Nagpur.	New Admn. Bldg., 5th Floor, Civil Lines, Nagpur.	0712- 2548522
34.	Addl. Nagpur Dist. Forum	New Admn Bldg., 3rd Floor Civil lines Nagpur-440001.	0712-2546884
35.	Wardha Dist. Forum	Sewagram Road, Near Yashwant College, Wardha- 442001.	07152- 243550
36.	Bhandara Dist. Forum	Before Akhil Sabhagriha, Ganeshpur, Bhandara- 441904.	07184-254467
37.	Gondia Distt. Forum	Collector Admn. Building, Room No. 214, Gondia	07182-232250
38	Chandrapur Dist. Forum	"Grahak Nyay Bhawan", Near Bachat Saphlya Bhavan, Collector Compound, Chandrapur- 442401.	07172-251010.

Sl. No.	*States/District Forum*	*Address*	*Phone/ Fax No.*
39.	Gadchiroli Dist. Forum	District Complex, barrack No. 1, room Nos. 17,18,19 & 20, Gadchiroli- 442605.	07132-222735
		MANIPUR No information	
		MEGHALAYA	
1.	Shillong District Forum	East Khasi Hills, Shillong	0364-2224003 0364-2223394 (Fax)
2.	Nongstoin District Forum	West Khasi Hills, Nongstoin	03654-280221 03654-280331 (Fax)
3.	Jowai District Forum	Jaintia Hills, Jowai	03652-220721 03652-220865 (Fax)
4.	Nongpoh District Forum	Ribhoi District, Nongpoh	03638-232221 03638-232503 (Fax)
5.	Williamnagar District Forum	East Garo Hills, Williamnagar	03658-220226 03658-220272 (Fax)
6.	Tura District Forum	West Garo Hills, Tura	03651-223835 03651-222226 (Fax)
7.	Baghmara District Forum	South Garo Hills, Baghmara	03639-222292 03639-222225 (Fax)
		MIZORAM	
1.	Aizawl	Tuikhuahtlang, Aizawl- 796001	0389-2329202
2.	Lunglei	Office of the Deputy Commissioner, Lunglei - 790701	0372-2324020

Sl. No.	States/District Forum	Address	Phone/ Fax No.
3.	Saiha	Office of the Deputy Commissioner, Saiha - 796901	0835-22024
4.	Serchhip	Office of the Deputy Commissioner, Serchhip - 796181	0389-22285
5.	Lawngtlai	Office of the Deputy Commissioner, Lawngtlai - 796891	03835-232805
6.	Champhai	Office of the Deputy Commissioner, Champhai - 796321	03831-234402
7.	Kolasib	Office of the Deputy Commissioner, Kolasib Office of the Deputy Commissioner, Kolasib - 796081	03837-21063
8.	Mamit	Office of the Deputy Commissioner, Mamit - 796441	0389-2565221
		ORISSA	
1.	ANGUL District Forum	Plot No. 1013 (P) At/PO/Distt - Angul, PIN - 759 122	06764-231454(O)
2.	BALASORE District Forum	Plot No.778, Srikanthapur, PO/Dist. Balasore, PIN - 756 001.	06782-263910(O)
3.	BARGARH District Forum	At-Back side of Civil Court Near Ranibandh, Ward No. 10 Po/Dist. Bargarh PIN - 768028.	06646-31532(O)
4.	BHADRAK District Forum	Naripur Chhak PO/Dist. Bhadrak. PIN - 756100.	06784-241942(O)

Sl. No.	*States/District Forum*	*Address*	*Phone/ Fax No.*
5.	BOLANGIR District Forum	Near Children Park At/PO/Dist. Bolangir. PIN - 767001.	06652-233350(O)
6.	BOUDH District Forum	Boudh Kunja Nivas, PO/Dist. Boudh PIN - 762014.	06841-222419(O)
7.	CUTTACK District Forum	Sector - 1, C.D.A. Colony, Near Sati Choura Chhak, Cuttack - 753014.	0671-2366339(O)
8.	DEOGARH District Forum	Deogarh Near Post Office, Plot No. 231/1337 PO/Dist. Deogarh - 762014.	26879(O)
9.	DHENKANAL District Forum	Parikh Sahi Mahabir Bazar PO/Dist. Dhenkanal - 759001.	24279(O)
10.	Gajapati (Paralekhemundi) District Forum	Jengaon Street PO-Paralakhemundi Dist. Gajapati - 761201.	23127(O)
11.	GANJAM District Forum (Behrampur)	Nehru Nagar - 9 PO-Gosani Nuagaon, Dist. Ganjam- 760003.	200860(O)
12.	JAGATSINGHPUR District Forum	At/Po/Dist. Jagatsinghpur PIN - 754103.	06724-220106
13.	JAJPUR District Forum	At Babel Bazar PO/ Distt Jajpur-755 001.	06728-223498
14.	JHARSUGUDA District Forum	Jharsuguda Near Collectorate PO-O. M.P. Line Dist. Jharsuguda PIN - 768204.	06645-270699
15.	Kalahandi (BHAWANI PATNA) District Forum	At/Po :- Bhawanipatna Dist. Kalahandi - 766001.	06670-231008

Sl. No.	*States/District Forum*	*Address*	*Phone/ Fax No.*
16.	KENDRAPARA District Forum	Plot No. 209, At-Santa Sahi Dist. Kendrapara, Near Police Station. Pin – 754211	06727-232030
17.	KEONJHARGARH District Forum	At/Po-Keonjhar Dist. Keonjhar. PIN – 758001.	06766-253390
18.	KHURDA District Forum	Plot No. 1159, at Jagamara, PO – Khandagiri, Near Khandagiri Chhak, Dist. Khurda – 751002.	0674-2350122
19.	KORAPUT District Forum	Koraput At Jeypore At/Po-Jeypore, Dist. Koraput – 764004.	06852-230792
20.	MALKANAGIRI District Forum	Old S.B.I. Building, Po/Dist. Malkanagiri – 764045.	06861-230337
21.	MAYURBHANJ District Forum	At/Po :- Baripada, Dist. Mayurbhanj – 757001.	06792-257574
22.	NABARANGPUR District Forum	Old Sanskrati Bhawan, In the RCD High School Playground Po/Dist-Nabarangpur – 764059.	06858-232780
23.	NUAPADA District Forum	Nuapada Rajpur, Near Bhagabat Temple Po/Dist. Naupada- 766 105.	06678-223624
24.	NAYAGARH District Forum	Nayagarh Po/Dist.- Nayagarh – 752064.	06753-252913
25.	PHULBANI District Forum	At/PO/Dist- Phulbani – 762 001	06842-254363
26.	PURI, District Forum	H.No. 336, Matimandap Sahi, Dwarkanath Das Lane, PO/Dist. Puri-752 001.	06752-224781

Sl. No.	*States/District Forum*	*Address*	*Phone/ Fax No.*
27.	RAYAGADA District Forum	New Colony,PO/ Dist-Rayagada –765 001	06855-223025
28.	SAMABALPUR District Forum	At-Nari Seba Sadan, Building, Municipality Chowk, PO/Dist. Sambalpur – 768 001	0663-2410037
29.	SONEPUR District Forum	At-Sonepur Town, PO/ Dist. Sonepur – 767 017	06654-220401
30.	SUNDARGARH-I Disrict Forum	At/PO/Dist- Sundargarh – 770001	06622-273234
31.	SUNDARGARH-II	Rourkela, Qr.No.C/13, Rourkela – 2, Distt. Sundargarh – 269 002	0661-2642989
		PONDICHERRY	
	Pondicherry	District Consumer Forum, No.3, D.P. Thottam, Muthiapet, PONDICHERRY	
		PUNJAB	
1	Amritsar District Forum	SCO No.10, Ist floor, District Shopping Centre, Ranjit Avenue, Bank of India Bldg., Amritsar	95183-2504499 95183-2506833 (Resi)
2	Bathinda District Forum	Near Bus Stand, Bhatinda	95164-22158559 5164-2214855 (Resi)
3	Faridkot District Forum	Judicial Court Complex, Faridkot	951639-2535529 51639-255057 (Resi)

Sl. No.	*States/District Forum*	*Address*	*Phone/ Fax No.*
4	Fatehgarh District Forum	District Court Complex, Fatehgarh Sahib	951763-232101 0172-596563 (Resi)
5	Ferozepur District Forum	Shaheed Bhagat Singh Stadium, Indore Game Complex, New Railway Bridge, Ferozepur City-155002	951632-243303 951632-247305 (Resi)
6	Gurdaspur District Forum	New PWD, Rest House Road, Gurdaspur	951874-234971 951874-237237 (Resi)
7	Hoshiarpur District Forum	B-17/813, Manwata Nagar, Sutheri Road, Opp. Dr. Kapila's Hospital, Hoshiarpur.	951882-221522 951822-246800 (Resi)
8	Jalandhar District Forum	Room no.217-220, IInd floor, Administrative Complex, Jalandhar.	95181-2222360 95181-2232127 (Resi)
9	Kapurthala District Forum	Bldg. No.B-XVII-23, Ist floor, Fateh Bazar, Opp. Old Hospital, Amritsar Road, Kapurthala.	951822-231886 951822-220766 (Resi)
10	Ludhiana District Forum	Guru Theg Bahadur Market, Near Clock Tower, Ludhiana.	95161-2747108 95161-230422 (Resi)
11	Mansa District Forum	Sardar Sita Singh Bldg., Opp. New District Court Complex, Mansa.	951652-228649
12	Moga District Forum	D.C. Complex, Opp. Geet Cinema, Moga.	951636-235400 51636-230397 (Resi)

Sl. No.	*States/District Forum*	*Address*	*Phone/ Fax No.*
13	Muktsar District Forum	District Court Complex, Kotakapuras Road, Mukatsar.	951633-260129 951632-268229 (Resi)
14	Nawan Shahr District Forum	Chhokran Mohalla, Nawan Shahr.	951823-222681
15	Patiala District Forum	239, Shah Bldg., Passy Road, Patiala.	95175-2305407 95175-2307838 (Resi)
16	Ropar District Forum	Room no.4, Ist floor, Court Complex, Mini Secretariat, Ropar.	01881-220295 01881-226295 (Resi)
17	Sangrur District Forum	Ist floor, Old Treasury Office Bldg., Opp. District Court Complex, Sangrur.	951672-231432 951672-230432 (Resi)
		RAJASTHAN	
1.	Ajmer DF	Collectorate Premises, Ajmer, Rajasthan-305001	0145 – 2425228 Fax : 2425228
2.	Alwar DF	Collectorate Premises, Alwar, Rajasthan-301001.	Telefax : 0144 – 2337627
3.	Banswara DF	D.J. Collectorate Premises, Banswara, Rajasthan-327001.	Telefax : 02962-240160
4.	Barmer DF	Collectorate Premises, Barmer, Rajasthan-344001	Telefax : 02982 – 221519
5.	Bundi	Collectorate Premises, Bundi, Rajasthan-323001	Telefax : 0747-2442464
6.	Bharatpur DF	Room No. 53, Collectorate Premises, Bharatpur, Rajasthan-321001.	Telefax : 05644-225090
7.	Bhilwara	IInd Floor, Collectorate Premises, Bhilwara, Rajasthan –311001.	Telefax : 01482-222833

Sl. No.	States/District Forum	Address	Phone/ Fax No.
8.	Bikaner	New Court Premises, Public Park, Bikaner, Rajasthan-334001.	Telefax : 0151-2523346
9.	Baran	Collectorate Premises, Baran, Rajasthan-325205	Telefax : 07453-230624
10.	Churu	Collectorate Premises, Churu, Rajasthan-51394	Telefax : 01562-251394
11.	Chittorgarh	Collectorate Premises, Chittorgarh, Rajasthan-312001	Telefax : 01472-241710
12.	Dungarpur	Collectorate Premises, Dungarpur, Rajasthan-314001.	Telefax : 02964-232171
13.	Dholpur	Bari Sepau Road, Dholpur, Rajasthan-328001	Telefax : 05642-221382
14.	Dausa	Collectorate Premises, Dausa, Rajasthan-303303.	Telefax : 01427-223217
15.	Hanumangarh	G.P.F. Office Grieph Road, Hanumangarh Jn., Rajasthan-335512	Telefax : 01552-261140
16.	Jaipur-I	Court Premises, CBI Court Bldg., Banipark, Jaipur-I, Rajasthan-302006.	Telefax : 0141-2200138
17.	Jaipur-II	Mini Secretariat, Banipark, Jaipur-II, Rajasthan-302106	Telefax : 0141-2202872
18.	Jodhpur	High Court Premises, Jodhpur, Rajasthan-342001	Telefax : 0291-2545502
19.	Jaisalmer	Collectorate Premises Jaislmer, Rajasthan-345001.	Telefax : 02992-250012

Sl. No.	*States/District Forum*	*Address*	*Phone/ Fax No.*
20.	Jalore	Collectorate Premises, Jalore, Rajasthan-3433001.	Telefax : 02973-223241
21.	Jhalawar	Near Bhawami Natya Shala, Jhalaware, Rajasthan-326001.	Telefax : 07432-230661
22.	Jhunjhunu	Collectorate Premises, Jhunjhunu, Rajasthan, 303301.	Telefax : 01592-232982
23.	Kota	Collectorate Premises, Kota, Rajasthan-342001.	Telefax : 0744-2329200
24.	Nagaur	Manasar Road, Collectory Circle, Nagaur, Rajasthan-3341001.	Telefax : 01582-242421
25.	Pali	Room No. 116, Collectorate Premises, Pali, Rajasthan-306401.	Telefax : 02932-222361.
26.	Rajsamand	Collectorate Premises, Rajasamand, Rajasthan-313326.	Telefax : 02952-221726
27.	Sikar	Shiv Singh Pura Navalgarh Road, Sikar, Rajasthan-3332001.	Telefax : 01572-249637
28.	Sawai Madhopur	Collectorate Premises, Sawai Madhopur, Rajasthan-322001.	Telefax : 07462-220592
29.	Sirohi	Swaroop Vilas, Sirohi, Rajasthan-307001.	Telefax : 02972-220652
30.	Sri Ganganagar	Old Hospital Premises, Sri Ganganagar, Rajasthan, Rajasthan-335001.	Telefax : 0154-2444416
31.	Tonk	Collectorate Premises, Tonk, Rajasthan-304001.	Telefax : 01432-246550

Sl. No.	*States/District Forum*	*Address*	*Phone/ Fax No.*
32.	Udaipur	District & Session Judge, Udaipur, Rajasthan-313001.	Telefax : 0294-2411743.
33.	Karauli	Court Premises, Karoli, Rajasthan-322241	Telefax : 07464-250084
		SIKKIM	
1.	District Forum (East District)	District Consumer Disputes Redressal Forum, Secretariat Annexe-I, Sonam Tshering Marg, Gangtok Sikkim	03592-21168 Fax : 03592-202248
2.	District Forum (North)	Office of the District Civil Supplies and Officer, Food & Civil Supplies and Consumer Affairs Department, Govt. of Sikkim, Mangan-737116, North Sikkim.	
3.	District Forum (South).	Office of the District and Session Judge(S/W) Govt. of Sikkim, Namchi-737126, Souty Sikkim	03595-264358 250779 Fax : 03592-263360
4.	District Forum (West)	Office of the District and Session Judge (S/W) Govt. of Sikkim, Gayalshing-737111, West Sikkim.	03595-50405
		TAMILNADU	
1.	**Chennai South, DCDRF**	No. 212, R.K. Mutt Road, III floor, Mylapore, Chennai – 600 004.	044-24938699

Sl. No.	*States/District Forum*	*Address*	*Phone/ Fax No.*
2.	**Chennai North, DCDRF**	No. 212, R.K. Mutt Road, Ist floor, Mylapore, Chennai - 600 004.	044-24952458
3	**Chengleput DCDRF**	Sub-Collector Office Compound, G.S.T. Road, Melamaiyur Village, Chengalpattu	04114-27428832
4	**Coimbatore DCDRF**	Collectorate Campus, Coimbatore-641018	0422-2300152
5	**Cuddalore DCDRF**	102, Pudupalayam Main Road, Cuddalore-607002	04142-215926
6	**Dindigul DCDRF**	D.Nos. 95 & 96, Pensioners' Street, Near Arya Bhawan, Dindigul-624001	0451-2433055
7	**Erode DCDRF**	Erode Commercial Complex, Surampatty Naal Road, Erode-638009.	0424-2250022
8	**Karur, DCDRF**	Municipal Building, Azad Road, Karur 639 002.	04324-260193
9	**Krishnagiri DCDRF**(clubbed with Salem DCDRF)	Taluk Office Campus, Salem - 636002	0427-2213279
10	**Madurai, DCDRF**	District Court Campus Madurai-625001	0452-2533304
11	**Nagapattinam DCDRF**	543, Public Office Road, Vellipalayam, Nagapattinam-611001	04365-247668
12	**Nagercoil DCDRF**	55, Old No.36/1, Ist floor, President Sivathanu Road, South of S.L.B. Hr.Sec. School, Nagercoil,	04652-229683

Sl. No.	*States/District Forum*	*Address*	*Phone/ Fax No.*
13	**Namakkal DCDRF**	3/152, Jeeva Complex, Triciiy Main road, Namakkal : 637001.	04286-224716
14	**PERAMBALUR DCDRF**	Lakshmi Illam, 345, Rover Nagar, Ist Floor, Ellambalur Road, Perambalur : 621212.	04328-276700
15	Pudukkottai DCDRF(Clubbed with Dindigul DCDRF)	D.Nos. 95 & 96, Pensioners' Street, Near Arya Bhawan, Dindigul-624001	0451-2433055
16	**Ramanathapuram** DCDRF	Collectorate Complex (MeetingHall) Ramanathapuram-623501	– –
17	**Salem DCDRF**	Taluk Office, Campus Salem : 636002.	0427-2213279
18	Sivagangai DCDRF	10/25, Thirupathur Road Sivagangai-630561	04575-241591
19.	Srivilliputhur, DCDRF	Court Hall No. 5, Virudhnagar District Court Complex, Srivilliputhur - 626125	04563-260380
20.	**Thanjavur DCDRF**	Elango Commercial Complex, Court Road, Needhi Nagar, Thanjavur - 613 002	04362-272507
21	**The Nilgiris DCDRF**	NCMS Complex, Udhagamandalam-643001	0423-2451500
22	**Theni DCDRF**	1st Floor, Combined Court Building, Lakshipuram, Periakulam Road, Theni-625523	04546-269801
23	**Tiruchirapalli DCDRF**	63A, St.Mary's Complex, Ist floor, Bharathidasan Salai, Tiruchirapalli-62001	0431-2461481

Sl. No.	*States/District Forum*	*Address*	*Phone/ Fax No.*
24	**Tirunelveli DCDRF**	D.No. 4/993, 2nd Street, Shanthi Nagar, Bel Amrose Colony, Palayamkottai, Tirunelveli : 627002.	0462-2572134
25	**Tiruvallur DCDRF**	1-D, C.V. Naidu Salai, 1st Cross Street, Tiruvallur-602001	04116-264823
26	**Tiruvannamalai** DCDRF (Clubbed with Vellore DCDRF)	District Court Campus, Sathuvachari, Vellore - 632009	0416-2254780
27	**Tiruvarur DCDRF**	52, Kumara Koil Street Tiruvarur-610001	04366-224353
28	**Tuticorin DCDRF**	2/263, 10th St., Valli Illam, P&T Colony, Tuticorin-628008	– –
29	**Vellore** DCDRF	District Court Campus, Sathuvachari, Vellore - 632009	0416-2254780
30	**Villupuram DCDRF** (Clubbed with Chengleput DCDRF)	Sub-Collector Office Compound, G.S.T. Road, Melamaiyur Village, Chengalpattu	04114-27428832
		TRIPURA	
1.	District Forum, West Tripura, Agartala.	District Judge's Court Complex, Agartala.	
2.	District Forum, South Tripura, Udaipur.	District Judg's Court Complex, Udaipur.	

Sl. No.	States/District Forum	Address	Phone/ Fax No.
3.	District Forum, North Tripura, Kailashahar.	District Judg's Court Complex, Kailashahar.	
		UTTARANCHAL	
1.	**Almora**	Choughan Pata, Almora-263601	05962-230190
2.	**Bageshwar**	District Court Compound, Bageshwar – 263 642	05963-220394
3.	**Champawat**	District Court Compound, Champawat-246401	05965-230878
4.	**Chamoli**	District Court Compound, Gopeshwar Chamoli-246401	01372-252191
5.	**Dehradun**	District Court Compound, Dehradun-248001	-
6.	**Haridwar**	Collectorate Compound, Room No. 319, 2nd Floor, Roshanabad, Haridwar 249401	01334-239314
7.	**Nainital**	District Court Compound, Nainital-263002	05942-2378040
8.	**Pauri Garhwal**	District Court Compound,Pauri Garhwal-246001	01368-222596
9.	**Pitthorgarh**	District Court Compound, Pithorgarh-262505	05964-224894
10.	**Rudraprayag**	District Court Compound, Rudraprayag-246171	01364-233284

Sl. No.	*States/District Forum*	*Address*	*Phone/ Fax No.*
11.	**Tehri Garhwal**	District Court Compound, Tehri Garhwal-249148	01376-232356
12.	**Udhamsingh Nagar**	Collectorate Compound, Rudrapur, Udhamsingh Nagar-263153	05944-244432
13.	**Uttarkashi**	District Court Compound, Uttarkashi-249193	01374-222287
	UTTAR PRADESH		
1.	**Moradabad-I District Forum**	Civil Court Club Compound, Moradabad - 244001	0591-2425826
2.	**Moradabad-II Disrict Forum**	Civil Court Club Compound Moradabad - 244001	0591-2428660
3.	**Ram Pur District Forum**	Room No. 35, Collectorate Compound, Ram Pur - 244901	0591-2353707
4.	**Bijnor District Forum**	Collectorate Compound, Near Krishi Bhawan, Bijnor - 246701	01342-260890
5.	**J.P. Nagar District Forum**	District Court Compound, J. P. Nagar - 244221	05922-259066
6.	**Lucknow-I, District Forum**	2 - A/1, Rana Partap Marg, Lucknow-226001	0522-2616246
7.	**Lucknow-II District Forum**	2 - A/1, Rana Partap Marg, Lucknow-226001	0522-2230743
8.	**Hardoi District Forum**	Dharamshala Road, Hardoi - 241100	05852-232776
9.	**Unnao District Forum**	Room No. 43, Collectorate Compound, Unnao - 209801	0515-2820780

Sl. No.	States/District Forum	Address	Phone/ Fax No.
10.	**Raebareli District Forum**	House No. 213, Sarojini Sadan, Field Hostel Road, Raibareli - 229001	0535-2702454
11.	**Sitapur District Forum**	Collectorate Compound, Sitapur - 261001	05862-245579
12.	**Lakhimpur Kheri District Forum**	Civil Court Compound, Lakhimpur Kheri-262701	05872-255614
13.	**Agra-I District Forum**	Civil Court Compound Agra - 282002	0562-2526477
14.	**Agra-II District Forum**	Civil Court Compound Agra - 282001	0562-2263021
15.	**Firozabad District Forum**	Civil Court Compound Firozabad - 283203	05612-285075
16.	**Hathras District Forum**	Room No. 9 Collectorate Campus Hathras-204101	0571-2610810
17.	**Aligarh District Forum**	Tehsil Koal Parishad Aligarh - 202001	0571-2511960
18.	**Etah District Forum**	IIIrd Floor, Civil Court Campus, Etah - 207001	05742-230399
19.	**Mathura District Forum**	Collectorate Compound, Opp. SSP Office, Mathura - 281001	0565-2407495
20.	**Mainpuri District Forum**	Civil Court Compound Mainpuri - 205001	05672-235460
21.	**Kanpur Nagar District Forum**	15/261 New Civil Lines Kanpur Nagar - 208001	0512-2330466
22.	**Kanpur Dehat District Forum**	Civil Court Compound, Civil Lines, Kanpur Dehat - 208001	0512-2305638
23.	**Etawah District Forum**	Civil Court Compound Etawah - 206001	05688-256537
24.	**Farrukhabad District Forum**	Civil Court Campus Farrukhabad - 209625	05692-235408

Sl. No.	*States/District Forum*	*Address*	*Phone/ Fax No.*
25.	**Meerut District Forum**	Collectorate Compound, Meerut - 245001	0121-2662865
26.	**Ghaziabad District Forum**	Room No. 202, Collectorate Campus, Raj Nagar, Ghaziabad - 201001	0120-2826770
27.	**Bulandshahar District Forum**	Civil Court Compound Bulandshahar - 203001	05732-281682
28.	**Gautam Budh Nagar District Forum**	C - 27 Sector - 12, Civil Court Compound, Noida, Gautam Budh Nagar	0120-2543232
29.	**Saharanpur District Forum**	Civil Court Compound, Saharanpur - 251003	0132-2722220
30.	**Muzaffarnagar District Forum**	Civil Court Compound, Muzaffarnagar - 251001	0131-2409044
31.	**Faizabad District Forum**	Mohda Civil Lines Faizabad - 224001	05278-225970
32.	**Barabanki District Forum**	Civil Court Compound Panchayat Bhawan, Barabanki - 225001	05248-227088
33.	**Sultanpur District Forum**	D.S.O. Office, Sultanpur - 228001	05362-227534
34.	**Ambedkar Nagar District Forum**	102, Meeranpur, Akbarpur, Ambedkar Nagar - 224122	05271-246907
35.	**Gonda District Forum**	Civil Court Compound, Gonda - 271001	05262-232486
36.	**Bahraich District Forum**	Collectorate Compound Zila Panchayat Bhawan Bahraich - 271801	05252-238895
37.	**Shravasti District Forum**	Near Old Tehsil, Bhinga, Shravasti	05250-222680

Sl. No.	*States/District Forum*	*Address*	*Phone/ Fax No.*
38.	**Balrampur District Forum**	District Court Compound, Balrampur - 271201	05263-236036
39.	**Varanasi District Forum**	Pcf Plaza Building, IInd Floor, Room No. 10, Ment House, Nadesar, Varanasi - 221001	0542-2509593
40.	**Jaunpur District Forum**	Civil Court Compound, Jaunpur – 222001	05452-260467
41.	**Chandauli District Forum**	Munsab Katra G.T. Road, Chandauli - 232104	05412-260260
42.	**Ghazipur District Forum**	Civil Court Compound, Ghazipur - 233001	0548-2220218
43.	**Bareilly District Forum-I**	202 - B Civil Lines Bareilly – 243001	0581-2429497
44.	**Bareilly District Forum -II**	202 - B Civil Lines Bareilly – 243001	0581-2511357
45.	**Badaun District Forum**	Collectorate Campus Badaun – 243601	05832-266053
46.	**Sahajahanpur District Forum**	Civil Court Compound Sahajahanpur – 242001	05482-233433
47.	**Pilibhit District Forum**	Civil Court Compound, Pilibhit – 262001	05882-256438
48.	**Gorakhpur District Forum**	Charuchandrapuri Gorakhpur – 273001	0551-2200791
49.	**Maharajganj District Forum**	Near Sarojininagar District Hospital Maharajganj – 273303	05523-222431
50.	**Deoria District Forum**	Collectorate Compound, Deoria - 274001	05568-222504

Sl. No.	*States/District Forum*	*Address*	*Phone/ Fax No.*
51.	**Padrauna (Kushinagar).**	North Sahabganj, Near Gaushala, Padrauna/ Kushinagar - 274403	05564-240062
52.	**Basti District Forum**	Collectorate Compound, Basti - 272001	05542-245917
53.	**Sidarthnagar District Forum**	Sisahnia Ward No. 6 House No. 7 Behind Police Station Sidarthnagar	05544-222528
54.	**Jhansi District Forum**	372/36 A Civil Lines Jhansi – 284001	0510-2449293
55.	**Lalitpur District Forum**	District Court Compound, Lalitpur – 284403	05176-273800
56.	**Jalaun District Forum**	District Court Compound, Jalaun – 285123	05162-252420
57.	**Banda District Forum**	District Court Compound, Banda - 210001	05192-285148
58.	**Hamirpur District Forum**	Zilla Panchayat Parishad, Hamirpur – 210301	05282-222245
59.	**Mahoba District Forum**	Law Chamber Collectorate Campus Mahoba – 210427	05281-255444
60.	**Chitrakoot District Forum**	District Court Compound, Chitrakoot - 210204	05198-235757
61.	**Azamgarh District Forum**	Harioudh Kala Bhawan Azamgarh – 276001	05462-227097
62.	**Mau District Forum**	Civil Court Compound Mau – 284204	0547-2224225

Sl. No.	States/District Forum	Address	Phone/ Fax No.
63.	**Ballia District Forum**	District Court Compound, Ballia - 277001	05498-222172
64.	**Allahabad District Forum**	Civil Court Compound, Allahabad - 211002	0532-2548598
65.	**Fatehpur District Forum**	District Court Compound, Fatehpur - 223601	05180-223620
66.	**Pratapgarh Disrict Forum**	DSO Office, Pratapgarh - 230001	05342-223503
67.	**Kaushambi District Forum**	District Court Compound Kaushambi	05331-232815
68.	**Mirzapur District Forum**	Behind City Club, New Basti Ramaipatti Mirzapur - 231001	05442-253127
69.	**Sonbhadra District Forum**	Collectorate Compound Sonbhadra	05444-223996
70.	**Sant Ravidas Nagar District Forum**	Collectorate Campus, Sant Ravidas Nagar - 221401	05414-251028
		WEST BENGAL	
1.	**State Commission**	31, Belveder Road, Bhabani Bhavan, Alipore, Kolkata-27.	033-2479/ 4916033-2479/ 0378(F)
2.	**CDF Kol. Unit–I**	8B, Nelie Sengupta, Sarani, 7th Floor, Kolkata-700087.	033-2252-0634
3.	**CDF Kol. Unit-II**	8B, Nelie Sengupta, Sarani, 7th Floor, Kolkata-700087.	033-2252-0312
4.	**CDF Alipore**	24 PGS(S), 18, Judges Court Road, Alipore, Kolkata-27.	033-2479-4350

Sl. No.	*States/District Forum*	*Address*	*Phone/ Fax No.*
5.	**Barasat CDF**	24 PGS(N), 2 No., Barrackpore Road, Maya Bhavan (1st Flr), PO Nabapally, Barasat	033-2542-5131
6.	**Jalpaiguri**	PO Jalpaiguri, Old Court, Near D. M. Office, District Jalpaiguri.	03561-225395
7.	**Coochbehar CDF**	Sri D.K. Dutta, 2nd Floor, B.S. Road (Opp. Site of the CMO Health Office, Coochbehar-736101	03582-222023
8.	**Maldah CDF**	Maldah Sevaniketan, Atul Ch. Kr. Market, PO & Distt. Maldah-732101.	03512-251472
9.	**Birbhum CDF**	C/o House of Abdur Rashid, Chandnipara, Behind Deaf & Dumb School, P.O. & P.S. Suri, Distt. Birbhum	03462-255559. (Telefax)
10.	**Howrah CDF**	Red Court Bldg., Rishi Bankim Ch. Road, Howrah-711101.	033-2660-0892
11.	**Hooghly CDF**	C/o Khadya Bhawan, PO Chinsurah, Hooghly-712102	033-2680-4768
12.	**Murshidabad CDF**	Murshidabad Cantonment Road, Behrampur, Murshidabad	03482-253207
13.	**Purulia CDF**	Collectorate Compound, P. O. & Distt. Purulia.	03252-224001
14.	**D.Dinajpur CDF**	Distt. Judges Office, Dakshin Dinajpur at Balurghat, Balurghat – 733 101	03522-271050

Sl. No.	States/District Forum	Address	Phone/ Fax No.
15.	**U. Dinajpur CDF**	PO Raigunj, (Super Market Complex), Block - I, First Floor U. Dinajpur	03523-252006
16.	**Nadia CDF**	170, Don Bosco Road, Austin Memorial House, P.O. Krishnanagar, Nadia	953472-257788
17.	**Siliguri CDF**	Kshudiram Basu Brianna Kendra, (2nd Floor), Hill Cart Road, Pradhannaar, Siliguri-724403.	0353-2517190
18.	**Midhnapore CDF**	At the house of Nemia Kundu, Mohatabpur, PO & Dt. Midnapore	03222-266694
19.	**Bankura CDF**	Dist. Judge, Kuchkuchia Road, PO 7 Dt. Bankura	953242-241317
20.	**Burdwan CDF**	Muchipara, G.T. Road, PO Sripally, Distt. Burdwan - 713103	0342-2545861
21.	**Darjeeling CDRF**	New Bldg, CAPT N. Sherpa 24, Mahatih Chand Road, Darjeeling-734101.	0354-2252305
22.	Purba Mednipore	President, DCDRF A. Abasbari, PO Tamluk, Purba Mednipore	953228-270125

XXXIV
SUGGESTED READING MATERIAL ABOUT CONSUMER RIGHTS

Meaning and Concept

Every individual is a consumer, regardless of occupation, age, gender,community or religious affiliation. Consumer rights and welfare are now an integral part of the life of an individual and we all have made use of them at some or the other point in our daily routine.

Every year 15th March is observed as **"World Consumer Rights Day"**. It commemorates a historic declaration (1962) by former US President John F. Kennedy of four basic consumer rights:

- The right to safety
- The right to be informed
- The right to choose
- The right to be heard

This declaration eventually led to the international recognition of the fact that all citizens, regardless of their incomes or social standing, have basic rights as consumers. Another significant day is 9 April 1985, when the General Assembly of the United Nations adopted a set of guidelines for consumer protection and the Secretary General of the United Nations was authorized to persuade member countries to adopt these guidelines through policy changes or law. These guidelines constituted a comprehensive policy framework outlining what Governments need to do to promote consumer protection in the following areas:

- Physical safety
- Protection and promotion of consumer economic interests
- Standards for safety and quality of consumer goods and services
- Measures enabling consumers to obtain redressal
- Measures relating to specific areas (food, water, and pharmaceuticals) and
- Consumer education and information programme

Now it is universally accepted that the consumer has a right to be provided with all relevant information in order to avoid exploitation and make a considered choice in availing of products and services from the market. These rights are well-defined, both on international and national platform and several agencies like the Government as well as voluntary organisations are constantly working towards safeguarding them.

In India, 24th December is celebrated as "National Consumer Rights Day", since the Consumer Protection Act, 1986 was enacted on this day. The Consumer Protection Act was enacted in 1986 based on United Nations guidelines with the objective of providing better protection of consumers' interests. The Act provides for effective safeguards to consumers against various types of exploitations and unfair dealings, relying on mainly compensatory rather than a punitive or preventive approach. It applies to all goods and services unless specifically exempted and covers the private, public and cooperative sectors and provides for speedy and inexpensive adjudication.

The rights under the Consumer Protection Act, 1986 flow from the rights enshrined in Articles 14 to 19 of the Constitution of India. The Right to Information Act (RTI), which has opened up governance processes of our country to the common public also has far-reaching implications for consumer protection.As per the Act, a '**Consumer**' has been defined as:

- Any person who buys goods for consideration, and

any person who uses goods with the approval of the purchaser.

- Any person who hires any service(s) for a consideration and any beneficiary of such services, provided the service is availed with the approval of the person who had hired the service for a consideration.

Moreover, the consideration for either the goods or services may be either paid or promised, or partly paid or promised, or provided under a system of deferred payment. The Act envisages the promotion and protection of the following rights of consumers:

Right to Safety

Means right to be protected against the marketing of goods and services, which are hazardous to life and property. The purchased goods and services availed of should not only meet their immediate needs, but also fulfil long term interests. Before purchasing, consumers should insist on the quality of the products as well as on the guarantee of the products and services. They should preferably purchase quality marked products such as ISI, AGMARK, etc.

Right to be Informed

Means right to be informed about the quality, quantity, potency, purity, standard and price of goods so as to protect the consumer against unfair trade practices. Consumer should insist on getting all the information about the product or service before making a choice or a decision. This will enable him to act wisely and responsibly and also enable him to desist from falling prey to high pressure selling techniques.

Right to Choose

Means right to be assured, wherever possible of access to variety of goods and services at competitive price. In case of monopolies, it means right to be assured of satisfactory quality and service at a fair price. It also includes right to basic goods and services. This is because unrestricted right of the minority to choose can mean a denial for the majority of its fair share. This right can be better exercised in a competitive market where a variety of goods are available at competitive prices.

Right to be Heard

Means that consumer's interests will receive due consideration at appropriate forums. It also includes right to be represented in various forums formed to consider the consumer's welfare. The consumers should form non-political and non-commercial consumer organizations which can be given representation in various committees formed by the Government and other bodies in matters relating to consumers.

Right to Seek Redressal

Means right to seek redressal against unfair trade practices or unscrupulous exploitation of consumers. It also includes right to fair settlement of the genuine grievances of the consumer. Consumers must make complaint for their genuine grievances.Many a times their complaint may be of small value but its impact on the society as a whole may be very large. They can also take the help of consumer organisations in seeking redressal of their grievances.

Right to Consumer Education

Means the right to acquire the knowledge and skill to be an informed consumer throughout life. Ignorance of consumers, particularly of rural consumers, is mainly responsible for their exploitation. They should know their rights and must exercise them. Only then real consumer protection can be achieved with success.Thus, the concern of consumer protection is to ensure fair trade practices; quality of goods and efficient services with information to the consumer with regard to quality, quantity, potency, composition and price for their choice of purchase. Such a consumer protection policy creates an environment whereby the clients, customers, and consumers receive satisfaction from the delivery of goods and services needed by them.

CONSUMER COMPLAINTS REDRESSAL

Department of Consumer Affairs has been receiving a very large number of complaints from the consumers regarding shortfall in the supplies/expectations of the consumers. The complaints cover a wide range of subjects like supply of defective refrigerators, T.V. Sets, use of poor material by the builders in the construction of flats, non-refund of fixed deposit amounts by companies on maturity and complaint against unfair trade practice against service providers, etc.

Consumer Grievance Redressal Cell (CGRC) and Consumer Coordination Council (CCC)

The department had set up a Consumer Grievance Redressal Cell (CGRC) in February 2002, for providing services for redressal of complaints of the consumers belonging to the following categories:

- Sale of defective goods or deficient services and charging of higher prices, etc.
- General grievances including those received from the Cabinet Secretary and the PMO related to consumer matters.
- Attending to the consumer complaints appearing in the columns of the newspapers to the extent possible.

Also, complaints regarding delay in disposal of pending cases with the various districts/States/National Commission were received and processed and necessary follow up action were taken up as pro-active measures in order to redress their grievances to their satisfaction. The Redressal Cell had received 2272 complaints upto 31st March 2007. These complaints were forwarded to the Consumer Coordination Council (CCC) for redressal regarding replacement of goods, re-installation of telephone/electricity, rectification of wrong bills, possession of allotted flats, payment of amounts due to the investors on maturity, etc.

The Consumer Grievance Redressal Cell and Consumer

Coordination Council do not have any statutory powers to take action on the complaints of consumers. Hence, they forward the complaints to the concerned authorities to get the redressal.

Redressal Mechanism As per the Consumer Protection Act

- **Who Can File A Complaint**

A complainant in relation to any goods or services may be filled by-

- A consumer or
- Any voluntary consumer association registered under the Companies Act, 1956 (1of 1956)or under any other law for the time being in force or
- The Central Government or any State Government; or
- One or more consumers, where there are numerous consumers having the same interest or
- In case of death of a consumer, his legal heir or representative

A power of attorney holder cannot file a complaint under the Act.

- **What Constitutes a Complaint**

A complaint means any allegation in writing made by a complainant that-

- An unfair trade practice or a restrictive trade practice has been adopted by any trader or service provider
- The goods bought by him or agreed to be bought by him; suffer from one or more defects
- The services hired or availed of or agreed to be hired or availed of by him suffer from deficiency in any respect
- A trader or service provider, as the case may be, has charged for the goods or for the service mentioned in the complaint a price in excess of the price fixed by or under any law for the time being

in force or displayed on the goods or any package containing such goods or displayed on the price list exhibited by him by or under any law for the time being in force or agreed between the parties

- Goods which will be hazardous to life and safety when used or being offered for sale to the public
- Services which are hazardous or likely to be hazardous to life and safety of the public when used, are being offered by the service provider which such person could have known with due diligence to be injurious to life and safety

- **How to File a Complaint**

- A complaint can be filed on a plain paper. It should contain-
  - o The name description and address of the complaints and the opposite party
  - o The Facts relating to complaint and when and where it arose.
  - o Documents in support of allegations in the complaint
  - o The relief which the complainants is seeking
  - o The complaint should be signed by the complainants or his authorized agent.
- No lawyer required for filing the complaint
- Nominal court fee

- **Where to File a Complaint (depends upon the cost of the goods or services or the compensation asked)**

- District Forum: if it is less than Rs. 20 lakhs
- State Commission: if more than Rs. 20 lakhs but less then Rs. 1 crore
- National Commission: if more than Rs. 1 crore

- **Integrated Three Stage Consumer Complaint Redressal Mechanism**

This mechanism includes Consumer Online Research and Empowerment (CORE) Centre, National Consumer Helpline (NCH) and Consumer Voice at Level 1 and FICCI Alliance For Consumer Care at Level 2. While, at Level 3 is the Non Litigation Mechanism or Alternative Dispute Resolution (ADR).

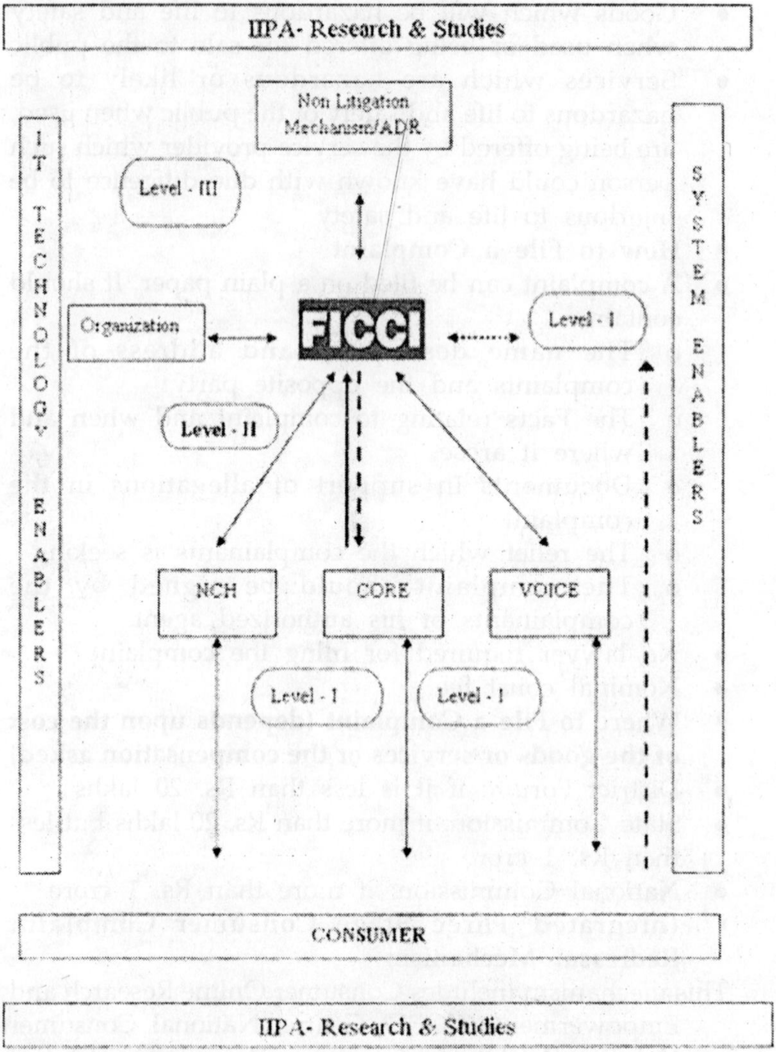

Integrated Three Stage Consumer Complaint Redressal Mechanism

- **Consumer Online Research and Empowerment (CORE) CentreA CORE Centre** has been set up in collaboration with Consumer Coordination Council (CCC) through signing of an MoU. It is intended to provide the most scientific and effective system of collection and dissemination of consumer related information to generate consumer awareness and empowerment of all sections of the society. It is the only authorized agency of the Department of Consumer Affairs to handle 'Online Consumer Complaints' for redressal through mediation. By accessing the online **Complaint Redressal System** in the CORE, the consumers can register themselves and lodge their grievance online.If the grievance/ complaint is still not redressed, complainant is advised that it is up to him to decide, whether he/ she would like to take the matter to the Consumer Court. For this, necessary support by way of indication of the procedure and the contact address of the nearest member organisation of CCC, who can provide assistance in this regard, is also provided to the complainant.
- **National Consumer Helpline (NCH)**A National Consumer Helpline project was launched by the Department of Consumer Affairs in coordination with Delhi University, Department of Commerce , at an approved cost of Rs. 3.12 crores. Under the helpline, consumers from all over the country can dial toll-free number 1800-11-4000 and seek telephonic for problems that they face as consumers. The helpline intends to deal with problems related to telecom, courier, banking, insurance, financial services, etc.
- **Consumer Voice -Voluntary Organization in Interest of Consumer Education**It is a voluntary action group, consisting of academicians, professionals and volunteers, channelising their energies towards creating informed consumers. It raises awareness in consumers not only about malpractices perpetuated

in the marketplace, but also about her/his rights. Mission of Voice is to promote right choices in a volatile and dynamic market place by providing consumer education for all through integrating experiential good practices and scientific knowledge for the safety and health of consumers and the environment. It provides legal to its subscribers for seeking grievance redressal under the Consumer Protection Act, 1986.

- **FICCI Alliance For Consumer Care (FACC)** FICCI, with the support of the Department of Consumer Affairs has taken the initiative of setting up a dedicated Centre called "FICCI Alliance for Consumer Care". FACC provides an interface between business and the consumer and facilitates prompt redressal of consumer grievances. It also facilitates a dialogue between the business and consumers for promotion of responsible business practices and consumer satisfaction. It has been set up with a goal of devicing a mechanism and providing a platform that facilitates prompt redressal of consumer complaints through voluntary self-regulation and consumer education.
- **FACC Dispute Resolution** A neutral body, which will have panel of professionally trained mediators, will be responsible for dealing with complaint redressal. The Centre will only facilitate communication between the company and the complainant to help both sides resolve the complaint. In many cases, mediation and conciliation may be available to help resolve the dispute. FACC's value to the business community is based on its neutrality. The system is not to act as an advocate for business or consumers, but to act as a mutually trusted intermediary, to resolve disputes, to facilitate communication and to provide information on ethical business practices. When FACC Board receives a complaint, it refers it to the business concerned for dealing with it and most companies would be happy

at the opportunity given to resolve the problem, since their patronage by the customer is preserved. At the same time FACC has no legal powers and it cannot force a company to respond, nor can they enforce any sanctions.

- **Non Litigation Mechanism or Alternative Dispute Resolution (ADR)**Alternative dispute resolution (ADR) consists of a variety of approaches to dispute resolution, many of which include the use of a neutral individual such as a mediator who can assist disputing parties in resolving their disagreements. ADR increases the parties' opportunities to resolve disputes prior to or during the use of formal administrative procedures and litigation (which can be very costly and time-consuming). ADR is generally classified into at least three subtypes: negotiation, mediation, and arbitration. The salient features of each type are as follows:
    - In negotiation, participation is voluntary and there is no third party who facilitates the resolution process or imposes a resolution.
    - In mediation, there is a third party, a mediator, who facilitates the resolution process (and may even suggest a resolution, typically known as a "mediator's proposal"), but does not impose a resolution on the parties.
    - In arbitration, participation is typically voluntary, and there is a third party who, as a private judge, imposes a resolution. Arbitrations often occur because parties to contracts agree that any future dispute concerning the agreement will be resolved by arbitration. In recent years, the enforceability of arbitration clauses, particularly in the context of consumer agreements (e.g., credit card agreements), has drawn scrutiny from courts. Although parties may appeal arbitration outcomes to courts, such appeals face an exacting standard of review.

- **Computerization and Computer Networking of Consumer Forums in the Country (Confonet)** This **scheme** has been launched through National Informatics Centre (NIC) as a turnkey project to be implemented from 2004-05. The objective of the scheme is to provide I.T solutions in order to achieve e-governance, transparency, efficiency of consumer fora and facilitate disposal of cases in a time bound manner. It will help in systematizing processing of various types of cases, data and generation of reports and also facilitate better administrative control for subsequent maintenance. It will enable consumers to file their complaints online and to see the status of their cases on the website. Under it, all consumer related websites (those of National Commission, State Commissions, District Fora, Department of Consumer Affairs, CORE Centre, National Consumer Helpline, etc) will be linked so that consumers can access any consumer related information from any of these websites.

THE BUREAU OF INDIAN STANDARDS (RECOGNITION OF CONSUMERS' ASSOCIATIONS) RULES, 1991

GSR 619(E) - In exercise of the powers conferred by Section 37 of the Bureau of Indian Standards Act, 1986 (63 of 1986), the Central Government hereby makes the following rules, namely:-

1. Short Title and commencement -

(1) These rules may be called the Bureau of Indian Standards (Recognition of Consumers' Associations) Rules, 1991.

(2) They shall come into force on the date of their publication in the Official Gazette.

2. Definitions - In these rules, unless the context otherwise requires:-

a. 'Act' means the Bureau of Indian Standards Act, 1986 (63 of 1986);
b. 'Form' means a Form appended to the Schedule to these rules;
c. 'Ministry' means the Ministry of Civil Supplies, Consumer Affairs and Public Distribution; and
d. 'Principal Officer' in relation to a consumer association means any individual who is specifically authorised in writing or by means of a resolution adopted by such consumer association in that behalf.

3. Application for recognition of consumers association-

(1) Every consumers association which is desirous of being recognised as a registered consumers association, -

a. shall have not less than fifty consumers as its members; and
b. shall make an application for such recognition in triplicate to the Bureau of Indian Standards in Form-I.

(2) Every application made under sub-rule (1), shall be accompanied by a bank draft of rupees one thousand.

(3) On receipt of an application made under sub-rule (1), the Bureau of Indian Standards shall note thereon the date of its receipt and shall forthwith communicate such date to the applicant.

(4) The Bureau of Indian Standards may, before issue of a certificate of recognition, require the applicant to furnish, within such period as may be specified by it, such additional information as may be considered necessary within a period of 30 days of the receipt of that letter by the applicant.

(5) On receipt of an application and such other additional information as may be sought under sub-rule (4), the Bureau of Indian Standards shall process the application and forward the documents to the Ministry of Civil Supplies, Government of India with its recommendations for their consideration.

(6) On receipt of the recommendations of the Bureau under sub-rule (5), the Ministry shall consider those recommendations and after satisfying itself that the applicant association is fit to be recognised, may recognise the association in this behalf.

(7) The certificate of recognition to be issued by the Ministry under sub-rule (6) shall be in Form-II.

(8) Where a certificate of recognition issued under these rules is lost, destroyed or mutilated, a duplicate may be issued on an application made in this behalf and on payment of a fee of rupees one hundred.

4. Payment of fees - The fees payable under those rules shall be paid in the form of a bank draft in favour of the Bureau of Indian Standards, New Delhi.

5. Refusal to grant certificate of recognition to consumer association - Where a certificate of recognition of a consumers association has been refused, the applicant shall be informed of the reasons for such refusal by the Bureau.

6. Copies of certificate of recognition to be furnished to certain authorities - Every consumer association which has been recognised as a 'registered consumers' association under these rules, shall furnish a copy of the certificate of recognition issued to it while filing a complaint under section 34(1) of the Act.

7. Verification of application - Every application made under these rules shall be duly verified by the principal Officer.

Telecom Regulatory Authority of India
List of Consumer Organizations/NGO registered with TRAI

Sl. No.	Name & Address of CO/NGO	Registration Number	Date of Regn.	Name of the contactperson / phone No.
1.	Voluntary Organization in Interest of Consumer Education(VOICE) F-71, Lajpat Nagar II,New Delhi	TRAI/CO/NGO/1/2001 - NO	25.01.2001	Mr. H.K. Awasthi Legal Coordinator Tel. No. 24619079/24619080 Fax. No. 4626189
2.	Consumer Care Society 1/A, 2nd Main, 36th Cross8th Block Jayanagar, Bangalore 560082	TRAI/CO/NGO/2/2001 - NO	02.03.2001	Sh. G.S. Gundu Rao Tele: 6341515/6717338 / 6636532
3.	Bombay Telephone Users' AssociationRoom No. 7, Petit Municipal High School, Municipal Compound, Waterfield Road,Bandra West, Mumbai - 400 050.	TRAI/CO/NGO/3/2001 - NO	02.03.2001	Sh. Achintya Mukherjee Hon. Jt. Secretary Tele: (022) 26439292 / 20582233
4.	Chandigarh Telecom District Telephone Subscribers Association (CTSA) House No.1339, Sector 15. Punchkula, Haryana	TRAI/CO/NGO/4/2001 - NO	13.03.2001	Shri R.K.Verma, President, Tele: (0172) - 2606487 / 2609898

Sl. No.	Name & Address of CO/NGO	Registration Number	Date of Regn.	Name of the contactperson / phone No.
5.	Grahak Sahayak Gurgaon C-153, Sushant Lok Gurgaon 122 002	TRAI/CO/NGO/5/2001 - NO	19.04.2001	Shri Jeet K Wadhwa Hony. Hon. General Secretary Tel : 26385208 Fax: 26351386
6.	Surya Foundation 170, Sector-A, Pocket-C, Vasant Kunj, New Delhi - 110 070.	TRAI/CO/NGO/6/2001 - NO	23.04.2001	Shri M.P. Agarwala Tel : 25582994/ 25573681
7.	Citizen consumer and Civic Action Group (CAG) Old No. 7, New No. 8, 4th Street, Venkateshwara Nagar, Adayar, Chennai - 600 020	TRAI/CO/NGO/7/2001 – NO	26.04.2001	Ms Shohba Iyer, Coordinator Tel: 24460387/24914358 Fax: 24914358 E-mail : cag@xlweb.com
8.	Consumer Guidance Society of India,'J' Block, Azad Maidan,Mahapalika Marg, Opp. Cama Hospital Mumbai - 400 001.	TRAI/CO/NGO/8/2001 – NO	21.05.2001	Shri Surender U. Kanstiya, Chairman Tel: 022 – 2621612 Fax : (022)-2659715
9.	Consumer Protection Council 501/B, 5th Floor Shaily Navrangpura Ahmedabad 380 009	TRAI/CO/NGO/9/2001 – NO	29.5.2001	Shri Vinod R.Shah, Chairman Tel : 27541472 Fax: 27542371 **E-mail cpc_ ahmedabad@hotmail.com**

Sl. No.	Name & Address of CO/NGO	Registration Number	Date of Regn.	Name of the contactperson / phone No.
10.	Consumer Protection Association Jai Somnath, Himmat Nagar Sabarkantha, Gujarat 3833001	TRAI/CO/NGO/10/2001 - NO	20.7.2001	Dr. Niranjan Nath President Tel: (02772) 240636
11.	OrissaConsumers' Association Debajyoti Upobhokta Kalyan Bhavan, Biswanath Lane, Cuttack-753 002	TRAI/CO/NGO/11/2001 - NO	14. 8.2001	Shri K.N. Jena Gen. Secretary Tel: 2617597
12.	Kerala Consumer Service Society 'PRATIBHA' Ashoka Road Kochi - 682 017	TRAI/CO/NGO/12/2001 - NO	26.9.2001	Dr. T. Balachandran President Tel. : (0484) - 2330188
13.	Balakedarara Vedike (R) Consumers' Forum Brasam Building Nehru Maidan SAGAR-577 401 Karnataka	TRAI/CO/NGO/13/2001 - NO	2.11.2001	Shri K.N. Venkatagiri Rao Secretary Tel: (08183) - 26473/ 37717 / 27465
14.	All India Chamber of Consumers 64/2/3, Grahak Bhavan, Begbera Colony, Jhamshedpur - 831 002	TRAI/CO/NGO/14/2001 - NO		Shri B.N. Pandey General Secretary Tel. : (0657) - 2494671

Sl. No.	Name & Address of CO/NGO	Registration Number	Date of Regn.	Name of the contactperson / phone No.
15.	Consumer Coordination Council 62, Qutab View Apartments, Shaheed Jigsingh Marg, New Delhi - 110 016.	TRAI/CO/NGO/1/2002 - NO	14.02.2002	Mr. Bejon Misra Vice Chairman Tel : 22712678 E-mail : ccdel@del13.vsnl.net.in
16.	Akhil Bhartiya Upbhokt Congress 302, Transit Hostel, South TT Nagar, Bhopal - 462 003	TRAI/CO/NGO/2/2002 - NO	14.02.02	Shri B.D. Sharma Regional President & Principal Officer, Tel.: 2772286
17.	Federation of Consumer Associations West Bengal, 52-A, Shakespeare Sarani, 5th Floor, Kolkata - 700 017.	TRAI/CO/NGO/3/2002 - NO	06.03.02	Shri Pradeep Kumar Datta Executive Officer, Tel.:(033) - 22807425/22800711 Fax : 22805927
18.	Telecom Users Group of India A-98, Malviya Nagar, New Delhi - 110 017.	TRAI/CO/NGO/4/2002 - NO	05.06.02	Shri Anil Prakash Tel/Fax : 26716363
19.	Palakkad District Consumers Association KIITS College, Court Road Palakkad - 678001	TRAI/CO/NGO/01/2003 - NO	13.05.03	Sh. P.A. Surendran General Secretary Tel : 0491-522320/570652

Sl. No.	Name & Address of CO/NGO	Registration Number	Date of Regn.	Name of the contactperson / phone No.
20.	Consumer Unity and Trust Society D-217, Bhaskar Marg, Bani Park,Jaipur - 302016	TRAI/CO/NGO/02/2003 - NO	22.05.03	Shri S.M. Mathur Secretary Tel : 0141 - 207482 207486/203998 (FAX)
21.	Consumer Guidance Society 45, Veerpaneni Plaza Pata MataVijayawada - 520010	TRAI/CO/NGO/03/2003 - NO	22.05.03	Ch. Divakar Babu Secretary
22.	Consumer RightsEducation & Awareness Trust 239, 5th C Main, Remco Layout Vijaynagar, Bangalore-560 040	TRAI/CO/NGO/01/2004 - NO	22.02.04	Shri Y.G. Muralidharan Secretary Tel : 080- 2357280/23403170 Fax : 23303973 E-mail : creatorg@sify.com
23.	Federation of Consumer Organisations- Tamil Nadu & Pondicherry, S -1 Beacone Street Mylapore, CHENNAI- 600 004 Tamil Nadu E-mail : fedcotdurai@yahoo.com	TRAI/CO/NGO/02/2004 - NO	07.04.04	Prof. P. Duraisingam Chairman 2/84, Melachatram Street, Parmakudi - 623 707 Tel : 04564-227405 Fax : 228448Mob : 9443381816
24.	PTC India Foundation Suite 306-307, Competent House7, Nangal Raya Business Centre New Delhi- 110 046	TRAI/CO/NGO/03/2004 - NO	27.04.04	Air Commodore(Retd). N.K.Chhibber, Secretary General Tel :28522640, 28521854 Fax : 28521854, 28522640

MAJOR CONSUMER NGOS IN INDIA

(The following is NOT legal advice and is purely for informational purposes only. Consumerdaddy is not competent to give any legal advice. For legal advice please contact a competent lawyer. Any reliance that you place on this information is at your own risk. Consumerdaddy does not guarantee the accuracy of this information and is not responsible for any consequences, actions, lack of actions, results or lack of results that you may or may not face from following information in this article.)

Contents

Consumer Coordination Council (CCC)
Consumer Guidance Society of India
Citizen Consumer and Civic Action Group
Association for Consumers Action on Safety and Health
Consumer Education and Research Centre
Consumer Protection Council
Consumer Unity and Trust Society
Consumers Association of India
Consumers' Forum
Mumbai Grahak Panchayat
VOICE Society
Grahak Shakti

Non-Governmental Consumer Organizations are non-profit, non-political (in most cases), non-regulatory, independent advocacy groups promoting consumerism in India. Although they lack statutory powers, they form a critical support network for you when you are a victim of corporate malpractice and/or deceit. Imagining you alone against a corporate powerhouse with 50,000 employees, 50 lawyers, and Rupees 500 Crores at their disposal isn't exactly a comforting thought. With consumer organizations to assist, you don't have to worry; you are not alone in your fight for justice... you have the support of powerful and determined social organizations that can organize protest rallies against corporate entities (no matter how powerful they are), or lobby the government or other statutory agencies to take notice of your grievance.

Consumer organizations improve your awareness of your consumer rights and advice you on the legal recourse you can take when your consumer rights are violated. This article provides you information about the salient consumer protection and advocacy groups in India today. If you notice that any of their addresses are outdated, please inform us by writing to Consumerdaddy(at)yahoo(dot)com.

Consumer Coordination Council (CCC)

Established in 1993 under the Societies Registration Act 1860, Consumer Coordination Council (CCC) has been a stalwart proponent of good governance. In 1996, CCC launched a national campaign on citizens' charter to implement transparency, accountability, standards of service and a public grievance redressal system at the government level. CCC has made notable achievements in influencing the making of laws, governmental policy decisions, and providing administrative infrastructure for protecting consumer interest. It also serves as an umbrella organization for all other consumer NGOs in India.

Contact Us

Phone +91 9426201611

Fax+91 120 240 4273

Address Consumer Coordination Council (CCC), NITS Complex A 20-21, Sector 62 Noida, Uttar Pradesh 201 307

Website http://www.cccindia.net

Email cccdel@del3.vsnl.net.in

Consumer Guidance Society of India

Consumer Guidance Society of India (CGSI) was founded in 1966 to eliminate all possible forms of consumer exploitation. It is one of the oldest consumer organizations in the country and has been instrumental in lobbying the government to pass a consumer protection act. It has been a member of Consumers International for several years and

70% of the consumer complaints received by it have been resolved. CGSI has been instrumental in promoting consumerism by publishing its flagship monthly periodical "Keemat", performing product testing, providing consumer education at the grass root level such as schools, and giving legal guidance to consumers with grievances. It won the national award for consumer protection in 1991 for its long, dedicated and effective services to consumers.

Contact Us
Phone +91 22 2262 1612
Fax+91 22 2265 9715
Address Consumer Guidance Society of India Block 'J', Mahapalika Marg Mumbai, Maharashtra 400 001
Website http://www.cgsiindia.org
Email cgsibom@mtnl.net.in

Citizen Consumer and Civic Action Group

Established on October 7, 1985, Citizen Consumer and Civic Action Group (CAG) has grown out to be one of the country's leading consumer advocacy groups. Instrumental in running campaigns for greater access to information, improved functioning of public utilities, greater transparency and accountability in governmental and private sector functioning, and protection of our open spaces and natural environment, CAG plays a vital role in the growth of consumerism in our country. CAG specializes in attending issues that affect the common man's life such a lack of hygiene, pollution of our natural resources, inaccessible healthcare facilities, corruption and lack of accountability for the government revenue from tax sources. CAG has been a member of Consumers International since 1990.

Contact Us
Phone +91 44 2446 0387
Fax+91 44 2491 4358
Address Citizen Consumer and Civic Action Group 9/5, II Street, Padmanabha Nagar, Adyar Chennai, Tamil Nadu 600 020

Website http://www.cag.org.in
Email contact@cag.org.in

Association for Consumers Action on Safety and Health

Association for Consumers Action on Safety and Health (ACASH) is a consumer organization that focuses on health-related consumer issues. It has programs aimed at the general public promoting consumer rights and overall dispersion of information regarding consumer safety. Founded by a group of doctors, lawyers and other eminent personalities, ACASH today helps consumers in India through education & awareness, training, developing IEC (Information, Education and Communication) material, networking, advocacy and lobbying and follow-up action. A member of Consumers International since 1990, ACASH is also a member of Globalink, International Network of Women Against Tobacco (INWAT), International Baby Food Action Network (IBFAN), International Lactation Consultant Association (ILCA), World Alliance for Breastfeeding Action (WABA), Health Action International (HAI), Breastfeeding Promotion Network of India (BPNI), All India Drug Action Network (AIDAN), Bureau of Indian Standards (BIS) and Voluntary Health Association of India (VHAI).

Contact Us
Phone +91 22 2388 6556 / 2388 7354
Fax +91 22 2388 7340

Address Association for Consumers Action on Safety and Health Lawyers Chambers, Room #21, R S Sapre Marg Mumbai, Maharashtra 400 002

Website http://www.acash.org
Email acashorg@vsnl.com

Consumer Education and Research Centre

Consumer Education and Research Centre (CERC) protects consumer interest in India through consumer research, campaigns through media, creation / monitoring

/ enforcement of effective consumer laws, consumer advocacy and information dissemination. An apolitical outfit, CERC has research facilities recognized by the Indian government, and the United Nations has approved CERC as an NGO. CERC's mission includes environmental protection, creating transparency and accountability in the public and private enterprises and agencies in our country, resolving individual consumer complaints, ensuring consumer safety through product research, consumer education, awareness campaigns and product test results dissemination.

Contact Us

Phone +91 79 2748 9945/ 2748 9946 / 2745 0528 / 2743 8752 / 2743 8753 / 2743 8754

Fax+91 79 2748 9947

Address Consumer Education and Research Centre 'Suraksha Sankool', Thaltej, Sarkhej-Gandhinagar Highway Ahmedabad, Gujarat 380 054

Website http://www.cercindia.org

Email cerc@cercindia.org

Consumer Protection Council

Not to be confused with the governmental bodies established as per the Consumer Protection Act 1986, the Consumer Protection Council (CPC) is a consumer organization that is non-affiliated to any statutory agency. Instituted in Ahmedabad, the CPC has been instrumental in undertaking consumer issues such as consumer safety, traffic safety and pedestrian safety. It has effectively and successfully pursued legal battles against governmental agencies when they neglect or fail to carry out their duties to the tax payers. CPC has been a member of Consumers International since 1986.

Contact Us

Phone +91 79 2754 1472

Fax+91 79 2754 2786

Address Consumer Protection Council 501/B, 5th Floor, 'SHAILY', Opp. Loha Bhavan B/h. Old Gujarat High Court, Navrangpura Ahmedabad, Gujarat 380 009

Website None
Email cpc_ahd@yahoo.co.in

Consumer Unity and Trust Society

Consumer Unity and Trust Society (CUTS) originated from a rural background in Rajasthan. It operates five program centers in India, an advocacy center in New Delhi, and resource centers in several international locations. CUTS's consumer work is focused on consumer protection and consumer safety. With about 20,000 square feet office space, 140 employees, and affiliation to / recognition from major national and international consumer agencies, CUTS is truly equipped to be the champion of consumer causes in our country. It publishes a monthly 'Gram Gadar' which has been effective in ensuring justice for oppressed social masses. CUTS has been a member of Consumers International since 1990.

Contact Us
Phone +91 141 228 2821
Fax+91 141 228 2485
Address Consumer Unity and Trust Society D-217, Bhaskar Marg, Bani Park Jaipur, Rajasthan 302 016
Website http://www.cuts-international.org
Email cuts@cuts.org

Consumers Association of India

Consumers Association of India (CAI) was established on the world consumer rights day to be a powerful lobby for the consumer. It has successfully and determinately taken up the mission to spread awareness among consumers, educate them about their responsibilities and rights and to ensure that the consumers' voices can be heard. In the past six years, CAI has successfully settled over 98% of the 7500 complaints it has received through arbitration. For the remaining 2% CAI has supported the consumer in pursuing the complaint through the Indian legal system. CAI has been a member of Consumers International since 2003.

Contact Us

Phone +91 44 2449 4576

Fax+91 44 2449 4578

Address Consumer Association of India 3/242, Rajendra Garden, Vettuvankeni Chennai, Tamil Nadu 600 041

Website http://www.cai-india.org

Email cai.india1@gmail.com

Consumers' Forum

Consumers' Forum is one the consumer organizations that existed in India long before the Consumer Protection Act 1986 was passed. The mission of the organization, at its start, was to promote consumerism by making aware, training and educating the consumers on their rights. This was particularly necessary when there were no stalwart laws in our country to protect the consumers. The forum provides free advice to consumers, conducts brain storming sessions on matters related to consumer protection and ensures the representation of consumers in national, state and district level consumer courts and legally mandated consumer protection councils. Consumer Forum has been a member of Consumers International since 1996.

Contact Us

Phone +91 11 2588 7833

Fax+91 11 4248 8331

Address Consumers' Forum 12/25 Ground Floor, West Patel Nagar New Delhi, Delhi 110008

Website http://www.consumer.org.in

Email Not available

Mumbai Grahak Panchayat

Mumbai Grahak Panchayat (MGP), or Bombay Consumer Forum, started as an agitation against the increase of consumer prices near festival season for fair and free distribution of consumer goods. The distribution system that flourished was registered under the Indian Societies

Registration Act 1960 and Indian Public Trust Act 1950 in the name of MGP. MGP promotes consumerism by bringing the consumer to the forefront of the logistics and supply chain of consumer goods as decision makers, executors and monitors. MGP's primary objectives include organizing the consumers for common causes, educating them and protecting consumer interest through legal and other means.

Contact Us

Phone +91 22 2628 1832 / 1839

Fax+91 22 2625 0916

Address Mumbai Grahak Panchayat Grahak Bhavan, Sant Dnyaneshwar, Marg Road Behind Cooper Hospital, JVPD Market, Vile Parle (West) Mumbai, Maharashtra 400 056

Website Not available

Email mgpanchayat@hotmail.com

VOICE Society

Voluntary Organization in Interest of Consumer Education (VOICE) strives to be the voice of and for the consumer that the governments and other statutory / regulatory bodies of the country seldom hear. The primary focus of this NGO is to establish informed consumers in India. Information dispersed to consumers through VOICE includes corporate negligence / misconduct on issues such as consumer safety or customer satisfaction, your rights as a consumer to get value for your money, and the recourse that can be taken if your consumer rights are defied. Founded by students and teachers of the University of Delhi in 1983, it was registered as charitable public trust in 1986, the same year the consumer protection act came into being.

Contact Us

Phone +91 11 2437 9078 / 79 / 80

Fax+91 11 2437 9081

Address VOICE Society 441, Jangpura, Bhogal, Mathura Road New Delhi, Delhi 110 014

Website http://www.consumer-voice.org

Email legal@consumer-voice.org

Grahak Shakti

Grahak Shakti works towards creating consumer awareness by organizing various programs, street plays and on shows such as 'Hello Geleyere'. The organization has undertaken a number of surveys like the one on spurious drugs in coordination with the Drugs Control Department – Government of India. Its campaign on credit cards and effective liaison with the regulator was an effective way to warn the erring bankers to conduct business ethically. It also participated in joint raids in coordination with the Department of Legal Metrology and some oil companies to check malpractices related to weights and measurement, adulteration and pilferage.

Contact Us

Phone +91 9448366360

Fax+91 8023145998

Address Grahak Shakti, No. 57,18th Cross, 4th Main Chitrakoot Apartment, Flat No. 19, Malleswaram, Bangalore, Karnataka - 560055

Website http://www.grahakshakti.org

Email grahakshakti@gmail.com

WORLD CONSUMER DAY
(15TH MARCH)

Every year World Consumer Day is celebrated on 15th MARCH to make aware the people that for every rupee they spend are valuable. So they must be financially literate and save their money.

In public interest Government also through its Department of Food Supplies & Consumer Affairs educate the people through public advertisements to Know their rights and responsibilities as consumers as under:

KNOW YOUR RIGHTS

Right to Safety - To be protected against the sale of goods & services which are spurious/hazardous to life.

Right to Information - To know the quality, quantity, weight and the price of goods/services being paid for, so that you are not cheated by unfair trade practices.

Right to Choose - To be assured wherever possible, access to a variety of goods and services at competitive price.

Right to be Heard - To be heard and be assured that your interest will receive due consideration at appropriate fora.

Right to Seek Redressal - To seek legal redressal against unfair or restrictive trade practices or exploitation.

Right to Consumer Education - To have access to consumer education.

KNOW YOUR RESPONSIBILITIES

Obtain full information regarding quality and price before making any purchase.

Be careful about false and/or misleading advertisements.

Purchase goods having quality marks like ISI/Agmark etc. as and where available for safety and quality.

Obtain proper receipt/cash memo for purchase made and guarantee/warranty card duly signed by the seller, wherever applicable.

Approach Consumer Forum for redressal of consumer grievances against sale of defective goods or deficient services or adoption of unfair or restrictive trade practices.

Safeguard yourself against adulteration, over-pricing, counterfeiting, spurious goods and expired products. Become a vigilant and aware customer is an empowered consumer.

Issued in public interest by

DEPARTMENT OF FOOD SUPPLIES & CONSUMER AFFAIRS

Government of NCT of Delhi, 'K' Block, Vikas Bhawan, I.P. Estate, New Delhi.

WORLD CONSUMER RIGHTS DAY

is also celebrated by insertion of advertisement in public interest by

Ministry of Consumer Affairs, Food and Public Distribution

Department of Consumer Affairs, Government of India
Krishi Bhawan, New Delhi=110001
Today on
WORLD CONSUMER RIGHTS DAY
I have resolved to exercise my Consumer Rights
Today, Tomorrow and Everyday!

- ✓ I will check MRP and insist on bill for my purchase.
- ✓ To assess its Quality properly, I will make sure to know what it contains.
- ✓ I will make sure that goods/service provided to me is safe.
- ✓ I will choose only that which is right for me.

- ✓ I will ensure that my complaint, if any, is heard properly by its seller and manufacturer.
- ✓ I will seek assistance from the Consumer Forum, if my complaint is not properly redressed.

Why don't you do the same?

To locate the Consumer Forum in your Area, log on to www.ncdrc.nic.in

Jago Grahak Jago

National Consumer Helpline No. (1800-11-4000 Toll Free)

(From BSNL/MTNL Lines) or 011-27662955,56,57,58 (Normal Call Charges Apply)

(9.30 am to 5.30 p.m. - Monday to Saturday)

Bibliography

1. Adil, M.S., Consumer protection: law, practice and procedure / by M.S. Adil.– New Delhi: JBA, 2006. 562 p.

2. Agarwal, V. K., Consumer protection: law and practice, consumer protection amendment act, 2002 (62 of 2002) / by V. K. Agarwal.—5th ed.– New Delhi: B.L.H., 2003. 1059p.

3. Agarwal, V. K. Consumer protection: law and practice: a commentary on the consumer protection act, 1986 alongwith central rules and regulations and state rules / by V. K. Agarwal.—6th ed.– New Delhi: B.L.H., 2008. 1101p.

4. Agarwal, V.K., Consumer protection in India with special reference to restrictive and unfair trade practices / by V.K. Agarwal. – New Delhi: Deep and Deep, 1989. 646p.

5. Agarwal, V.K. Consumer protection: law and practice / by V.K. Agarwal.-New Delhi: B.L.H., 1993. 658p.

6. Aggarwal, Sukhdev, Commentary on the consumer protection act, 1986 / by Sukhdev Aggarwal, Parveen Aggarwal and Sanjay Lohia.—2nd ed.– Delhi: The Bright Law House, 2003. 831p.

7. Ahmad, Farooq Consumer protection in India: problems and prospects / by Farooq Ahmad.— New Delhi: APH Pub., 1999. 456p.

8. Arora, Renu, Consumer grievances redressal / by Renu Arora.— New Delhi: Manak, 2005. 240 p.

9. Bakshi, P.M. Consumer protection law / by P.M. Bakshi.— New Delhi: Ashoka Law House, 2005. 2014p.

10. Banerjee, A.K. Digest on consumer protection laws: cases and materials / by A.K. Banerjee and S.K. Awasthi.— Allahabad: Ashoka Law House, 1992. 536p.

11. Barowalia, J.N. Commentary on the consumer protection act, 1986 / by J.N. Barowalia.—2nd ed.— Delhi: Universal Law, 2002. 1263p.

12. Batra. Satish K. Consumer behaviour: text and cases / by Satish K. Batra and S.H.H. Kazmi.— New Delhi: Excel Books, 2004. 536p.

13. Blackstone's statutes commercial and consumer law: 2005-2006 / edited by F.D. Rose.—14th ed.— Oxford: Oxford Univ. Press, 2005. 791p.

14. Chaudhary, Ram Naresh Prasad Consumer protection law: provisions and procedure / by Ram Naresh Prasad Chaudhary.— Delhi: Deep and Deep, 2005 324p.

15. Consumer behaviour and consumer protection in India /edited by Meenu Agrawal.— New Delhi: New Century, 2006. 309p.

16. Consumer protection act with rules and regulations.— New Delhi: Taxmann, 2002. v.p.

17. The consumer protection law and rights of consumers / edited by Santosh Khanna.— Delhi: Vidhi Bharati Parishad, 2002. 147p.

18. Consumer protection law mannual (as amended by consumer protection (amendment) act 2002): with

practice mannual.-New Delhi: Taxmann Allied Services, 2003. 267p.

19. Consumer protection movement in India: problems and prospects / edited by S.S. Chahar.— New Delhi: Kanishka, 2007. 400p.

20. Consumer rights in service sector / edited by V.N. Viswanathan.— New Delhi: Concept, 2008. 234p.

21. Consumerism: global and Indian perspectives / edited by J.S. Panwar, Navin Mathur and Darshana R. Dave.— Jaipur: RBSA Pub., 2006. 224p.

22. Devanbu, P. Consumer protection organisations in India and Australia.— Madras: IIPA, 1993. p.35-39. [In] Selected papers from IIPA seminars. B3096 Se48

23. Digest National Commission and Supreme Court on Consumer Protection Law (2003 - Aug. 2008) / by National Consumer Disputes Redressal Commission.— Delhi: D.L.T Publications, 2008. 2 vols.

24. Dobson, Paul Sale of goods and consumer credit / by Paul Dobson.—5th ed.— Delhi: Universal Law Publishing, 2003. 456p.

25. Gambhir, Cheena Consumer protection administration: organisation and working / by Cheena Gambhir.— New Delhi: Deep & Deep, 2007. 206p.

26. Giri, H.N. Consumers, crimes and the law / by H.N. Giri.— Delhi: Ashish, 1987. 349p.

27. Girimaji, Pushpa Consumer rights for everyone / by Pushpa Girimaji.— New Delhi: Penguin, 1999. 460p.

28. Grover, S.K. Trademark/brand duplication and consumer protection / by S.K. Grover.— New Delhi: Deep & Deep, 1996. 270p.

29. Guidelines and rules for grant of financial assistance under consumer welfare fund / by Department of Consumer Affairs, Ministry of Consumer Affairs, Food

and Public Distribution.— New Delhi: Department of Consumer Affairs, Ministry of Consumer Affairs, Food and Public Distribution, n.d. 19p.

30. Gupta, Rakesh Case laws on medical negligence / by Rakesh Gupta and Vandana Singh.— New Delhi: Indian Institute of Public Administraation, 2005. 137p.

31. Gurbax Singh Digest of consumer protection cases / by Gurbax Singh.— Jaipur: Bharat Law, 1995. 1314p.

32. India. Ministry of Consumer Affairs, Food, and Public Distribution. Department of Consumer Affairs Report of working group on consumer protection: eleventh plan (2007-2012), vol.1 / by Department of Consumer Affairs, Ministry of Consumer Affairs, Food, and Public Distribution, India.— New Delhi: The Author, 2006. 73p.

33. Introducing human rights: an overview including issues of gender justice environmental and consumer law / by South Asia Human Rights Documentation Centre.— New Delhi: Oxford University Press, 2006. 261p.

34. Jain, N.K. Consumer protection: law and practice / by N.K. Jain.— New Delhi: Regal, 2008. 296p.

35. Jan, Rifat Consumerism and legal protection of consumers: with a critical and explanatory commentary and latest case law / by Rifat Jan.— New Delhi: Deep & Deep, 2007. 495p.

36. Kaushal, Anoop K. Consumer protection law / by Anoop K. Kaushal.— Delhi: Universal Law, 1996. 274p.

37. Kaushal, Anoop K. Medical negligence and legal remedies with special reference to consumer protection law / by Anoop K. Kaushal.—3rd ed.— Delhi: Universal Law, 2004. 412p.

38. Kaushal, Anoop K. Universal's medical negligence and legal remedies with special reference to consumer protection law / by Anoop K. Kaushal.—3rd ed.— Delhi: Universal Law, 2005. 412p.

39. Landmark judgement on consumer protection / compiled by NCDRC Bar Association.— Delhi: Universal Law, 2003. 613p.

40. The law of consumer protection: an exhaustive commentary on consumer protection act, 1986 (68 of 1986) / edited by D.P. Wadhwa and N.L. Rajah.— New Delhi: Wadhwa, 2006. 1698p.

41. Majumdar, P. K. Law of consumer protection in India: as amended by act no. 62 of 2002 (w.e.f. 15.3.2003) / by P. K. Majumdar.—5th ed.— New Delhi: Orient, 2004. 1775p.

42. Modi's medical jurisprudence and toxicology / edited by K. Mathiharan and Amrit Patnaik.—23rd ed.— New Delhi: Lexis Nexis, 2005. 794p.

43. Murthi, R.K. Primer for consumer activists / by R.K. Murthi.— New Delhi: Reliance, 1995. 232p.

44. Murthy, P. V. V. Satyanarayana Consumer justice (a manual for consumer forum members) / by P. V. V. Satyanarayana Murthy.— New Delhi: Indian Institute of Public Administration, 2006. 328p.

45. National commission and supreme court on consumer cases 1986 2002, part iv / edited by Swarn Bhatia Nijhawan.— Delhi: International Law Book Company, 2002. 6832p.

46. National commission and supreme court on consumer cases 1986 1996, part ii / edited by Swarn Bhatia Nijhawan.—Delhi: International Law Book Company, 1996. 3259p.

47. National commission and supreme court on consumer cases 1986 2002, part vi / edited by Swarn Bhatia Nijhawan.—Delhi: International Law Book Company, 2005. 10008p.

48. National commission and supreme court on consumer cases 1986 2006, part vii / edited by Swarn Bhatia

Nijhawan. – Delhi: International Law Book Company, 2006. 11568p.

49. National commission and supreme court on consumer cases 1986 2007, part viii / edited by Swarn Bhatia Nijhawan. – Delhi: International Law Book Company, 2008. v.p.

50. National commission and Supreme Court on consumer cases, 1986-2004 / edited by Swarn Bhatia Nijhawan. – Delhi: International Law Book Company, 2004. v.p.

51. National consumer service / By Central Bharat Sewak Samaj.-New Delhi: Central Bharat Sewak Samaj, 1964. 13p. (Non - official price intelligence service).

52. Nayar, Rajendra Kumar Consumer protection law in India: an eco-legal treatise on consumer justice / by Rajendra Kumar Nayak.– Bombay: Indian Law Inst., 1991. 695p.

53. Nigam, Shalu Consumerism, medicine and the law: emerging voices from India / by Shalu Nigam.– New Delhi: Om Pub., 2004. 391p.

54. Nijhawan, Swarn Bhatia National commission and Supreme Court on consumer cases, 1986-2002 / by Swarn Bhatia Nijhawan.– Delhi: International Law Book Company, 2004. v.p. Contents: pt.4, v.p.

55. Nijhawan,Swarn Bhatia National commissilon and supreme court on Consumer cases 1986-2006 / by Swarn Bhatia Nijhawan.– Delhi: International law book company, 2006. v.p. Contents: part 7. T34403x54 N582/ 7/86-2006

56. Panta, Murali Prasad Business, consumer and the government: an economic and legal perspectives (India and Germany) / by Murali Prasad Panta.– New Delhi: Mittal, 2001. 349p.

57. Pavleen Consumer decision-making / by Pavleen.– New Delhi: Deep & Deep, 2006. 227p.

58. Rao, Mamta Public utility services under the consumer protection act / by Mamta Rao.— New Delhi: Deep & Deep, 1999. 394p.

59. Saha, Tushar Kanti Law of tort and consumer justice / by Tushar Kanti Saha.-New Delhi: Kanishka, 2001. 187p.

60. Saraf, D.N. Law of consumer protection in India / by D.N. Saraf.—Bombay: N.M. Tripathi, 1990. 259p.

61. Saxena, Anurag Consumer protection in India: a study of implementation strategies / by Anurag Saxena.— New Delhi: Indian Institute of Public Administration, 2004. 138p. An APPPA M.Phil dissertation, 2003-04 (Guide: Prof. S.S. Singh).

62. Shah, M. B. Landmark judgments on consumer protection / by M. B. Shah — Delhi: Universal Law, 2005. 262p.

63. Shah, M.B. Landmark judgments on insurance: under the consumer protection act (October 2003 to July 2004) / by M.B. Shah — Delhi: Universal Law, 2004. 196p.

64. Sharma, Deepa Consumer grievance redressal: under the consumer protection act / by Deepa Sharma.— New Delhi: New Century, 2002. 272p.

65. Singh, Gurjeet, The law of consumer protection in India: justice within reach / by Gurjeet Singh.— New Delhi: Deep and Deep, 1996. 542p.

66. Singh, Jagdish Medical profession and consumer protection act / by Dr. Jagdish Singh.— Jaipur: Bharat Law, 1994. 132p.

67. Singh, S.S. Evaluation of the effectiveness of the implementation of the consumer protection act, 1986 / by S.S. Singh and M.K. Balachandran.— New Delhi: Indian Institute of Public Administration, 1994. 81p. (IIPA Working Paper, 1994: 4).

68. Sivaprakasam, P. Consumer empowerment: rights and responsibilities / by P. Sivaprakasam and S. Rajamohan.— New Delhi: Kanishka, 2001. 314p.

69. Sobti, Renu Medical services and consumer protection in India: (cases reviewed up to April 2001) / By Renu Sobti.— Delhi: New Century, 2001. 320p.

70. Tyagi, S.P. Medical negligence / by S.P. Tyagi.— Delhi: Vinod Pub., 2004. 922+p.

71. Uppal, R.K. Consumer protection through mass awareness: new challenges and opportunities / edited by R.K. Uppal and Rimpi Kaur.— New Delhi: Mahamaya, 2007. 655p.

72. Vats, R.M. Consumer and the law / by R.M. Vats.— Delhi: Universal Book, 1994. 254p.

73. Vats, R.M. Law relating to electricity with special reference to consumer protection law / by R.M. Vats.— Delhi: Universal Law, 2002. 358p.

74. Vats, R.M. Law relating to telephones with special reference to consumer protection act / by R.M. Vats.— 2nd ed.— Delhi: Universal Law, 1999. 386p.

75. Venkatesha, H.R. Consumer protection in India: a study of Karnataka state / by H.R. Venkatesha.— Jaipur: University Book House, 2005. 336p.

76. Verma, S.K. A treatise on consumer protection laws / by S.K. Verma and M. Afzal Wani.— New Delhi: The Indian Law Institute, 2004.

77. Vohra, Munish Consumer behaviour / by Munish Vohra.— New Delhi: Anmol, 2006. 471p.

78. Wadhwa, D. P. The law of consumer protection / by D. P. Wadhwa and N. L. Rajah.—2nd ed.— Haryana: Lexis Nexis, 2009. 2 vols. Contents: v.1. 1422+p.; v.2. pp. 1423-2271.